*Studies in Central and Eastern Europe*

Edited for the International Council for Central and East European Studies by **Roger E. Kanet**, University of Miami, USA

*Titles include*:

Thomas Bremer (*editor*)
RELIGION AND THE CONCEPTUAL BOUNDARY IN CENTRAL
AND EASTERN EUROPE
Encounters of Faiths

Joan DeBardeleben (*editor*)
THE BOUNDARIES OF EU ENLARGEMENT
Finding A Place for Neighbours

Graeme Gill (*editor*)
POLITICS IN THE RUSSIAN REGIONS

Roger E. Kanet (*editor*)
RUSSIA
Re-Emerging Great Power

Rebecca Kay (*editor*)
GENDER, EQUALITY AND DIFFERENCE DURING AND
AFTER STATE SOCIALISM

Stanislav J. Kirschbaum (*editor*)
CENTRAL EUROPEAN HISTORY AND THE EUROPEAN UNION
The Meaning of Europe

Katlijn Malfliet, Lien Verpoest and Evgeny Vinokurov (*editors*)
THE CIS, THE EU AND RUSSIA
Challenges of Integration

John Pickles (*editor*)
STATE AND SOCIETY IN POST-SOCIALIST ECONOMIES

Stephen Velychenko (*editor*)
UKRAINE, THE EU AND RUSSIA
History, Culture and International Relations

*Forthcoming titles include*:

John Pickles (*editor*)
GLOBALIZATION AND REGIONALIZATION IN POST-SOCIALIST
ECONOMIES
Common Economic Spaces of Europe

Stephen White (*editor*)
MEDIA, CULTURE AND SOCIETY IN PUTIN'S RUSSIA

Stephen White (*editor*)
POLITICS AND THE RULING GROUP IN PUTIN'S RUSSIA

Stephen Hutchings (*editor*)
RUSSIA AND ITS OTHER(S) ON FILM
Screening Intercultural Dialogue

**Studies in Central and Eastern Europe**
**Series Standing Order ISBN 0–230–51682–3 hardcover**
(*outside North America only*)

You can receive future titles in this series as they are published by placing a standing order. Please contact your bookseller or, in case of difficulty, write to us at the address below with your name and address, the title of the series and the ISBN quoted above.

Customer Services Department, Macmillan Distribution Ltd, Houndmills, Basingstoke, Hampshire RG21 6XS, England

# State and Society in Post-Socialist Economies

Edited by

John Pickles
*Department of Geography, University of North Carolina,
Chapel Hill, NC 27599-3220*

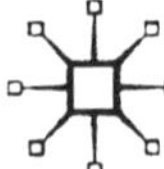



First published in 2008 by
PALGRAVE MACMILLAN
Houndmills, Basingstoke, Hampshire RG21 6XS and
175 Fifth Avenue, New York, N.Y. 10010
Companies and representatives throughout the world

PALGRAVE MACMILLAN is the global academic imprint of the Palgrave
Macmillan division of St. Martin's Press, LLC and of Palgrave Macmillan Ltd.
Macmillan® is a registered trademark in the United States, United Kingdom
and other countries. Palgrave is a registered trademark in the European
Union and other countries.

ISBN-13: 978–0–230–52214–5 hardback
ISBN-10: 0–230–52214–9 hardback

This book is printed on paper suitable for recycling and made from fully
managed and sustained forest sources. Logging, pulping and manufacturing
processes are expected to conform to the environmental regulations of
the country of origin.

A catalogue record for this book is available from the British Library.

A catalog record for this book is available from the Library of Congress.

10   9   8   7   6   5   4   3   2   1
17   16   15   14   13   12   11   10   09   08

Printed and bound in Great Britain by
CPI Antony Rowe Chippenham and Eastbourne

# Contents



## Part 1   Economic Governance, the State and Varieties of Capitalism

## Part 2   Social Mobilization and Economic Transformation

# List of Illustrations

# List of Tables

# Acknowledgements

I am very grateful to Roger Kanet who worked tirelessly and with great patience to help develop this book and to bring it successfully to the Palgrave Macmillan Studies in Central and Eastern Europe Series. Robert Jenkins (Director of the Center on Slavic, East European and Eurasian Studies at the University of North Carolina at Chapel Hill) helped frame the book and offered insightful comments on the chapters. Jennifer Pyclik was immensely helpful in carrying out careful and thorough copy-editing of the original manuscripts. I am particularly indebted to Dennis Arnold, Annelies Goger, Christian Sellar and Tim Stallmann. They stepped in at very short notice to help with the review and correcting of the proofs.

Review and editing on *State and Society in Post-Socialist Economies* was carried out from spring through winter 2006, and final editing was completed over the winter break 2006–7. My wife, son, and parents were again kind enough to put up with John 'doing' another book in the precious summer and winter holidays which could otherwise have been put to different uses. I am reminded of this 'otherness' of our lives, particularly on the day that I print the final manuscript for the publisher, because today I learned of the passing of Allan Pred. For over four decades Allan was one of the world's leading geographers, a constant voice for social justice, an inveterate writer of wonderful books dealing with the ambiguities of Swedish social democracy, and a friend. He and Michael Watts first introduced me to the complex dialectics of Walter Benjamin, illuminating new possibilities for thinking about European socialisms and post-socialisms. I dedicate this book to his memory.

# List of Abbreviations

| | |
|---|---|
| BEA | Bureau of Economic Analysis |
| BATA | Bulgarian Association of Travel Agents |
| CEE | Central and Eastern Europe |
| CEO | Chief Executive Officer |
| CEFIR | Centre for Economic and Financial Research |
| CIS | Commonwealth of Independent States |
| ČMKOS | *Českomoravská konfederace odborových svazů* Czech–Moravian Confederation of Trade Unions |
| COMECON | Council for Mutual Economic Assistance |
| ČSOP | *Český svaz ochranců přirody* Czech Nature Protectors' Union |
| CSR | Corporate Social Responsibility |
| DFI | Direct Foreign Investment |
| EBRD | European Bank for Reconstruction and Development |
| ECE | East Central Europe |
| EMU | European Monetary Union |
| ERT | European Round Table |
| EU | European Union |
| FDI | Foreign Direct Investment |
| GDP | Gross Domestic Product |
| IER | Institute for Economic Research (Hitotsubashi University, Tokyo, Japan) |
| IET | (or IEPP in Russian) – Institute for the Economy in Transition |
| IFI | International Financial Institutions |
| IMF | International Monetary Fund |
| IPF | Investment Privatization Funds |
| JSC | Joint-Stock Company |
| KIWNS | Klausian Welfare National State |
| KOZ SR | *Konfederácja Odborových Zväzov Slovenskej Republiky* Confederation of Trade Unions of the Slovak Republic |
| MNC | Multinational Corporation |
| MSZOSZ | *Magyar Szakszervezetek Országos Szövetsége* National Confederation of Hungarian Trade Unions |
| NGO | Non-Governmental Organization |

| | |
|---|---|
| OECD | Organization for Economic Cooperation and Development |
| OPT | Outward Processing Trade |
| OPZZ | All-Poland Alliance of Trade Unions |
| OSCE | Organization for Security and Cooperation in Europe |
| PDC | Producer-Driven Commodity Chain |
| PWPR | Porterian Workfare Postnational Regime |
| R&D | Research and Development |
| REB | Russian Economic Barometer |
| SITC | Standard International Trade Classification |
| SME | Small and Medium-sized Enterprise |
| SU HSE | State University – Higher School of Economics (Russian University, Moscow) |
| TsEMI | Central Econometrical Institute |
| TNC | Transnational Corporation |
| TTPP | Think Tank Partnership Programme |
| UNDP | United Nations Development Programme |
| US AID | US Agency on International Development |
| USD | US Dollar |
| USSR | Union of Soviet Socialist Republics |
| VoC | Varieties of Capitalism |

# Notes on Contributors

**Massimo Congiu** is a journalist for *Il Movimento* and has worked for many years with trade unions on economic reform in post-socialist societies.

**Sandrine Devaux** is a faculty member in the Group of European Political Sociology at the University of Robert Schuman, Strasbourg. Her research focusses on democratization and transitions, socialization, and political militancy in post-communist states. She has published on Czech community life, on youth organizations, and on the revival of the associative sector.

**Jan Drahokoupil** is a research fellow at Max Planck Institute for the Study of Societies in Cologne, Germany. He earned his PhD at the Department of Sociology and Social Anthropology of the Central European University in Budapest. His recent publication projects include *Neoliberal Governance and Beyond*, a volume co-edited with Bastiaan van Apeldoorn and Laura Horn (forthcoming in Palgrave in 2008).

**Tatiana G. Dolgopyatova** is chief researcher at the Institute for Industrial and Market Studies and professor in the Department of Microeconomic Analysis at the State University – Higher School of Economics. Her doctorate of economics (1997) is from Moscow State University and her areas of research include institutional transformations and enterprises' economic behaviour, private sector development including small business matters, business restructuring and corporate governance. She has long practice in conducting directors' and entrepreneurs' in-depth interviews, face-to-face and mail surveys. She has participated in a number of research and technical assistance projects supported by the EBRD, the IBRD, OECD, US AID and Russian Ministries and foundations, and has about 200 publications including about 25 papers published in Austria, Croatia, England, Finland, France, Germany, Japan, Poland, and the USA. In 1995 she published the book *Russian Enterprises in Transitional Economy: Economic Problems and Behaviour* (in Russian, 290 pages) and has edited several books, including *Russian Industry: Institutional Development* (SU-HSE publishing house, 2003). Tatiana G. Dolgopyatova, Dr of Economics, Professor, Department of Microeconomic Analysis and Chief

Researcher, Institute for Industrial and Market Studies State University – Higher School of Economics, Slavyanskaya Square 4, bld.2, of. 501, Moscow 109074, Russia.

**Kristen Ghodsee** has a PhD from the University of California at Berkeley and is an assistant professor at Bowdoin College. Her articles on gender in Bulgaria have been published in journals such as *Signs, Gender and Women's Studies Quarterly, The International Journal of Politics, Culture and Society, L'Homme: Zeitschrift für Feministische Geschichtswissenschaft* and *Human Rights Dialogue.* She is also the author of *The Red Riviera: Gender, Tourism and Postsocialism on the Black Sea* (Duke University Press, October 2005). In 2005–6 she was a fellow at the Woodrow Wilson International Center for Scholars and in 2006–7 she is a fellow at the Princeton Institute for Advanced Study where she is working on her second monograph: *The Miniskirt and the Veil: Gender, Eastern Aid and Islamic Revivalism on the Edge of Europe.*

**Béla Greskovits** is Professor of Political Science at the Central European University, where he teaches courses on the politics of development. He is author of *The Political Economy of Protest and Patience. East European and Latin American Transformations Compared,* Central European University Press 1998, and numerous articles and book chapters on the politics of economic reforms. His current research focus is the political economy of major industries, and the varieties of East European capitalism. In 1998-9 he was holder of the Luigi Einaudi Chair at the Institute for European Studies at Cornell University. In 2003–4 he was Visiting Professor of Social Studies at Harvard University.

**Åse B. Grødeland** is a researcher at the Norwegian Institute of Urban and Regional Research, where she has been involved in and directed major research projects on informal networks and economies of corruption in post-socialist countries. In 2001 she co-edited *A Culture of Corruption?: Coping With Government in Post-Communist Europe* with William Lockley Miller and Tatyana Y. Koshechkina.

**Kiryl Haiduk** is a PhD candidate at the Department of International Relations and European Studies of the Central European University in Budapest, Hungary. Prior to this, Mr Haiduk has been working for the ILO Moscow Office within the framework of the Project aimed at assisting independent and democratic trade unions of Belarus. He has also held two fellowships at the Centre for Policy Studies of the Open Society in Budapest, doing research on the consequences of the EU eastward enlargement and macroeconomic policies and the role of labour unions in transition. Recent publications include 'Belarusian Economic at a Crossroads' (a book written in co-authorship and published by the ILO in 2005) and a contribution 'The Political Economy of Post-Soviet Offshorisation' for an edited volume 'Global Finance in the New Century' to be published by Palgrave in 2006.

**Jurgita Maciulyte** was born in 1970 in Siauliai, Lithuania. She entered Vilnius University in 1988 and studied geography at the Department of General Geography, Faculty of Natural Sciences until 1992. She obtained a master's degree (Geographer – spatial planner) in 1993 at the Toulouse Le Mirail University and defended her doctoral thesis 'Agrarian transformation in Lithuanian rural territories' at Montpellier Paul-Valéry University in 1999, where she obtained a PhD in social geography. She was involved in postdoctoral researches at the LADYSS laboratory of social sciences in the French national research centre in Paris from 2001 to 2003. At present she works as an associated professor at the department of Geography and Spatial Planning in Vilnius University. Her main fields of interest are local and regional development in post-Soviet space, transformations of rural territories, and sustainable development in rural areas.

**Satoshi Mizobata** is currently Professor at the University of Kyoto, Kyoto Institute of Economic Research. He gained his PhD in Economics at the University of Kyoto. His books include *Economic and Management System in Russia* (Houritsubunka, 1996), *The Economics of Transition* (Sekaishisousha, 2002), *Big business in Russia* (Bunrikaku, 2003, with Ia. Pappe). He is managing editor of *The Journal of Comparative Economic Studies*.

**John Pickles** is the Earl N. Phillips Distinguished Professor of International Studies and Professor of Geography at the University of North Carolina at Chapel Hill. His main research interests are in regional economic transformation in Eastern Europe, ethnicity, violence and economic change, and critical theory and cultural studies. He has published numerous articles in these fields, as well as several monographs, the most recent of which are: *A History of Spaces: Cartographic Reason, Mapping, and the Geo-Coded World* (Routledge, 2004); *Environmental Transitions: Transformation and Ecological Defence in Central and Eastern Europe* (with Petr Pavlinek, Routledge, 2000); *Theorizing Transition: The Political Economy of Post-Communist Transformations* (edited with Adrian Smith, Routledge, 1998); *Bulgaria in Transition* (edited with Krassimira Paskaleva, Phillip Shapira, and Boian Koulov, Ashgate, 1998); *Ground Truth: The Social Consequences of Geographical*

*Information Systems* (edited, Guilford Press, 1995); and *Phenomenology, Science, and Geography: Space and the Social Sciences* (Cambridge University Press, 1985). He is currently working on the integration of Central and Eastern European apparel production networks into EU and broader global value chains.

**Arjan Vliegenthart** (1978) studied political science and history at the Vrije Universiteit (Amsterdam) and the Freie Universität (Berlin). Arjan Vliegenthart was junior lecturer at the department of political science of the VU from 2003 until 2005. Currently he is working within the framework of the Amsterdam Research Centre for Corporate Governance Regulation (ARCCGOR) at the Vrije Universiteit on his PhD on the political dimension of the developments in corporate governance regulation in Central and Eastern Europe, i.e. the former Visegrád group.

# 1
# The Spirit of Post-Socialism: 'What Is to Be Understood by It?'

*John Pickles*

In the title of this study is used the somewhat pretentious phrase, 'the spirit of capitalism'. What is to be understood by it?

If any object can be found to which this term can be applied with any understandable meaning, it can only be an historical individual, i.e., a complex of elements associated in historical reality which we unite into a conceptual whole from the standpoint of their cultural significance....

Such an historical concept, however, since it refers in its content to a phenomenon significant for its unique individuality...must be gradually put together out of the individual parts which are taken from historical reality to make it up. Thus the final and definitive concept cannot stand at the beginning of the investigation, but must come at the end....This is a necessary result of the nature of historical concepts which attempt for their methodological purposes not to grasp historical reality in abstract general formulae, but in concrete genetic sets of relations which are inevitably of a specifically unique and individual character.

Max Weber (1905)[1]

The habit of looking at the last ten thousand years as well as at the array of early societies as a mere prelude to the true history of our civilization which started approximately with the publication of the Wealth of Nations in 1776, is, to say the least, out of date.

Karl Polanyi (1944)[2]

## Introduction

*State and Society in Post-Socialist Economies* deals with the reform economies of post-socialist Europe and with the ways in which the various projects of communism that emerged across the region in the twentieth century have been and still are being dismantled and replaced by alternative visions, institutions and practices of capitalist market economies and democratic polities.

These transformations have now been underway for at least two decades and, in that time, the region has experienced several rounds of intense institutional rupture and reorganization. The complex structures of communism have been dismantled. Economies that collapsed are now being rebuilt. *Nomenklatura* power has morphed into or given way to democracy movements, diverse practices of civil society, new economic elite formations and new configurations of class, gender and interest. Massive economic recession has further opened sectors of the economy to rapid internationalization and, more recently, European Union accession and enlargement have enabled a relatively painless integration of many Central and Southeast European countries into the wider regional economies of Europe.

1989 remains an important marker of these transformations; a ruptural moment that has shaped so much thinking about state socialism and post-socialism.[3] The 'transitology' that emerged with the ending of communism was a kind of global dream that shaped post-socialist realities in very specific ways.[4] Throughout the 1980s, individualistic and anti-bureaucratic theories of Hayekian neoliberalism had played a prominent role in shaping the thinking of the anti-communist opposition. Consequently, transition theorists, political leaders and policy-makers throughout the region were already predisposed to thinking of post-socialism as a process of economic convergence toward a natural market economy and a political return to Europe. For many in the region, Milton Friedman typified this public role of Hayekian neoliberal thought. As Larry Summers wrote in his 2006 *The New York Times* obituary for Friedman: 'Ask reformers in any one of the countries behind what we used to call the Iron Curtain where they learned to contemplate alternatives to communism during the closed era before the Berlin Wall fell and they will often tell you about reading Milton Friedman and realizing how different their world could be.'[5]

This form of transitology was also, of course, a kind of return to the modernization theories of the 1960s in which 'transition' was interpreted to be part of an inexorable global developmental continuum which was flattening the earth and subsuming cultural and regional differences. In this global dream, indigenous belief systems, religious, ethnic, linguistic and cultural identity claims were interpreted to be parochial obstacles to effective liberalization and democratization, to be 'swept away by trans-national forces of modernization, secularization and the ultimate triumph of a free enterprise-driven global economy'.[6] By contrast, the institutions, values and practices of Western political economy were assumed to be universal, superior and hence the only feasible alternative.[7]

Other scholars and policy-makers struggled to contrast theories of modernization and convergence with alternative models of economic transformation.[8] Rudolf Tökés has referred to these modernization logics as 'synthetic overviews', exemplified by Samuel Huntington's *The Third Wave*, in which Huntington treats the collapse of communist regimes as part of a global scheme of 'waves of democratization'.[9] An alternative reading is given by what he calls 'ambitious South-East "transitology" studies'. This approach attempts to understand Soviet and East European political and economic outcomes in terms that marked the end of authoritarian rule in other parts of the world, particularly in Latin America and Southern Europe. Others focus more directly on specific pathways of development within the post-socialist world, developing comparative analyses of 'varieties of capitalism' across the region.[10] Finally, Tökés identifies the work of mainly younger social scientists whose focus is less concerned with the general, analytical categories of abstraction and analysis that typify these first three approaches, and instead is 'seeking to make distinctions between generic and unique factors in pre- and post-Communist contexts that contributed to the fall of the old regimes'.

The chapters in *State and Society in Post-Socialist Economies* draw on several of these traditions of writing, but as a whole the collection also aims to contribute to this last goal of mediating the general and the unique drivers of post-socialist transformation. It deals with these themes of transformation in three ways. First, the volume deals with the changing patterns of economic governance. In so doing, it attempts to take seriously the specificities of individual and regional economic practices and the concrete conditions in which specific forms of governance emerge and are sustained. Second, all the chapters exemplify forms of grounded theory that attempt – each in its own way – to avoid inscribing a standard set of assumptions about how post-socialism works. Instead, each chapter focuses on the concrete actors and relations that are shaping the kinds of market institutions that are being composed and recomposed in 'transitional' economies. Thus, instead of an attempt to define the how each case approximates what Weber called 'a final and definitive concept' of what a market economy is or should be, the author of each chapter seeks to show the actual effects of specific practices, institutions and actors in their complex social and institutional settings and geographies. Third, this volume draws on the research and writing of scholars working on or from the region who are engaged in this rethinking of economic governance, including authors from the EU, Central and Eastern Europe, Russia, the US and Japan.[11] In recent years, a great deal of attention has been paid to the changing practices of economic governance in post-socialist Europe and this has been stimulated further by EU enlargement and its consequences for the wider economic policies of the region.[12] The diversity of the authors' scholarly and national backgrounds further exemplifies the multivariate nature of post-socialist transformations.

In addressing the diverse forms of economic governance in post-socialist societies, *State and Society in Post-Socialist Economies* also focuses on the dialectic between market harmonization and economic regional differentiation. In so doing, it pays particular attention to the roles played by state and non-state actors in shaping these outcomes. For the regulation theorist Alain Lipietz, these complex interbedded processes of economic change and social and political regulation produced what he has called 'chance stabilizations'; differentiated regimes of accumulation with corresponding modes of social regulation and norms of social consumption that are both converging with broader patterns of political economy in and across Europe, but are also quite distinct in their details, forms and practices.[13] While for some these details may be dismissed as residual forms that will pass away or may be interpreted as barriers to normalization that need to be addressed, for Lipietz and the authors in this volume these specificities matter. How we answer Weber's question of what we understand by 'the spirit of capitalism' requires grounded explanations of this double movement of simultaneously occurring processes of institutional convergence and concrete specificities that shape diverse and complex social and regional differences. Post-socialism is being produced by these dialectics of globalization and localism, by what Grabher and Stark have referred to as the *legacies, linkages* and *localities* of post-socialist transformation.[14] In this sense, the book contributes to what I refer to below as 'fourth wave transition studies', and it is to these that I now turn.

## Fourth wave transition studies and the role of society in economic regulation

In what we might think of as first wave transition studies, the political economy of post-socialism was marked most clearly by the wholesale acceptance of policy programs involving political and economic liberalization, privatization and institutional reform (particularly through shock therapy and structural adjustment). Scholarly and policy research centred around neoclassical economics, reform was institutionally led often by major transnational actors such as the European Bank for Reconstruction and Development, the IMF, and the World Bank, and attempts were made to apply economic reforms wholesale and quickly across the region.

In the second wave, and partly as a consequence of the combined effects of legacies of rigid bureaucratic planning structures and the devastating consequences of economic globalization, countries across the region experienced intense economic recessions in virtually every sector of the economy. The result was a scale of economic collapse that was deeper and longer lasting than had occurred in the Great Depression of the 1920s–30s. During this phase, scholarly and policy writing focused increasingly on social inequality, access to state disbursements and the needs for investments in social capital to facilitate the transition to an effective liberal market economy.

In the third wave of transition studies, the devaluation of capital stock and the rush to dispose of assets on national and world markets resulted in a rapid increase in foreign direct investment (FDI), particularly into the more resource-rich economies of Central Europe. FDI brought with it changes in managerial skills, harmonization of finance and banking procedures and many opportunities for technically trained and bilingual entrepreneurs. Aggregate gross output and living standards increased, while geographically and socially uneven development deepened or became more visible. Scholarly and policy writing was heavily focused on lead sectors of industry, on policies of harmonization and economic integration and on regional analyses of political 'successes' (Central Europe) and 'laggards' (Southeastern and Eastern Europe).

In what I am here referring to as the fourth wave of transition studies, the flourishing of regional economies in Central Europe was helped by accession agreements with the European Union, and this in turn exacerbated the regionally differentiated nature of economic and political reforms. War in the Balkans was paralleled by integration of production and banking systems in Poland, Hungary and the Czech Republic, by financial crisis and ongoing economic decline in Bulgaria and Romania and by political struggle for control over the Russian state. Thus, through the late 1990s to the present, perhaps one overriding characteristic of economic life across the region has been the emergence of different governance regimes: the return of an oligarchic, bureaucratic centralism in Russia, the vigorously liberal regimes and open economies of countries like Slovakia, the resurgence of reformed socialist and social democratic parties in Central Europe and the unstable political alliances and stop-start economic reforms of countries like Bulgaria and Romania. These patterns of political economic transformation have become clearer in recent years and, not surprisingly, they have generated tendencies among scholars and policy-makers to think much more seriously about the ways in which the economy is structured by historical legacies, social practices and cultural norms.

At the heart of this 'fourth wave' is a questioning of the logics and theories of 'transition studies' themselves, an attempt to think outside of modernist logics of linear transformations and the centrality they have accorded to the mechanisms of markets, liberalization and liberal polities for the social re-engineering of the post-socialist economy. From the side of cultural studies, social theory, poststructuralism and post-colonialism, contemporary social sciences are now suspicious of the use of meta-narratives to explain social and economic processes, and political economy itself has developed a thorough-going critique of transitology and the logics of reform via the technologies of international financial institutions (IFIs). In their place have emerged new forms of regional economic analysis that seek to more fully integrate the role played by the concrete specificities of state rule and economic practice, and to do so in much more complex and contingent ways.[15] The recombinant forms of rule emerging in post-socialist societies thus require that we pay much more attention to the specificities of daily practice, the concrete logics of institutional norms and the diverse forms that are generated in the struggle over the allocation of social surplus. This fourth wave of transition studies thus interrogates the complexities of the social economy, its historical legacies, the ways in which it is recomposing social and class relations and the resulting recombinant and hybrid forms of regional, national and transnational systems of governance that now shape the diverse economies of the region.

## The chapters

*State and Society in Post-Socialist Economies* comprises twelve original essays by authors from Western, Central and Eastern Europe, Russia, the US and Japan who have been shaping recent debates about economic governance, regime theory and the various roles played by state and society in the transformation of post-socialist economies. It takes as its central concern the important relationships between the state and society in shaping the nature of economic lives and practices in post-socialist and post-soviet regions. As a whole, the collection illustrates some of the key ways in which scholarly disciplines and policy fields have attempted to address post-socialist economic regimes and governance systems.

Part 1 deals with the emergence of overlapping and diverse governance regimes and the importance of understanding economic reform in terms of differentiated forms of capitalist development. The chapters address the ways in which these regimes and varieties of capitalism have produced differentiated economic outcomes and experiences across the region. Béla Greskovits provides a detailed assessment of country- and sector-specific indices of production and significance, demonstrating the value of a 'varieties of capitalism' approach for regional economic analysis. His analysis focuses on the emerging socio-economic regimes of the ten Eastern European Member and Candidate States of the EU and poses three important questions. What is the pattern that these new capitalisms exhibit? Which factors account for the emergence of variation? What are the implications for social conditions, macroeconomic stability and developmental prospects? The chapter traces the legacies of state socialism, the market reforms of the 1990s and the location decisions of transnational corporations. These factors led to varied types of integration into global and European systems of production via particular leading export sectors that produced specific transnational varieties of capitalism in Eastern Europe.

Arjan Vliegenthart turns to the role of transnational actors in shaping the structures of corporate governance in Central and Eastern Europe. He focuses particularly on the role of the EU in the reforms in the Czech Republic. While much of the varieties of capitalism literature focuses on two primary types of economic governance in the region, either the Anglo-Saxon or the continental European model of corporate governance, Vliegenthart suggests that in Central and Eastern Europe we are not seeing convergence around either one of these models. Instead, he suggests, a specific type of capitalism is emerging. Focusing on the crucial role foreign investment has played in Czech economic reforms, he argues that foreign banks and corporations now own a large part of the Czech economy, exerting enormous influence over its corporate governance and regulation. In this regard, the EU has been a particularly important transnational actor in securing the climate for foreign investment, particularly through its efforts to lock in newly established property rights through corporate governance regulation.

Drawing on the work of Bob Jessop and regulation and regime theory, Jan Drahokoupil continues this work by developing an interesting periodization of the dominant state accumulation strategies in Central and Eastern Europe in the late 1990s. He documents how the crisis of what he calls the Klausian welfare national state emerged in the 1990s because of its dual commitment to neo-liberal reforms while fostering growth based on Czech national capitalism. This crisis has led to the emergence of an alternative regime, which he describes as the Porterian workfare postnational regime, aimed at attracting foreign capital to upgrade industry. This marks a moment of renewed convergence among the Visegrad-Four countries, each of which is now adopting this kind of development strategy.

Focusing more directly on patterns of corporate governance and drawing on surveys and in-depth interviews with managers and owners of Russian joint-stock companies between 1999 and 2005, Tatiana Dolgopyatova turns to the emergence of micro-models of corporate control in Russian companies. She shows how the adoption of new business practices has promoted the gradual separation of ownership and operational management, and how demands for institutional reform were used by shareholders to extend their control over the management of companies. The result has been a shift in the pattern of corporate governance from one based on the redistribution of corporate stock and the dispersal of employee property through voucher privatization to one with highly concentrated corporate ownership and insider control by dominant owners who participate directly in management or closely oversee hired managers.

Satoshi Mizobata extends Dolgopyatova's analysis of Russian corporate governance by focusing on the combined features of normalization and preservation in Russian businesses since the 1998 financial crisis. He pays particular attention to the simultaneous trends in enterprise restructuring and the impact of EU enlargement, suggesting that, while Russian corporate governance superficially appears to parallel similar forms in EU-oriented and globally oriented businesses, in practice

Russian governance models exhibit quite different features that continue to be influenced in important ways by the interests of specific institutional stakeholders and the specificities of Russian historical and cultural formations.

In Part 2 authors provide specific analyses of the role of state institutions and regulations in shaping social and economic outcomes. Here, state and society are interrogated for the ways in which they shape specific forms of economic regime and form of governance. Kiryl Haiduk focuses on the role of state institutions and social practices in shaping labour relations and reforms in Belarus, arguing that labour remains one of the key drivers of economic governance and institutional reform. By focusing on employment practices, wage-setting procedures and differential access in decision-making, the author argues that the dynamics of labour struggles and negotiation remain an important element in understanding the differentiated nature of economic practice in specific enterprises and sectors of the economy.

Haiduk begins by analysing the debates in contemporary political economy about the origins and dynamics of specific paths of development, contrasting a Keynesian Western European model with a Southern European authoritarian model. Within the Western European model, he distinguished between two specific forms. The first is the 'minimalist' Anglo-American model with its commitment to a liberal market economy. The second is the Continental European model of Germany and Sweden, for example, with their commitment to strong 'social partnership' and coordinated market economies. Haiduk argues that post-war Keynesianism in Western Europe did not depend on the use of government to direct decisions made in the private sector, but instead was based on social democracy as a medium of such policies. By contrast, in Southern Europe the state did act to direct public and private investments in specific ways. Consequently, prior to becoming EU members the Southern European states were characterized by less established mechanisms of social compromise and intense inequality in the distribution of wealth and incomes, characteristics that meant that social confrontation was an always present threat. This confrontation might cause social upheavals and strikes in a climate of uncertainty and unrest. The latter could be 'cooled down' by various means, from the populist-authoritarian methods of a Latin American type to the social-democratic methods of a Western European type. However, in the Southern European authoritarian states it was the absence of a considerable middle class, on the basis of which social democracy could be mobilized politically, that prevented alternatives to authoritarian orders emerging in Southern Europe. Here, macroeconomic regulation of demand had been embodied in a system of state corporatism that functioned by interest mediation and manipulation. Any 'genuine' Western European type of social compromise was very difficult under these circumstances.

Massimo Congiu draws on his experience as a journalist of trade union reform to illustrate the consequences of these conditions in terms of the challenges facing organized labour as market liberalization and the withdrawal of the state from direct control over the economy occurred after 1989. His chapter focuses on the broader consequences of EU membership for organized labour and trade union representation in the new member states. With changes in lead sectors within the economy and corresponding transformations in labour markets, trade unions are now struggling to redefine their role in these countries and they are doing so in an EU context in which social and market models of economic growth continue to be debated and where – at least in the more social democratic states – union membership has stabilized or is again increasing. The chapter documents changing patterns and consequences for organized labour of economic integration, foreign ownership and GDP growth across the region and assesses the likely consequences of membership in the European Union. It concludes with an assessment of two models of trade unionism corresponding to the two broad models of the EU: a social model and a market model.

While Congiu focuses on the effects on organization of labour movements across the region, Kristen Ghodsee turns to the impact of the collapse of communism on Bulgarian employees as they struggled to navigate the new rules in a labour market where the state no longer guaranteed full employment to all citizens. Ghodsee shows how privatization of the tourist industry and the introduction of domestic and international competition to once monopolistic enterprises had unexpected consequences for women employed in the industry. Contrary to the experience of women in many other important sectors in the post-communist economy, she shows that a large group of women benefited from the privatization and globalization of the industry because they were able to mobilize the education, skills and experience they had received before 1989 in the changed conditions after 1989. Moreover, state regulations regarding the management of hotels and restaurants after 1989 inadvertently favoured these women by requiring certain minimum levels of education to work in professional positions in the sector, types and levels of education and training that were disproportionately female before 1989.

The roles played by institutional and economic legacies of state socialism after 1989 are also the focus of the two chapters on the political economy of environmental reform by Jurgita Maciulyte and Sandrine Devaux. In dealing with Lithuania, Maciulyte demonstrates that the socioeconomic divisions between urban and rural areas that deepened in the USSR have persisted since independence and continue to shape the implementation of EU environmental legislation, the successes of ecological reform and the quality of lives in different places. The environmental governance regimes resulting from preparation for EU accession have been and continue to be shaped by the differential geographies of urban and rural legacies of the Soviet period.

In her study of environmental activism in the Czech Republic, Sandrine Devaux similarly traces the significance of pre-1989 social and institutional investments in shaping post-1989 environmental politics. Rejecting the epochal significance of 1989 as a break from command to market economies and from authoritarianism to democracy, she develops instead an institutional and historical analysis of the ways in which the Czech ecological movement emerged *in and through* the institutions created by communist governments as they attempted to forge conservative ideologies of environmental conservation and nature awareness. Devaux traces the histories of institutional investment in nature and ideological awareness as part of a broader national consciousness through the work of biology and geography departments in the Academy of Sciences to state management institutions, showing how each operated as a kind of 'incubator' for gradually more radical forms of political and ecological activism. What Pavlinek and Pickles (2000) had earlier called the politics of ecological defence here similarly emerges in and through the institutions, preparing the ground for what emerged in 1989 as a broadly based and institutionally secure environmental movement.[16] Institutional investments by the state, the need for trained professionals in the service of the state and the growing importance of a national (including Soviet) model of nature appreciation and preservation all served in this way as crucial legacies and resources through which Western standards of economic and environmental regulation were mobilized to oppose the structure and practices of the central state.

The book concludes with a chapter by Åse Berit Grødeland that deals with the ways in which the negative consequences of reform and the opportunity structures it has created have similarly encouraged individuals and groups to work in and through informal social 'networks' and personal 'contacts' to help each other (often to achieve their legal rights), to derive economic or political benefit (often in the absence of effective institutional development), and to consolidate interpersonal and group obligations. Grødeland draws on interviews carried out as part of a three-year project investigating informal relations in politics, the judiciary and in public procurement practices in the Czech Republic, Slovenia, Bulgaria and Romania, and focuses on how such relations, networks and contacts are used to specific ends as forms of social capital. Here Grødeland extends a line of interesting research on the social dynamics of informality that has emerged in recent years, often dealing with grey, shadow or illegal economic networks, but also with the important political and economic roles of economies 'beyond the economy', or what elsewhere have been called informal economies, the economy of jars or economies of influence and reciprocity. These include accounts of non-monetarized exchange systems, economies of reciprocity, remittance-based economies and household economies.[17] But in this chapter he asks: (a) whether the 'culture of informality' has evolved in response to transition and the problems caused by it, or whether it has its roots in pre-transition political culture, and (b) whether – if the 'culture of informality' is a response to transition – is it less extensive in countries that have joined the EU in 2004 and fully implemented the *acquis communautaire* (here the Czech Republic and Slovenia) than it is in the new member states Bulgaria and Romania?[18] Surprisingly, the use and density of informal practices seem not to be related to the level of institutional reform in a country, although the types of informal requests being made are. Perhaps even more surprising is that many of the efforts to mobilize social contacts and informal networks seem to be directed at obtaining information or rights that are legally available to citizens, but about which they know little. Moreover, these typically mobilize the same contacts and networks that people used under communism, and again mainly to deal with mundane everyday needs and tasks rather than more significant political and economic 'favours'.

In one way or another, all the chapters show that political and economic practices are highly diverse, operating in the most quotidian of ways. Sometimes these seek to circumvent legal practices and institutional norms (such as with corruption) and sometimes they are part of a complex set of social adjustments that enable the institutions to operate at all. The former practices of corruption have become crucial challenges to reform societies and their economies, particularly as what David Harvey has called 'accumulation by dispossession' has been enabled by institutional upheaval, elite transformation and – in some cases – by war. In these cases, informal practices may have destabilizing political and economic effects. As a result, they have been the focus of much international policy concern and attention. But in a broader sense – as Grødeland shows clearly – the significance of the broader practices of informality that sustained (or, as Gerald Creed has suggested, domesticated) communism are now being reworked at all levels to domesticate the institutions and practices of capitalism.[19]

## Conclusion

I began this chapter with Max Weber's and Karl Polanyi's reflections on the question of what we are to understand by the 'spirit of capitalism' because, in many ways, Weber's and Polanyi's concerns are our own. What precisely is to be understood by capitalism? How are we best to approach this question in a region in which the struggles to reorder collectivist economies along more liberal lines have been so contested, across which they have produced so broad a diversity of social and regional consequences, and in which patterns of institutional convergence and divergence continue to change the form and significance of the state and other forms of social practice and regulation?

As Weber stresses, these questions necessitate that we attempt 'not to grasp historical reality in abstract general formulae, but in concrete genetic sets of relations which are inevitably of a specifically unique and individual character'. Polanyi is more direct; the modernist model of transition to capitalism as the unfolding of some kind of historical destiny or necessary evolution of economic principles is simply out-of-date. Instead of understanding economic development as a universal path of history (itself a parochial European project),[20] Polanyi draws our attention to the socially contested nature of economic practices, to what he calls their 'double movement' through which social and institutional struggles to territorialize the economy and homogenize political rule always generate their own counter-movements of dissidence and divergence.[21]

All the investigations in this volume problematize – to varying degrees – modernist notions of post-communist transitions, focusing instead on the concrete forms and practices of transformation and adjustment through which struggles over economic governance and the distribution of social surplus are actually occurring. Thus, one way of understanding the 'spirit of post-socialist capitalisms' is in terms of this restless double movement of the economy and the complex forms and practices it generates, be they found in competition among leading and lagging sectors of industry, institutionalization of the state and modes of social regulation, foreign direct investment and transnational actors, corporate governance, organized labour, environment and economy, gendered transitions or informal economic and political practices. From their own specific theoretical perspective, each of these chapters helps us answer Weber's challenge about how we are to understand capitalism – or, in our case, how we are to understand post-socialist capitalisms – which 'attempt for their methodological purposes not to grasp historical reality in abstract general formulae, but in concrete genetic sets of relations which are inevitably of a specifically unique and individual character'.

## Endnotes

1. Max Weber, 'Chapter 2. The Spirit of Capitalism', *The Protestant Ethic and the Spirit of Capitalism*, 1905, London: Routledge, 2001.
2. Karl Polanyi, *The Great Transformation*, New York: Rinehart & Company, 1944, p. 45.
3. For a review, see J. Pickles and A. Smith, eds, *Theorising Transition: The Political Economy of Postcommunist Transformation*, London and New York: Routledge, 1998.
4. R. L. Tökés, '"Transitology": Global Dreams and Post-Communist Realities', *Central Europe Review* 2(10), 13 March 2000, http://www.ce-review.org/00/10/tokes10.html. His comments are directed specifically to political science, but I think they can be usefully thought of more generally in terms of post-socialist transformation studies.
5. L. H. Summers, 'The Great Liberator', *The New York Times*, 19 November 2006. http://gustavojalife.blogspot.com/2006/11/new-york-times-19-november-2006-great.html
6. R. L. Tökés, 'Transitology', 2000, http://www.ce-review.org/00/10/tokes10.html.
7. This was, of course, what Francis Fukuyama saw as the moment at which history ended and the struggles over ideologies had been finally settled; liberal democracies and economies would now flourish in the absence of the threat of any return to state centrism and dreams of collective ownership (F. Fukuyama, *The End of History and the Last Man*, New York: Harper, 1993).
8. See, for example, R. L. Tökés, 'Transitology', 2000, http://www.ce-review.org/00/10/tokes10.html.
9. In *The Clash of Civilizations and the Remaking of World Order*, Huntington wrote:

    It is my hypothesis that the fundamental source of conflict in this new world will not be primarily ideological or primarily economic. The great divisions among humankind and the dominating source of conflict will be cultural. Nation-states will remain the most powerful actors in world affairs, but the principal conflicts of global politics will occur between nations and groups of different civilizations. The clash of civilizations will dominate global politics. The fault lines between civilizations will be the battle lines of the future (New York: Simon and Schuster, 1996, p. 184).

10. See, for example, Lucien Cernat's *Europeanization, Varieties of Capitalism and Economic Performance in Central and Eastern Europe* (London: Palgrave, 2006) which is focused particularly on institutional variables and economic performance. Ekiert and Hanson develop a comparative approach to the social, cultural, and geographical constraints and opportunities facing post-communist reformers, but its primary focus is in mapping the ways in which post-communist societies have successfully institutionalized democratic politics and capitalist market economies (G. Ekiert and S. E. Hanson, eds, *Capitalism and Democracy in Central and Eastern Europe: Assessing the Legacy of Communist Rule*, Cambridge University Press, 2003).

11. See also A. Seleny, *The Political Economy of State-Society Relations in Hungary and Poland: from Communism to the European Union* (Cambridge: Cambridge University Press, 2006). Several other works also deal with one or other aspect of economic governance and social transformation, but each also is more focused on specific economic policy implications, rather than on the analysis of the role of state and society in economic reform. An example is H. W. Hoen, ed., *Good Governance in Central and Eastern Europe: the Puzzle of Capitalism by Design* (London: Edward Elgar, 2001). From a more institutional perspective, J. Ahrens, *Governance and Economic Development: a Comparative Institutional Approach* (London: Edward Elgar, 2002) is focused directly on trying to identify ways of constructing effective market-enhancing governance structures and the necessary incentives for markets to operate. The World Bank Policy Research Dept, J. C. Brada, and I. Singh, *Corporate Governance in Central Eastern Europe: Case Studies of Firms in Transition* (New York: M. E. Sharpe, 1998), is another such volume, focused more directly on firm-level studies and microeconomic policies without the broader social and political economic contexts developed in this volume. Also see P. Cooke, P. Boekholt and F. Todling, *The Governance of Innovation in Europe: Regional Perspectives on Global Competitiveness* (New York: Continuum, 2000).

12. If post-socialist integration into the global economy in 1989 was what Guy Standing has called the first technocratic revolution orchestrated by international financial institutions, 2004 perhaps marked the first bureaucratic revolution wrought through the accounting, monitoring and penalizing practices of the *acquis communautaire* and institutional harmonization. G. Standing, 'The babble of euphemisms: re-embedding social protection in 'transformed' labour markets', in A. Rainnie, A. Smith and A. Swain, eds, *Work, Employment and Transition: Restructuring Livelihoods in Post-Communism*, London and New York: Routledge, 2002, pp. 35–54.

13. A. Lipietz, *Mirages and Miracles: The Crises of Global Fordism*, London: Verso, 1987.

14. G. Grabher and D. Stark, *Restructuring Networks in Post-Socialism: Legacies, Linkages and Localities*, Oxford: Oxford University Press, 2006.

15. J. Pickles and A. Smith, eds, *Theorizing Transition: The Political Economy of Postcommunist Transformations*, London and New York: Routledge, 1998.

16. P. Pavlinek and J. Pickles, *Environmental Transitions: Transformation and Ecological Defense in Central and Eastern Europe*, London and New York: Routledge, 2000.
17. See B. A. Cellarius, *In the Land of Orpheus: Rural Livelihoods and Nature Conservation in Postsocialist Bulgaria*, Madison: University of Wisconsin Press, 2004; G. Creed, *Domesticating Revolution: From Socialist Reform to Ambivalent Transition in a Bulgarian Village*, State College, PA.: The Pennsylvania State University Press, 1998; J. Pickles and A. Smith, eds, *Theorizing Transition: The Political Economy of Postcommunist Transformations*, London and New York: Routledge, 1998; A. Smith and A. Stenning, 'Beyond household economies: articulations and spaces of economic practice in post-socialism', *Progress in Human Geography*, 30(2), 2006, 190–213; and A. Smith, 'Informal work and the diverse economies of post-socialism', in E. Marcelli and C. Williams, eds, *The Informal Work of Developed Nations* (2007 forthcoming).
18. Å.B. Grødeland, 'Red Mobs', 'Yuppies', 'Lamb Heads' and Others: Contacts, Informal Networks and Politics in the Czech Republic, Slovenia, Bulgaria and Romania, *Europe-Asia Studies*, 59 (2), 2007, 217–52.
19. Every post-socialist citizen is aware of the significance of information and influence and the sheer necessity of mobilizing these contacts and informal networks in trying to be effective as a political or economic actor. See J. K. Gibson-Graham, *The End of Capitalism (as we know it): a feminist critique of political economy*, Oxford and New York: Blackwell, 1996; reprinted by the University of Minnesota Press, Minneapolis, 2006; A. Smith and A. Stenning, 'Beyond household economies: articulations and spaces of economic practice in post-socialism', *Progress in Human Geography*, 30(2), 2006, 190–213; A. Smith, 'Informal work and the diverse economies of post-socialism', in E. Marcelli and C. Williams, eds, *The Informal Work of Developed Nations* (2007 forthcoming).
20. For a parallel contemporary argument about the geographical specificity of universal Enlightenment claims to reason, see I. Buruma, *Murder in Amsterdam: the Death of Theo van Gogh and the Limits of Tolerance*, New York: Penguin Press, 2006.
21. I take the term 'territorialization of rule' from M. Biggs, 'Putting the state on the map: Cartography, Territory, and European State Formation', *Comparative Studies in Society and History*, 41(2), April 1999, 374–405.

# Part 1

# Economic Governance, the State and Varieties of Capitalism

# 2
# Leading Sectors and the Variety of Capitalism in Eastern Europe[*]

*Béla Greskovits*

## Introduction

State socialism is widely seen as a system that had been remarkably successful in creating and maintaining uniform economic and political structures and institutions in a large number of initially very different societies. From this perspective it is puzzling that, once the system fell apart, its pieces, which shared its unifying legacy as a point of departure and were exposed to the same exogenous shocks of the collapse, entered, in a patterned rather than random way, radically different trajectories of capitalist development. Thus, instead of a single post-socialist economy, diverse forms of capitalism have been emerging.

Focusing on the ten Eastern European member and candidate states of the EU, this chapter asks three questions. What is the pattern that these new capitalisms exhibit? What accounts for the emergence of variation? And what are the implications of these diverse outcomes for social conditions, macroeconomic stability, and developmental prospects? Earlier literature on the diverse experience of post-socialist countries pointed to the importance of initial political choices, the differences in institutional legacies or the orientation and preferences of domestic elite groups.[1] While these factors certainly mattered, my own contribution stresses the importance of the types of integration into global and European systems of production via particular *leading export sectors,* and explores how these industries shaped Eastern Europe's *transnational variety of capitalism.*[2] I define leading export sectors as major industry groups that share factor intensity, product character, and significantly contribute to exports.

In the second section, I identify the leading sectors that mark the European integration of the new Eastern European member and candidate economies. Briefly, the Visegrád countries export mainly cars, machinery and equipment, electrical and electronics products. In contrast, the Baltic States' and Southeastern Europe's leading sectors are textiles and apparel, footwear, wood and wood products, or agriculture, energy, mining, and steel and iron. Based on these specializations, I define four types of leading sector by the organization, ownership, and governance of their particular transnational production systems, and term them *heavy-basic, heavy-complex, light-complex, and light-basic* types. In the third section I investigate the *origins* of these four types and the *dynamics* of their emergence. In the fourth section, I characterize the four polar types of capitalist political economies rooted in the leading sectors by the origins of dominant transnational actors, links to their home and host economies, and by ownership, organization and governance forms. In the fifth section I analyse the *impact* of the above configurations on three aspects of the Europeanization of these new socioeconomic systems. Each is important for the ways in which it is shaping regionally and sectorally differentiated patterns of political and economic integration. a) How much do they facilitate the eastward extension of the European social model? b) How do they help to adopt the macroeconomic stability culture required by the Stability and Growth Pact and the European Monetary Union? And c) to what extent do they open up opportunities for industrial upgrading, for new models of a knowledge-based society, and states' capacity to assist these developments?

## Eastern Europe's specialization in the new European division of labour

It is often said that, as it enlarges, the EU becomes more not less heterogeneous in terms of the levels of economic and social development of its member states. Divergence in income per capita, social equity, work and living conditions has received a great deal of attention from academics and policy-makers. At the same time, it is also evident that, in another respect, the eastern and western parts of Europe have been converging. During the 1990s, the former socialist economies underwent a process of rapid and thorough internationalization. Between 1990 and 1999, average yearly growth of exports was 6.7 per cent with the bulk of exports increasingly being shipped to the EU-15 countries. Measured by the share of exports in GDP, Eastern

European states became as open as or even more open than the Western European countries. The proportion of foreign-owned banks in Central and Eastern Europe in 2000 exceeded 50 per cent, a degree of foreign penetration that is unprecedented in the west. These forms of economic integration (or penetration) were matched by foreign direct investment inflows to the candidate countries which, between 1989 and 2000, were equivalent to about 1200, USD per capita.[3]

**Production and export profiles, and leading sectors**

By 2003, post-socialist economies occupied markedly different positions in the emerging new European division of labour. To highlight these differences, I define a framework based on the factor intensity of production. First, I differentiate between production processes that are intensive in physical capital (e.g., buildings, productive infrastructure, machinery and equipment) and others which are not. Second, I separate human capital-intensive processes (relying on skilled and white-collar labour and research and development) from those that are less intensive. Combined, these attributes define a four-fold typology of production intensity. These are those that have: a) only physical capital, b) both physical and human capital, c) only human capital, and d) neither physical nor human capital, but unskilled labour. In the following, these factor-combinations are referred to respectively as a) heavy-basic, b) heavy-complex, c) light-complex, and d) light-basic profiles.

To give these profiles empirical content, I use typical factor intensities adapted from the EBRD's *Transition Report 1999*[4] and categorize each item in the 2-digit SITC export product classification as belonging to one of the above types. The resulting aggregates I term 'sectors'. In industry terms the heavy-basic sector is also resource-intensive and includes agriculture, mining, energy, and metallurgy. The heavy-complex sector includes car-manufacturing, airplane, ship-building, heavy machinery and equipment industries, and chemicals. The light-complex sector is exemplified by the electronics and electrical industries, and light machinery. Finally, the light-basic sector includes all the light industries, such as textiles and apparel, footwear, toys, wood, simple wood products and furniture. For any country and year, the sectors' size is given by aggregate export volumes relative to total exports. Finally, a sector is 'leading' if it contributes to 25 per cent or more of total exports. Table 2.1 reveals strong divergence in the sectors that lead the integration of East European countries into circuits of European and global economies.

*Table 2.1*   Leading sectors in Eastern Europe in 2003 (per cent of total exports)

| | Heavy-basic | Heavy-complex | Light-complex | Light-basic |
|---|---|---|---|---|
| **Visegrád states and Slovenia** | | | | |
| Hungary | 18 | 29 | 42 | 11 |
| Czech Republic | 27 | 32 | 25 | 16 |
| Slovak Republic | 30 | 40 | 13 | 17 |
| Slovenia | 26 | 27 | 25 | 22 |
| Poland | 32 | 31 | 15 | 22 |
| **Baltic and Southeastern European states** | | | | |
| Estonia | 29 | 15 | 22 | 34 |
| Lithuania | 37 | 24 | 11 | 28 |
| Romania | 27 | 15 | 12 | 46 |
| Bulgaria | 42 | 13 | 10 | 35 |
| Latvia | 26 | 7 | 9 | 58 |

*Source*: author's own calculation based on the COMTRADE database of the United Nations Statistics Division. Available from <http://intracen.org/tradestat/sitc3–3d>.

Heavy-basic industries are agriculture, oil, gas, electricity, coal, stone, non-ferrous metals, paper, rubber, plastic, ferrous metals (SITC-classification: 0, 1, 4, 22, 29, 21, 23, 25, 27, 28, 32–35, 64, 66–68).

Heavy-complex industries are chemicals (except pharmaceuticals), transport and heavy industrial machinery, railways, planes, etc. (SITC-classification: 50–59 excluding 54, 71, 73, 74, 78, 79).

Light-complex industries include pharmaceuticals, electronics, electrical, light machinery (SITC-classification: 54, 72, 75, 76, 77, 87, 88).

Light-basic industries include wood, simple wood products, textiles, clothes, footwear, furniture, etc. (24, 26, 60, 61, 63, 65, 80–85, 89). Adapted from EBRD *Transition Report* 1999: 179.

The integration of the Visegrád economies – the Czech Republic, Hungary, Poland, the Slovak Republic – and Slovenia is led either by both of the two more complex sectors or by at least one of them. Measured by the combined share of complex sectors, integration follows a clear-cut path in all these countries except Poland, where the share of complex sectors accounts for just less than half of total exports. In contrast, the integration paths of the Baltic states (Estonia, Latvia, Lithuania) and of Southeastern Europe (Bulgaria and Romania) are built on more basic industries. Neither the heavy nor the light variant of complex sectors could become leading in any of these countries, although the former came close to qualifying as a leading sector industry in Lithuania, and the latter in Estonia. With the exception of Hungary, the Visegrád states have a concentration in heavy sectors; the heavy-basic sector is leading in four countries, the light-basic sector is leading in none. In turn, the basic integration pattern in Estonia, Romania and Latvia is more on the light path, while in Lithuania and Bulgaria it is more on the heavy path.[5]

## The semi-core and the semi-periphery

Viewed in a global comparative context, the Visegrád countries export to the west what the west usually exports to 'the rest', while the export profiles of the Baltic and Southeastern European states resemble the pattern of less advanced countries. To paraphrase world-systems terminology, the Visegrád states seem to have adopted *semi-core* features.[6] Currently, there is only a handful of other relatively advanced developing countries that could join the elite club of major complex manufacturing exporters: five or six states in Southeast Asia, not more than three in Latin America, and none in all Africa. Therefore, it is important to stress how exceptional it is for reform economies to have such complex manufacturing export economies even if, for the time being, these are currently characterized by lower degrees of sophistication and skills than those in the developed western economies.

By contrast, the rest of the ex-socialist new member and candidate economies differ from the core economies not only in terms of the actual roles that go with their complex sectors, but also in terms of the relatively modest export contribution made by such industries. Unlike in the Visegrád states, even the relatively sizable heavy-complex and light-complex sectors of Lithuania and Estonia are rather 'one-dimensional' in the sense that the bulk of their output originates in a few industries or in a single industry (e.g., telecommunications assembly in Estonia). At the same time, even if their leading sectors are in the basic rather than the complex category, these countries are dominantly manufacturing exporters, which separates them from the major resource-intensive, that is *peripheral*, exporters of metals, oil, and cotton of the ex-Soviet Union (e.g., Kazakhstan, Azerbaijan, or Uzbekistan), which are not analysed in this study. Thus, as far as their export profile is concerned, the Baltic and Southeastern European states are *semi-peripheial*. Since any shift in the composition of manufacturing and exports from semi-peripheral to core status reflects a significant restructuring success, while semi-peripheral integration reflects a relative failure, it is important to understand why and how these successes and failures came about. Below I shall discuss the role of state socialist legacies, external factors and domestic policies in the divergence of the EU's newcomers' transnational integration.

## The dynamics of restructuring after the collapse of state socialism

Most analysts tended to explain the successes and failures of post-socialist economic transformation in terms of the policy choices that led to differences in the extent and effectiveness of economic liberalization, privatization, and market institution building in the 1990s. In contrast, the role of economic structural constraints and opportunities inherited from state socialism was usually considered less important. In the mainstream view, radical reformers were seen as the agents of success and gradualists or non-reformers were held responsible for failure.[7] Indeed, there was less debate on the actual developmental impact of market reforms – that was seen as largely uncontroversial – than on the political determinants of their implementation.[8] If marketization is the main path to economic development, then restructuring success and failure should closely reflect the degree to which economic liberalization, privatization, and market institution building have occurred. As a consequence, a high degree of institutional and policy convergence with the advanced economies should go hand in hand with improved positions in the European division of labour. Conversely, economies that are lagging behind in their export roles should be laggards in marketization too. However, in practice, it is surprising how little the available indicators of the results of market institution building support these hypotheses (Figure 2.1).

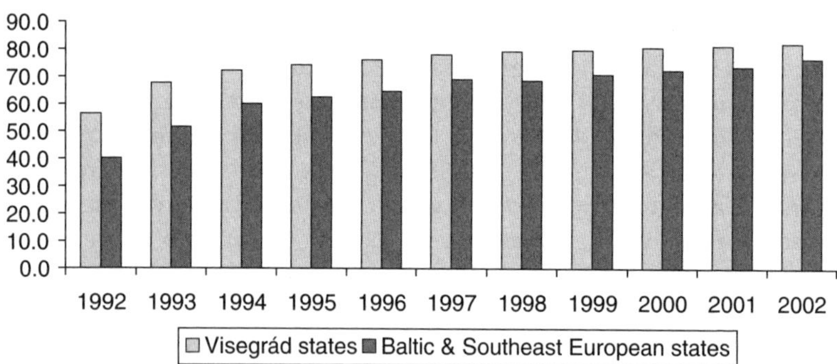


*Figure 2.1*   Average transition indicators (maximum=100)

*Source*: author's own calculation based on EBRD *Transition Reports*. Transition indicators measure advances in large- and small-scale privatization, price liberalization, foreign exchange and trade liberalization, competition policy, reform of banking sector, interest rates and non-banking financial institutions, and enterprise governance. EBRD grades the countries on these dimensions on a scale of 1–4.33. I calculated the averages for each country, and converted them into percentages where 100 per cent denotes a 'fully reformed', OECD-type, ex-socialist market economy.

Instead of divergence, by the early 2000s these measures show a great deal of *institutional similarity* between the Visegrád and the Baltic and Southeastern European group. The minor differences in the degree of reform fail to explain the much larger variation in the oucome of industrial restructuring. Instead, these data pose a puzzle: how can economies so similar in their institutional make-up still perform such radically different export roles in the single market? It is even more puzzling how states that all proved capable of initiating and implementing market-friendly policies and institutions can be so dissimilar in their ability to foster development through industrial restructuring.

## Thorough versus shallow paths of restructuring and transnational integration

To understand this puzzle it is important to recognize that in a market society states cannot restructure the economy on their own, but have to rely on economic actors. In concrete terms, 'much depends on how business-people react to the signals that government officials send: whether they invest and what they invest in'.[9] Success in Eastern European manufacturing industries ultimately depended on the decisions of western businesses to restructure by foreign direct investment (FDI) or by subcontracting production from eastern facilities and incorporating them into transnational systems of production. Such decisions greatly favoured the Visegrád economies over those in the rest of Eastern Europe, leading to significantly more FDI-led restructuring in the former than in the latter (Figure 2.2).

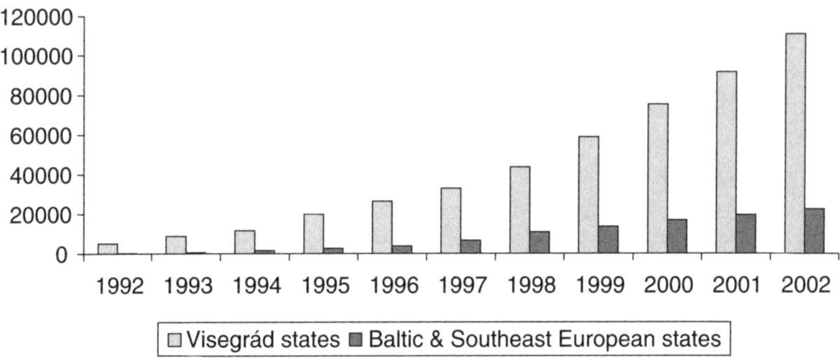


*Figure 2.2*   FDI stock (mln USD)

*Source*: author's own calculation based on EBRD Transition Reports, various volumes.

On the basis of the dramatically different magnitude of FDI attracted, the Visegrád economies seem to have followed a *thorough* path of transnational integration, while transnational integration in the Baltic and Southeastern European economies has been relatively *shallow*. To interpret these paths we have to better understand the main factors that motivated transnational business decisions as well as their dynamic interaction in the 1990s.

One way to learn about the motivation of foreign investors is to adapt product cycle theory to the conditions of FDI in post-Cold War Europe.[10] In this perspective, foreign direct 'investment will go first to those countries whose supply structures (proxied for example by factors of production) and demand structures (proxied for example by national income per capita) are most similar to those in the home country, and later to countries whose supply structures are less similar'.[11] Arguably, the initial export structure of the ex-socialist countries, and specifically the initial share of complex manufactures in total export, can serve as a good proxy for a congruent supply structure. Countries with a higher initial share of this kind of exports can be said to have *structural competitive advantages* over other countries.[12]

## Dynamic interplay of structural and institutional competitive advantages

Initially the Baltic and Southeastern European states did not significantly lag behind the Visegrád states in terms of complexity of their manufacturing industries. Although differences between individual national economies had existed in the early 1990s, from a structural viewpoint the Baltic and Southeastern European states had appeared to be competitive in attracting FDI. This is consistent with the findings of Csaba that in the COMECON division of labour the Baltic countries and the non-Soviet satellite states had exported significant volumes of complex manufactures to the (rest of) the USSR in exchange for energy, mining products, and basic manufacturing goods.[13] Consequently, while incongruent supply structures and the resulting initial structural disadvantages might have been important disincentives for FDI in most CIS countries, structural differences account for much less of the divergence within the 'west of the east'. In other words, at least in the western rim of Eastern Europe, structural congruence (and its absence) appears to be *as much the product as it is the cause* of FDI (Figure 2.3).

It is clear, however, that even the most congruent supply structure might fail to attract foreign investors in the absence of the kinds of *institutional* configurations that make it accessible and exploitable for

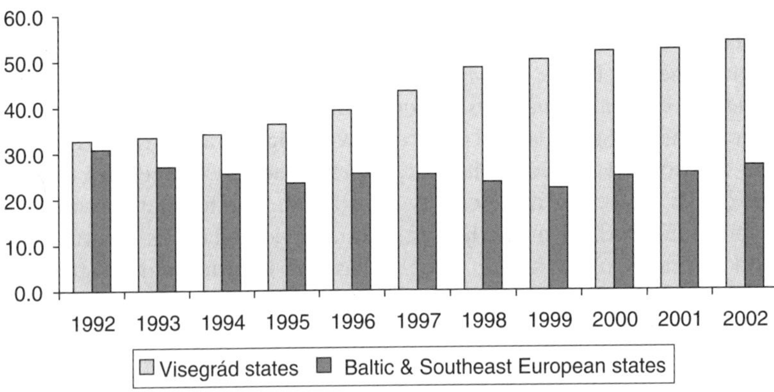



*Figure 2.3*   Complex exports (per cent of total exports)

*Source*: author's own calculation based on the COMTRADE database of the United Nations Statistics Division. See note to Table 2.1.

them. Countries that had gone further in removing the obstacles to foreign entry and in rebuilding their economic and political institutions by the time investment across the former Cold War borders was possible could develop *institutional competitive advantages* over other states. Clearly, in terms of initial institutional congruence with Western market democracies, the Visegrád group had been closer to the west than the rest of Eastern Europe (Figure 2.1). Interestingly, many of these advantages, including the originally more liberal regimes of foreign trade and foreign exchange, freer domestic prices, larger private sector, greater openness to FDI, longer traditions of subcontracting, and the earlier existence of a two-tier banking system, were no less the *inheritance of the Visegrád states' earlier market socialist experiments* than the structural advantages of relatively complex export sectors.

Thus, the proposition in much mainstream literature that the transition success stories resulted from rapid and radical market reforms, while the failures resulted from gradualist and cautious strategies, is not clearly confirmed by the data.[14] Instead, the majority of the Visegrád countries were able to build on the favourable institutional legacies of their long market-socialist experiments, while the Baltic and Southeastern European states had to build markets from scratch, an initial handicap that left its mark on their less convincing restructuring performance.

Notwithstanding their origins, the substantial initial institutional advantages of the Visegrád economies could indeed tilt the balance of investors' choices in their favour even if their competitors' economies had not yet been structurally disadvantaged. Thus, in the first years of transformation it was the *misfit between their relatively congruent supply structures and incongruent institutions* that propelled the semi-periphery onto paths that only later started to diverge significantly from those of the semi-core. However, this logic reversed itself by the second half of the 1990s, and even more clearly after 2000. Due to relatively radical reform efforts, the semi-periphery gradually worked off its institutional disadvantages and achieved a higher level of institutional congruence both with the west and with the Eastern European semi-core. However, this institutional catch-up seems to have been undervalued by foreign investors. Although FDI began to slowly enter the semi-periphery economies by the early 2000s, figures for accumulated FDI stock show that their integration into European networks continued to be relatively shallow (Figures 2.1, 2.2). What had gone wrong with restructuring in the semi-periphery?

Apparently, by the time these countries could work off their institutional disadvantages, *they had accumulated even more striking structural disadvantages*. If initially the Visegrád locations were preferred for their relative institutional advantages, in the subsequent period of increasing institutional convergence the same locations have been chosen for the substantial structural competitive advantages they acquired. That is, in the later years of transformation it is the *misfit between relatively congruent institutions and increasingly incongruent supply structures* that might account for the inferior restructuring performance of the semi-periphery.


### Further driving forces of divergence

There have been five additional meso- and micro-mechanisms that might have driven the dynamics of divergence: a) upgrading or atrophy of the complex sectors, b) the relative ease of adjustment in the basic sectors, c) disseminating technological and organizational knowledge, d) a 'follow the leader' phenomenon, and e) a 'follow the market/the user' phenomenon.

FDI allowed complex manufacturers in the Visegrád countries to gain access to the tangible and intangible factors of production needed to upgrade their activities and remain competitive even in the much more demanding single market. In contrast, deprived of the means of upgrading and restructuring because of an initial lack of FDI, the same sectors in the semi-periphery countries could not withstand the intense competition to which their radical efforts at marketization exposed them. These sectors lost large parts of their markets, factors of production, and policy influence.

Radical marketization also revealed the comparative advantages of the heavy-basic and light-basic sectors. In their World Bank/UNDP study of trade in the CIS countries, Michalopoulos and Tarr argue that:

> Adjustment is generally easier in labor- and natural resources-intensive industries…The more standardized nature of products in resource-based industries makes trade-reorientation easier. These goods rely on local raw materials, and therefore suffer least from trade disruption with the former Soviet Union. Minor changes in packaging or quality are often enough to meet Western standards.[15]

Similarly, trade liberalization that made cheap local labour accessible to foreign firms looking for transnational subcontractors helped the rapid adjustment of the light-basic sectors.

In considering the variety of patterns of FDI in Eastern Europe, Eichengreen and Kohl asked 'why countries differ in their ability to attract DFI and engage in technologically sophisticated OPT [Outward Processing Trade]'. Part of their answer is that 'higher-tech DFI and OPT, once started, have worked to disseminate technological and organizational knowledge and to attract additional DFI and OPT in a self-reinforcing circle'.[16]

Contributing to the persistence and strength of the above virtuous circles has been a more general transnational corporate strategy of 'follow the leader'. This strategy has been observed in all of the Visegrád countries and essentially means that transnational firms follow their competitors to new production locations while the first investors try to fend off further newcomers in part by enlarging their already existing facilities.[17] While their intensity might have differed in various industries, both strategies contributed to a self-propelling process of accumulating FDI in the originally preferred locations.

Moreover, major investors have been followed not only by competitors but also by suppliers, especially when major firms revealed their commitment to the new location by making substantial investments. This development highlights an important inter-sectoral relationship. To the extent that heavy-complex FDI (such as automotive industries) is increasing, it can provide expanding and relatively stable domestic markets for light-complex (such as electrical and electronics) suppliers.

# Sectoral variety of capitalist political economies

Which are the typical economic actors that have been empowered or disempowered by the divergent trajectories of transnationalization, restructuring, and economic development? Based on my earlier work, I differentiate among four contrasting types of post-socialist capitalist political economy by the origins, ownership, organization, and governance of dominant actors, their external and domestic links, and pattern of interaction.[18]

## Heavy-basic political economy

As a result of state-socialist forced industrialization most of the ex-socialist countries started their transnational integration path as heavy-basic political economies. This is the type that preserved many of the structural features of state socialism well into the 1990s. Each typically supplies standardized goods to oligopolistic world markets. Relative to other types, transnational production sharing is less advanced and less sophisticated. The type is dominated by large firms and large plants, specific equipment and infrastructure, which are less readily adapted to new productive activities. Hence these firms tend to experience difficulty and incur high costs in responding to market shifts in both the short and the long run. Typical owners and operators range from state managers to members of the domestic grand bourgeoisie, although by the late 1990s the role of foreign strategic owners became more pronounced, particularly in Slovakia, Bulgaria, and Romania. These heavy-basic political economies are characterized by organized and concentrated forces of unskilled labour, or workers with very specific skills that cannot be easily employed in other activities.

## Heavy-complex political economy

This political economy is transnationally controlled by the integrators – usually leading transnational corporations – on what Gereffi terms 'producer-driven global commodity chains' (PDC).[19] The core controlling component of this chain, the R&D unit, usually remains in the western home country, although by the late 1990s more and more R&D units were relocated to the Visegrád countries. The TNCs also maintained full equity-based control (typically 100 per cent ownership) over other core activities, e.g., final assembly plants, or manufacturing of crucial components, even if they were moved to the east.[20]

More labour- and less skill-intensive activities, e.g., parts production, are often subcontracted, but in Eastern Europe this usually goes to the first tier of foreign contract-manufacturers who followed the integrator to the new location. While domestic business may enter the peripheral tiers of the chain, ownership and control remain heavily foreign-dominated. Much of the workforce is relatively skilled, and in the core units occasionally trained and re-trained in-house. Labour organization is relatively strong, although some TNCs do not tolerate unions. Given their high fixed costs in large physical and human capital investments, the dominant actors of heavy-complex capitalism are relatively 'settled' and immobile across borders.

## Light-complex political economy

This type is either transnationally integrated by PDCs of the above type, or controlled by major contract manufacturer TNCs, acting as integrators of global commodity chains. The governance of the latter type of firms is closer to Gereffi's 'buyer–driven chains' (BDC).[21] Relative to the heavy-complex variant three differences occur. First, while PDC-type integrators own their local plants in this type as well, contract manufacturers often use non-equity-based methods of control, such as control of fashion design units, market access, or input channels. Second, in this type domestic capital has better chances to enter the production system even in relatively sophisticated roles. For example, in the Hungarian electrical and electronics industries a division of labour emerged between major TNCs and large-scale domestic businesses. Attracted by low labour costs and generous subsidies, TNCs relocated labour-intensive production segments to Hungary, while many domestic firms became their subcontractors or labour contractors. They supply their clients products, infrastructure, and often even plants equipped with either workers, or machinery, or both.[22] Third, for the generally less massive investment needs, the dominant transnational actors are less settled and more mobile across boundaries than in the heavy-complex type.

## Light-basic political economy

With respect to capital mobility the light-basic type is the extreme case since its transnational integrators are 'nomadic', that is characterized by very high cross-border mobility. Organization exhibits the features of the buyer-driven global commodity chains, 'where large retailers, branded marketers, and trading companies play the pivotal role in setting up decentralized production networks'.[23] Control is transnational, non-equity-based, and rests on privileged or monopolized access to markets, marketing, and fashion-design shops typically located in the integrators' western home countries. BDC-integrators rarely own production facilities in Eastern Europe; thus local investment is minimal and fixed costs are low. Production is partly or wholly subcontracted to many small or medium-size domestic firms, which employ large, fragmented, low-paid, usually female, labour forces. Typically, domestic capital is forced into cut-throat competition in prices and costs, and has little alternative to sweating workers. However, recent research on the textiles and apparel industries indicates that the prospects for upgrading are not uniformly bleak; rather countries perform differently in this respect.[24]

## The European social model in the east: Capitalisms with and without compromise[25]

Eastern Europeans expected that their countries' 'return to Europe' would help to bring their work and living standards closer to EU levels. Therefore, the extent to which the varieties of Eastern European capitalism are likely to facilitate the eastward extension of the European social model denotes a crucial aspect of these social systems. Europeanists defined the European social model as 'a specific combination of comprehensive welfare systems and strongly institutionalized and politicized forms of industrial relations', and often trace it to the postwar *historical compromise between capital and labour.*[26] How likely is it that the post-socialist variants of capitalism combine capital willing to accept and labour strong enough to press for a compromise?

Earlier literature identified the same attributes, intensity in physical and human capital, which constitute the meso-foundation of the above four ideal types, to be relevant both for capital's propensity to do a deal with workers, and for labour strength.

On the one hand, businesses' willingness for a compromise depends on how significant labour is for them as a *factor of production.* First, in his seminal article on the social bases of the second New Deal, Ferguson contrasts automated industries where labour cost is but a tiny fraction of total cost with the labour-intensive industries. He proposes that businessmen in the latter type 'could not afford higher social insurance, could not pay higher wages, could not accept a union. Where the workforce was already organized, they could not resist the pressure to attempt to undermine it. And a legislated minimum wage would usually constitute a direct threat to them'.[27] Second, in industries where competitiveness heavily depends on the *human capital* embodied in white-collar and skilled labour, employers are more likely to 'see benefits accruing to businesses from … an institutionalized system of labor relations, and from general conditions of good health, education, and living arrangements'.[28]

On the other hand, intensity in physical and human capital also affects two important factors of labour strength: the capacity for *collective action* and *market position*. First, as Shafer observes, workers' collective action is easier in capital-intensive industries where a few large firms employ concentrated labour forces with specific skills. 'Although distributional issues divide them, labour and management have grounds to cooperate.'[29] In contrast, '[c]ollective action by firms and workers is unlikely' in labour-intensive industries typically characterized by many small or medium size firms, which 'draw unskilled workers from mixed communities and employ them in tiny, dispersed sweatshops under the supervision of owners adamantly opposed to labour organization'.[30] Silver highlights another aspect of the industrial bases of workers' collective action capacities. For the vertical integration and the continuous flow of the production process in Fordist auto industry, workers could easily 'exploit their position within the complex division of labour … just a militant minority could stop production in an entire plant'.[31] In contrast, in the textile industry, where 'firms were small in size and production was vertically disintegrated … the damage done had no significant impact'.[32] Second, generally one can expect tighter labour markets for skilled than for unskilled workers, which enhances skilled labour's strength. Clearly, in the world of transnational production, cross-border capital mobility effectively counters even skilled labour's marketplace bargaining power. However, as mentioned above, businesses are *not uniformly mobile.* Rather, because of the associated fixed costs, their mobility is likely to be inversely related to their local investments in physical and human capital. In sum, high intensity in physical and human capital, and relative capital immobility stemming from it, predicts both capital's propensity, and labour's capacity, for a deal. Conversely, low intensity in physical and human capital, and its implication, high capital mobility, are likely to undermine business interest and labour capacity for a compromise.

These factors are not randomly distributed across the four ideal types but turn some of them, in the words of Hirschman, into 'a multi-dimensional conspiracy in favor' of, and others against, a compromise between capital and labour.[33] In concrete terms, the heavy-complex type which is intensive in both immobile physical and human capital is the more likely to produce the socioeconomic foundations of some kind of *solidaristic capitalism*. Its opposite the light-basic type, which is characterized by low physical and human capital intensity, and high cross-border mobility, produces *capitalism without compromise*. Ranking the two intermediate cases is no easy task, and may depend on many other factors, among them inter-sectoral relationships. For example, as indicated in the third section, the strong presence of a heavily invested 'settled' road vehicle industry might moderate the relatively high capital mobility of electrical and electronics industries (such as in the case of Hungary).

Sectoral features may have implications for the pattern of industrial relations, e.g., union density and collective bargaining coverage as well. Capital and skill intensity can indicate whether the dominant level of wage bargaining is at the intersectoral, sectoral, or company level. Furthermore, they are suggestive of the degree to which unions could recover from their initial weakness inherited from state socialism and exacerbated by the transformational recession.[34]

Finally, the propensity for a capital – labour compromise can predict workers' varied exposure to 'risks of illness, accident, aging, and the capriciousness of markets' and of unemployment, and their resulting demands for private and public remedies.[35] In general, this demand should be more pressing in capitalisms without compromise. However, to better understand Eastern European capitalisms' capacity to develop a European social model, it is also important to consider the impact of their constitutive features on the 'supply side' of available remedies, most importantly the pressure they might put on the existing, more or less robust, *welfare states* inherited from state socialism.[36] Although this is too complex an issue to be fully analysed in this essay, a few general propositions can be formulated. First, the path leading to heavy-complex capitalism may initially be very costly for the protection of *infant industries* (tax reliefs, customs protection, direct and indirect subsidies) offered, for example, to powerful automobile TNCs. This is especially the case in the climate of intense competition for these kinds of investments that is prevalent in Eastern Europe.

Moreover, the leading export businesses employ a relatively small fraction of the total labour force. Thus, while in the form of better wages, work conditions, job security, firm- and sector-based bonuses, leading sector labour may gain from the capital – labour compromise, the high costs of raising the 'infant' transplants are socialized. In extreme cases, the associated fiscal burden may undercut the welfare provisions provided to the rest of society, pensioners, marginalized minorities, and unemployed, and provoke strong discontent in their ranks.[37] The situation is even worse in the heavy-basic political economy. To the extent that a compromise within the leading sector emerges, it may result in a multi-class pressure group whose primary aim is to maintain inefficient firms, output, exports, and employment by protecting *sunset industries*.[38] In the extreme case, it is the least vocal and most marginalized groups of society who suffer most heavily. Despite state aid, the limited viability of such declining industries usually does not allow them to protect their own workers in the longer run.

Rather than the society at large, it is mainly the leading sector workers themselves who pay the costs in the light types of transnational capitalism in which competitiveness depends on high *labour-market flexibility*. These costs include precarious forms of employment, low wages, substandard work conditions, and job insecurity. Thus, in these types, pressures on the welfare state originate more in the social risks to which workers are exposed than directly in the crippling fiscal burden of infant-industry or sunset-industry protection. However, the light-complex and light-basic types are less likely to be trapped in the jobless growth pattern that often persists in the other two types. Instead, they tend to create more jobs but often of inferior quality. As a result, states have more autonomy to decide whether or not to remedy social risk exposure by retraining assistance, subsidized job creation, or temporary public works programs.


## European monetary integration in the east: The first shall be the last?[39]

How do the variants of East European capitalism perform in importing the *macroeconomic stability culture* fostered by the Stability and Growth Pact and the EMU?[40] Their performance seems no less varied than their potential to develop some aspects of the European social model. This is due to the varied forms and intensity of distributional conflicts exacerbated by the policies of preparation for EMU membership: currency appreciation, disinflation, high interest rates and fiscal austerity. Consistent with Frieden's sectoral approach, EMU's stability culture best fits the policy preferences of the dominant foreign players of the heavy-complex type and the needs of light-basic actors. Typically, the most important European TNCs, which also penetrated the Visegrád economies, export 'specialized and differentiated products in which quality, service and consumer loyalty – things related to market share – matter'. While these exporters are 'less likely to want a weak exchange rate and more likely to value currency stability', their preference for a stable currency is further buttressed by their need for predictability in their operations as major transnational investors.[41] At the same time, the fiscal austerity measures required for meeting the Maastricht criteria hardly touch their infant-industry subsidies. Therefore, they can afford neutrality in the intense political struggles around the budget deficit and government debt.

Quite to the contrary, most sensitive to nominal exchange rate levels are the exporters who sell 'in highly competitive markets' highly 'standardized products such as commodities, clothing, footwear and steel' (ibid.). However, exchange rate sensitivity is only a part of the reasons for their discomfort with the terms forced upon them by the preparations for EMU. In general, it is the *domestic members* rather than the foreign integrators of Eastern Europe's transnational systems of production who suffer most from currency appreciation, high interest rates, and disinflation. The core TNCs can compensate for the negative impact of appreciating currency either by forcing less favourable contractual terms onto domestic suppliers or by moving production to lower- cost locations.[42] Given their preference for financing trade or investment by euro-loans from their transnational 'house banks', the integrators are hardly affected by the high domestic interest rates either. In contrast, their domestic suppliers and subcontractors can less easily squeeze others (except their employees) or relocate (although the largest domestic contract manufacturers, such as the Hungarian electronics firm VIDEOTON, seem to 'follow their markets'). Usually domestic suppliers have to cope with the extra costs of increasing exchange and interest rates on their own. Similar is the situation of major domestic commodity and basic producers and traders who intensively use physical but not human capital.

National politics also influences various political economies' capacity to adopt the European stability culture. In some countries where the export economy is dominated by powerful 'anti-stability' actors, the competitive political system (as in Hungary) or the popularity of euro-sceptic parties (as in Poland) paved the way towards highly politicized distributional conflicts. In Hungary these struggles have been led by the *labour-intensive fraction of national export-bourgeoisie,* and have effectively undermined the prospects for a fast entry to EMU.[43] However, in other countries, which by the profile of their export economy seem no less predestined for similar distributional struggles, institutional factors, e.g., the currency boards of Estonia, Lithuania, and Bulgaria, or a social pact in Slovenia, have tamed the conflicts and facilitated the adoption of stability culture. Given these countries' semi-peripheral status, it remains to be seen how far the current outstanding macroeconomic performance is sustainable, especially if pressures for real convergence intensify. Ironically, EMU politics seems to have changed the performance ranking of Eastern Europe's capitalisms. *The first shall be the last* in the sense that the Visegrád countries, that had been widely considered as the front-runners of transformation, have become laggards in the race for the EMU and seem to have the biggest troubles with adopting its stability culture.

## Prospects for industrial upgrading and a knowledge-based society

After the collapse of state socialism Eastern Europe's inherited human capital (skills, R&D and innovation capacities, managerial and marketing networks and knowledge) *partly atrophied, partly became incorporated* into more or less promising functions and roles into human capital-intensive trans-European production systems. Which are the opportunities for further industrial upgrading and human capital-intensive development? In this process, what roles are played by states with their different levels of power to address countervailing social forces, with their own interests? In particular, to what extent are states operating as agents of restructuring and of a shift towards human capital-intensive development? I shall argue below that this capacity varies across the polar types of Eastern Europe's transnational capitalism.[44]

*Captured states*

In a heavy-basic political economy *the state is likely to become captured by a defensive and protectionist coalition* of the national heavy bourgeoisie and, as a junior member, their concentrated and organized labour. Under increasing competitive pressures these groups, whose hold on power stems less from entrepreneurship and flexibility than from a monopoly over natural resources, domestic capital sources, and sunset-industry subsidies, are threatened by foreign penetration and takeovers. Consequently, while liberalization, marketization, and privatization to privileged domestic owners might be consistent with their interests, they are likely to *vehemently oppose and resist any dramatic shift in their states' industrial and restructuring strategies.* In concrete, for reasons of traditionally close relations with state bureaucracy and strong capacity for collective action, they are in a good position to prevent a significant shift from sunset-industry protection to infant-industry protection and other policies fostering R&D, innovation, training and retraining. Effectively countering such adjustments, as well as TNCs' demands for more predictable and transparent legal – institutional – regulatory environment, they often succeeded in forcing foreign competitors to the sidelines in their own sector as well as other sectors of the economy. If this occurs, it leads to delays or deadlocks in restructuring and, in the extreme case, to a *post-socialist developmental trap.*

### Flexible developmental states localizing the global and globalizing the local

States in heavy-complex and light-complex political economies have fair chances to bring together, in a *coalition for industrial upgrading* and human capital-intensive development, transnational big business, domestic capital, white-collar labour, and professionals. As observed by Ó Riain in the Irish case, such coalitions are supportive to two kinds of developmental state roles and institutions. Flexible developmental states either attempt to *'localise the global'* by 'building local networks around global capital', or to *'globalise the local'* by 'taking local innovation networks global'.[45] The first opportunity seems to fit more the conditions of a heavy-complex, and the second the circumstances of a light-complex political economy. States can also combine these strategies in political economies that display both sectoral configurations simultaneously.

In a heavy-complex political economy, the PDC-integrators, who tend to fully control core operations, might be more ready to share control with national actors in peripheral (and typically smaller-scale) activities. Over time, these TNCs and the foreign suppliers who followed them to the new location will tend to outsource specific segments of production and service and thereby foster domestic firms' flexible specialization within their transnational systems. Furthermore, the high fixed costs of massive investment predict a permanent presence of large TNCs and their foreign networks in the host country, which in turn may improve state bureaucracies' position when bargaining with the 'domesticated' TNCs for enhanced labour training and re-training, transfer of technology, and managerial knowledge.[46] Conversely, by financial, organizational, and regulatory assistance, states may improve national businesses' own capacity for innovative sourcing, market research, marketing and design, and help them to enter the transnational networks in a position of relative strength.

The latter policies are also available to states in light-complex political economies. Moreover, this configuration may create especially favourable conditions for activities that are unintensive in physical but very intensive in human capital, such as the software industry. Domestic professional networks as well as highly skilled white-collar domestic labour trained and employed in TNCs can become an important source of entrepreneurial spin-offs. With state assistance, professionals and small knowledge-based firms can more easily maintain and develop connections to the global cutting edge in their field and reproduce, at internationally competitive standards, the national bourgeois element within, or connected to, the transnational light complexes. While the promising outcomes of the above type are far from granted, it seems easier for states to become agents of human capital-intensive development in complex political economies than in either of the basic types.

*Cornered states*

In a light-basic political economy the state is likely to be *cornered by a coalition of hyper-mobile transnational business with small-and medium-scale domestic capital* that is highly dependent on the opportunities to serve the former as subcontractor or labour contractor. Members of this coalition are tied together by their reliance on low-cost flexible production and its preconditions, e.g., low-wage unskilled labour, union-free environment, and flexible labour markets that allow maximum freedom in hiring, firing, and exploiting workers. Under competitive and restructuring pressures, mobile light-basic BDCs can easily decide to leave the national economy at little loss, since they are free from high fixed costs in physical and human capital. However, for their domestic subcontractors the exodus of their essential buyer-supplier contacts results in hard times. The more so because these kinds of transnational production systems might generally bring little in terms of training and knowledge transfer. To the contrary, earlier relationships with local and foreign suppliers, designers, wholesale and retail outlets may atrophy, leading to skill-deterioration, not upgrading.[47] Constrained by capital mobility, and at the same time by the limited and weakened developmental capabilities of national businesses, a state's role varies between damage control measures in case of massive capital flight and a peculiar type of a competition state whose developmental capacity is exhausted by the permanent effort to keep 'nomadic' BDC-integrators on board. At the extreme, the latter option may result in *a neoliberal developmental trap*: the consolidation of low wages, anti-labour regulation of industrial relations, poor work conditions, and ultimately a degradation of human capital. Alternatively, heightened competition may force local capital to upgrade their activities and expand to higher value-added segments of commodity chains.[48]

## Conclusion

I defined four variants of East European capitalism by their propensities for social compromise, macroeconomic stability, and industrial restructuring and upgrading, bounded by particular transnational leading sectors. As far as the solidaristic features of these capitalisms are concerned, I argued that these depend on the extent to which the leading sectors are likely to host a capital – labour compromise. Similarly, I tried to trace these capitalisms' macroeconomic stability to the emergence and sustainability of the required alliances among financial technocracies, business, and labour – all shaped by leading sector configuration and mediated by politics. Finally, I demonstrated how leading sector profiles strengthen or weaken Eastern European states' capacity to assist and contribute to human capital-intensive development.

So far I tried to advance these propositions at the level of polar types defined by just one sector. Limits of the present analysis should be noted. First, a more sophisticated analysis would require concepts about the interaction of several leading (and non-leading) sectors. To develop such concepts is the task of future research. Second, so far this concept can tell more about cleavages, likely policy preferences, clashes, compromises, constraints, risks, and opportunities, than actual outcomes. To judge about outcomes, concrete research questions have to be asked and answered in the particular political contexts of individual countries or country-groups. In this essay, my primary aim was to hint at the diverse contexts in which the transnational sectoral approach to the variety of Eastern European capitalism can be helpful. Before briefly summarizing my main propositions (Table 2.2), let me point out that neither the leading sectors that I defined, nor the variation of developmental trajectories, seem to be uniquely and exclusively Eastern European and post-socialist. Rather these sectors seem

*Table 2.2*   The variety of Eastern European capitalism

| Intensity in human capital | Semi-periphery | Semi-core | Semi-core | Semi-periphery |
|---|---|---|---|---|
| Intensity in physical capital | Heavy | Heavy | Light | Light |
| Variety of capitalism | Heavy-basic | Heavy-complex | Light-complex | Light-basic |
| Polar cases | Bulgaria | Slovak Republic | Hungary | Latvia/Romania |
| Major industries | Energy/ Steel and iron | Cars | Electrical/ Electronics | Wood/textiles and garment |
| Governance | State, national grand bourgeoisie | Transnational PDC | Transnational PDC/BDC | Transnational BDC, national petit bourgeoisie |
| Labour | Organized, defensive | Organized, accommodating | Skilled unorganized | Unskilled unorganized |
| Proximity to the European social model | Capitalism with unsustainable limited compromise | Capitalism with sustainable limited compromise | Capitalism with limited compromise | Capitalism without compromise |
| Transnational integration | Shallow | Thorough | Thorough | Shallow |
| Industry upgrading | Post-socialist developmental trap | Fair chances | Fair chances | Neoliberal developmental trap |
| State capacity to foster development | Captured state | Flexible developmental state | Flexible developmental state | Cornered state |

no less important in less advanced economies in other parts of the world: car manufacturing in Mexico, Brazil, South Africa, and Spain; electronics in Malaysia and Ireland; textiles and clothing in the Caribbean, Turkey and Portugal. It is the task of cross-regional comparative research to specify the extent to which the post-socialist pattern is but a variant subordinated to a general logic of late development.

In conclusion, there are reasons to doubt that the advanced societies evidently represent the future of less advanced economies either in a west-east context or specifically within the group of Eastern European new EU members and membership candidates. Rather, the shifts from less to more promising developmental trajectories are likely to pose serious challenges even after enlargement.

First, ironically, while the semi-peripheral states could surely attract more foreign investment had they more congruent supply structures, one cannot expect the foreign investors themselves to create the structural conditions of their relocation to the semi-periphery.

Second, while proper state policies are likely to be important, it is doubtful whether further marketization alone can bring about a breakthrough, especially in the light of already thorough marketization *without* industrial upgrading.

Third, I argued that state capacity to foster industrial upgrading and human capital-intensive development is, at least partly, subject to transnational leading sector constraints. State policies cannot readily substitute for the absent developmental capacity of economic actors. Instead, the less advanced the economy the likelier is it that the *state itself becomes part of the developmental problem* rather than its solution.

Given these difficulties, similar to Thomas Carothers' recent assessment of Third Wave democracies, I consider the variants of East European capitalism as *fairly permanent and self-sustaining configurations*, which for the foreseeable future represent 'a state of normality for many societies, for better or worse'.[49]

## Endnotes

* I presented an earlier version of the essay at the workshop 'Transition Process and Variety of Capitalism in the European Union. The Socio-Economic Models of the Central and Eastern European Countries' organized by GERPISA International Network on March 3–4 2005 in Paris. I am thankful to Bruno Amable, Bernard Chavance, Attila Havas, Yannick Lung, and other participants of the workshop, as well as Dorothee Bohle and Dieter Plehwe, for helpful comments and criticisms.

1. G. Eyal, I. Szelényi and E. Townsley, *Making Capitalism Without Capitalists. The New Ruling Elites in Eastern Europe*, London and New York: Verso, 1998; D. Stark and L. Bruszt, *Postsocialist Pathways: Transforming Politics and Property in East Central Europe*, Cambrige: Cambridge University Press, 1998; EBRD *Transition Reports 1994, 1999, 2000, 2001*, European Bank for Reconstruction and Development; V. Bunce, *Subversive Institutions. The Design and the Destruction of Socialism and the State*, Cambridge M. A., Cambridge University Press, 1999.

2. I borrow this term from D. Plehwe, 'Varieties of Transnational Capitalism?' paper presented at the 15th EGOS-Colloquium, Warwick, 1999. For the original application to Eastern Europe see Bohle (2000). In general, sectoral approaches focus on how major industries affect societal cleavages, state policies and politics (J. Kurth, 'The Political Consequences of the Product

Cycle: Industrial History and Political Outcomes', *International Organization*, 33(1), Winter 1979, 1–34; P. Gourevitch, *Politics in Hard Times*, Ithaca and London: Cornell University Press, 1986; J. Frieden, 'Classes, Sectors, and Foreign Debt in Latin America', *Comparative Politics*, October 1988, 1–20; J. Frieden, 'Invested Interests: the Politics of National Economic Policies in a World of Global Finance', *International Organization*, 45(4), Autumn 1991, 425–51; L. Sklair, *Assembling for Development: The Maquiladora Industry in Mexico and the United States*, London: Unwin Hyman, 1989; M. Shafer, *Winners and Losers. How Sectors Shape the Developmental Prospects of States*, Ithaca: Cornell University Press, 1994; G. Gereffi, 'Mexico's "Old" and "New" Maquiladora Industries: Contrasting Approaches to North American Integration', G. Otero, ed., *Neoliberalism Revisited*, Boulder, CO.: Westview Press, 1996, 85–105; T. Karl, *The Paradox of Plenty. Oil Booms and Petro-States*, Berkeley and Los Angeles: University of California Press, 1997. Recently, several collections of sectoral studies dealt with the role of electronics, machine tools, automobiles and other complex industries in advanced countries, and in the enlarging EU (J. Hollingsworth, P. Schmitter, and W. Streeck, *Governing Capitalist Economies. Performance and Control of Economic Sectors*, New York, Oxford: Oxford University Press, 1994; J. Zysman and A. Schwartz, *Enlarging Europe: The Industrial Foundations of a New Political Reality*, Berkeley and Los Angeles: University of California Press, 1998).
3.  EBRD *Transition Report 2002*, European Bank for Reconstruction and Development, p. 68.
4.  EBRD *Transition Report 1999*, European Bank for Reconstruction and Development, p. 179.
5.  Four countries specialize so heavily in one or another of the leading sectors that their cases easily lend themselves as empirical reference points for the elaborations of this paper as well as for future in-depth research. 'Heavy-metal' Bulgaria is an extreme case of the heavy-basic type given that energy, steel and iron, non-ferrous metallurgy and other industries that once formed state socialism's ' heavy core' still account for 42 per cent of its total exports. In 'VW-country' Slovakia heavy-complex industries, mostly automobiles, account for the largest sector of its kind in our sample: its size is 40 per cent. Hungary, which is often dubbed 'the general electric' country (both for the major role played by General Electric investments, and for the diverse array of exported electronics and electrical products), is the light-complex extreme case with a 42 per cent concentration. Finally, Europe's 'clothing (sweat)shop' Romania with 46 per cent of mainly garment and textiles share, and Latvia with a 58 per cent specialization in wood and garment industries, exhibit the light-basic polar type.
6.  I. Wallerstein, *The Capitalist World-Economy. Essays by Immanuel Wallerstein*, Cambridge University Press & Editions de la Maison des Sciences de l'Homme, 1979; F.H. Cardoso and E. Faletto, *Dependency and Development in Latin America*, Berkeley and Los Angeles: University of California Press, 1979.
7.  M. De Melo, C. Denizer, and A. Gelb, 'From Plan to Market. Patterns of Transition', Policy Research Working Paper 1564, Washington DC: The World Bank, 1996; M. De Melo, C. Denizer, A. Gelb, and S. Tenev, *Circumstance and Choice: The Role of Initial Conditions and Policies in Transition Economies*,

Washington DC: The World Bank: IFC, October 1997; M. Lavigne, 'Ten Years of Transition: A Review Article', *Communist and Post-Communist Studies*, 33, 2000, 475–83.

8. S. Fish, 'The Determinants of Economic Reform in the Post-Communist World', *East European Politics and Societies*, 12(1), 1998, 31–78; J. Hellman, 'Winners Take All. The Politics of Partial Reform in Postcommunist Transitions', *World Politics*, 50, 1998, 203–34.

9. E. Silva, 'Business Elites, the State, and Economic Change in Chile', in S. Maxfield and B. Schneider, eds, *Business and the State in Developing Countries*, Cornell Studies in Political Economy, Ithaca: Cornell University Press, 1997, 152–90 (p. 153).

10. R. Vernon, *Sovereignty at Bay: The Multinational Spread of U. S. Enterprises*, New York: Basic Books, 1971.

11. J. Kurth, 'The Political Consequences of the Product Cycle: Industrial History and Political Outcomes', *International Organization*, 33(1), Winter 1979, 1–34 (pp. 3–4).

12. Another aspect of structural competitive advantage, more important for those investors who target the domestic rather than foreign markets, is congruent demand structure. Initial demand structures had been more congruent with the west in the wealthier ex-socialist states where the recession following the systemic collapse had been milder too.

13. L. Csaba, *Kelet-Európa a világgazdaságban* (Eastern Europe in the world economy), K. J. K.: Budapest, 1984.

14. World Bank, *World Development Report 1996*, Washington DC: The World Bank/Oxford University Press, 1996.

15. C. Michalopoulos and G. Tarr, eds, *Trade in the New Independent States*, The World Bank/UNDP: Washington DC, 1994, pp. 127–8.

16. B. Eichengreen and R. Kohl, 'The External Sector, the State and Development in Eastern Europe', BRIE Working Paper 12, 1998. http://brie.berkeley. edu/~briewww/pubs/wp/wp128.htm (p. 2).

17. R. Vernon and L. T. Wells, Jr, *Economic Environment of International Business*, Prentice-Hall, inc.: Englewood Cliffs, New Jersey, 1981.

18. B. Greskovits, 'Beyond Transition: The Variety of Post-Socialist Development', in R. Dworkin *et al.*, eds, *From Liberal Values to Democratic Transition*, Budapest: Central European University Press, 2003, 201–25.

19. G. Gereffi, 'Global Production Systems and Third World Development', in B. Stallings, ed., *Global Change, Regional Response*, Cambridge: Cambridge University Press, 1997, 100–42 (p. 115).

20. R. Van Tulder and W. Ruigrok, 'European Cross-National Production Networks in the Auto Industry: How Eastern Europe is Becoming the Low End of European Car Complexes', paper presented at the Berkeley Roundtable on International Economy, 1997, http://www.ciaonet.org/conf/bri01/ bri01eb.html.

21. Gereffi, op. cit., p. 116.

22. D. Bohle and B. Greskovits, 'Capitalism Without Compromise? Strong Business and Weak Labor in Central-Eastern Europe's New Transnational Industries', *Studies in Comparative International Development*, Spring 2006.

23. Gereffi, op. cit., p. 116.

24. See A. Smith, R. Begg, M. Bucek, and J. Pickles, 'Global trade, European integration and the restructuring of Slovak apparel exports', *Ekonomicky*

*casopis* (Slovak *Journal of Economics*), 51(6), 2003, 731–48, and E. D. Yoruk, 'Patterns of Industrial Upgrading in the Clothing Industry in Poland and Romania', University College London, School of Slavonic & East European Studies, Centre For the Study of Economic and Social Change in Europe, Working Paper No. 19, March 1–36, 2001, for the differences between Poland and Romania. http://www.ssees.ac.uk/publications/working_papers/wp19.pdf

25. This section is based on D. Bohle and B. Greskovits, 'Capitalism Without Compromise? Strong Business and Weak Labor in Central-Eastern Europe's New Transnational Industries', *Studies in Comparative International Development*, Spring 2006.

26. J. Grahl, and P. Teague, 'Is the European Social Model Fragmenting?', *New Political Economy*, 2(3), 1997, reprinted in C. Pierson and F. G. Castles, *The Welfare State Reader*, Malden, MA: Polity Press, 2000, 207–33 (p. 220).

27. T. Ferguson, 'From Normalcy to New Deal: Industrial Structure, Party Competition, and American Public Policy in the Great Depression', *International Organization*, 38(1), Winter 1984, 41–94 (p. 49).

28. P. Gourevitch, *Politics in Hard Times*, Ithaca and London: Cornell University Press, 1986, 223.

29. M. Shafer, *Winners and Losers. How Sectors Shape the Developmental Prospects of States*, Ithaca: Cornell University Press, 1994, p. 14.

30. Ibid.

31. B. Silver, *Forces of Labor. Workers' Movement and Globalization Since 1870*, Cambridge: Cambridge University Press, 2003, p. 47.

32. Ibid., pp. 92–3.

33. A. Hirschman, 'A Generalized Linkage Approach to Development, with Special Reference to Staples', in *Economic Development and Cultural Change. Supplement. Essays in Honor of Bert Hoselitz*, Chicago: University of Chicago Press, 1977, 67–98 (p. 93).

34. S. Crowley and D. Ost, eds, *Workers After Workers States. Labor and Politics in Postcommunist Eastern Europe*, Lanham, Boulder, New York, Oxford: Rowman & Littlefield, 2001.

35. A. Martin and G. Ross, *The Brave New World of European Labor. European Trade Unions at the Millenium*, New York, Oxford: Berghahn Books, 1999, p. 1.

36. While differentiating between exposure to social risk and welfare state remedies I draw on M. Rhodes and M. Keune, 'EMU and Welfare States in East-Central Europe: The Political Economy of Adjustment', forthcoming in Kenneth Dyson, ed., *Enlarging the Euro-Zone: External Empowerment and Domestic Transformation in East Central Europe*, Oxford: Oxford University Press, 2006, forthcoming.

37. The 2004 Roma food riots in the Slovak Republic are a case in point.

38. This was a common phenomenon in Eastern Europe's basic heavy manufacturing industries after the collapse of state socialism.

39. This section is based on B. Greskovits, 'The First Shall Be the Last? Hungary's Road to the European Monetary Union', forthcoming in K. Dyson, ed., *Enlarging the Euro-Zone: External Empowerment and Domestic Transformation in East Central Europe*, Oxford: Oxford University Press, 2006, pp. 279–300.

40. K. Dyson, *European States and the EMU*, Oxford, UK: Oxford University Press, 2002.

41. J. Frieden, 'Real Sources of European Currency Policy: Sectoral Interests and European Monetary Integration,' *International Organization*, 56(4), Autumn 2002. 831–60 (pp. 839–40).
42. The recent mass exodus of low-end/low-wage garment, footwear, toys, electrical and electronics industries from the Visegrád countries to Southeastern or Eastern Europe is a case in point.
43. In Hungary, the intensity of these conflicts reflected businesses' existential discontent with a coming situation where currency depreciation combined with sweating poorly paid workers would less handily qualify as a winning strategy, while shifting to a new growth path would require gradual industrial upgrading that might not be eased by a fast-track EMU-entry strategy.
44. This subsection is based on B. Greskovits, 'Beyond Transition: The Variety of Post-Socialist Development', in R. Dworkin *et al.*, eds, *From Liberal Values to Democratic Transition*, Budapest: Central European University Press, 2003, 201–25, and draws on M. Shafer, *Winners and Losers. How Sectors Shape the Developmental Prospects of States*, Ithaca: Cornell University Press, 1994.
45. S. Ó Riain, 'The Flexible Developmental State: Globalization, Information Technology, and the "Celtic Tiger"', *World Politics*, 28(2), June 2000, 157–93 (p. 165).
46. T. Moran, 'Multinational Corporations and Dependency: A Dialogue for Dependentistas', *International Organization*, Winter 1978, 79–100.
47. G. Graziani, 'Globalisation of Production in the Textile and Clothing Industry: The Case of Italian FDI and Outward Processing in Eastern Europe', BRIE, Working Paper 128, 1998. http://brie.berkeley.edu/~briewww/pubs/wp/wp128.htm
48. Smith *et al.*, op. cit.
49. T. Carothers, 'The End of the Transition Paradigm', *Journal of Democracy*, 13(1), 2002, 5–21 (p. 18).

# 3
# Transnational Actors and Corporate Governance in ECE: the Case of the EU and the Czech Republic

*Arjan Vliegenthart*

## Introduction

> Our task is different. *We should not Europeanize issues,* but fight for the preservation of basic civil, political, and economic liberties. We need the institutional framework that makes them possible. We need unregulated markets; we need states to guarantee and safeguard the rule of law. The alternative is a non-state, post-democracy, and an administered society.
>
> Václav Klaus, President of the Czech Republic
> Speech at the Fraser Institute, November 2004

According to Vaclav Klaus, integration into the European Union does not go together with strong states and unregulated markets. This chapter contests the idea of a simple trade-off between integrating into the EU and leaving state power unabated. Though it will be argued that the character of the Czech state has fundamentally altered through its encounter with the European Union (EU), the Czech state, in interaction with transnational actors such as the EU, still plays a vital part in the shaping and regulating of the Czech economy. This chapter departs from the idea that what we are witnessing in the transitional economies of East Central Europe (ECE) is the transnationalization of the state, and in particular the transnationalization of governance. In discussing the politics of corporate governance regulation in the Czech Republic, it seeks to contribute to the discussion of state and society in ECE by challenging two fundamental premises that lie at the heart of most of the literature on the transition.

Firstly, it will argue that corporate governance regulation is based on political choices and not so much, as is often implicitly assumed, on rational 'best' policy options. The apolitical assumptions of the literature on corporate governance can be understood in the context of the dominant idea in ECE that economic transition requires a process of state retreat. From this point of view the transition envisages to 'depoliticize the economy'[1] in favour of *apolitical* market forces as a means of efficient allocation. This view is often implicitly and sometimes explicitly combined with the normative idea that state retreat is a positive development.[2]

However, the choice of *apolitical* market forces is already political. The choice of market forces in previously uncommodified spheres benefits some, whereas others lose. But this is not the only way in which politics influences the economic transition. Apart from framing the economic playing field, the state, through regulation, interferes in economic practices. This is particularly the case with corporate governance regulation. Corporate governance defined as 'the relationship among stakeholders in the process of decision making and control over firm resources (with the firm itself defined as a collection of resources embedded in a network of relationships among stakeholders)'[3] explicitly refers to the process of decision-making and control over firm resources and is thus directly related to the issues of power and the question of 'who gets what, when and how'.[4]

Secondly, this chapter challenges the idea that transition is a process that takes place within the borders of the nation-state, albeit simultaneously within different states. Most of the current accounts of the transition focus on the (comparison of) national contexts and their public and private national actors. Global forces in this process are either neglected or downplayed.[5] This is not to say that the latter approaches do not recognize the impact of transnational forces, but they downgrade their importance or explain their influence by domestic (or at 'best' regional) developments. This is an inadequate representation of the current developments in ECE. The task of developing a new institutional system from scratch has attracted considerable attention from international actors that considered ECE as a 'testing ground' for several new policies.[6] Where national institutions were in flux during the 1990s, transnational actors indeed played an important role in the establishment of the new institutional setting. Yet their role in the transition process is theoretically underdeveloped; the autonomy of national politics is implicitly taken for granted.

This chapter focuses on the changes in corporate governance regulation during the last few years from the perspective of a transnational political economy and links the developments in this field to the role of the Czech state vis-à-vis transnational actors. The empirical focus will be on the influence of the Czech entry into the European Union (EU) on the development of corporate governance regulation. Corporate governance constitutes one of the main policy factors affecting lock-in of the newly established property rights. During the second half of the 1990s the initial emphasis on privatization shifted towards 'reforming the reform',[7] i.e., a focus on the institutional underpinnings of the transition process. Problems that had arisen from the initial legislation were reconsidered and readdressed. In the Czech Republic, corporate governance issues have been of special economic and political interest after the economic recession during the second half of the 1990s. In these discussions EU conditionality and accession played an important role. In 1999, the Commission criticized the Czech achievements in this field and labelled the financial system a 'key weakness of the Czech economy', explicitly referring to the lack of adequate corporate governance regulation.[8] In several reports, it addressed the question of state-owned and controlled banks as a vital problem for good corporate governance and pressured the Czech government to privatize the banking sector.[9] As I will argue, most of the Czech regulation practices must be discussed in this light.

This chapter is divided into two parts. I will start out with a critique of the *Varieties of Capitalism* approach (VoC) that is increasingly finding its way into the literature on ECE. I will argue that based on its prioritization of the 'national', it does not come to terms with the question of how the different varieties are embedded in, and fundamentally co-determined by, transnational contexts and forces. It will be argued that issues of corporate governance should also be seen as a product of continuous interaction between domestic and transnational forces, in which the latter play a constitutive role. Section two contains an empirical account of these political struggles over these issues in the Czech Republic in the face of EU accession from the late 1990s until the early 2000s. This part substantiates the conceptual notions made in the previous section. It focuses on how the EU has evaluated the progress made by subsequent Czech governments in the field of corporate governance and influenced the domestic debates.

## On the type of capitalism in the Czech Republic

The Varieties of Capitalism approach (VoC) has increasingly attracted attention within the field of political economy. Departing from an interest 'in the differences in economic and political institutions that occur across countries',[10] a variety of scholars have set out to describe and characterize the different types of capitalism throughout the world. In most of the literature two types of capitalism are discerned. On the one hand there is the so-called Rhineland model[11] or coordinated market economy,[12] which is characterized by substantial governmental influence in the national economy. While pursuing industrial and macroeconomic policies, governments directly influence the behaviour of major players in their economies. With regard to corporate governance this model is characterized by cross-ownership and an important role of banks in the provision of investment capital. Stock markets play a subordinate role. Corporations are regarded as complex entities in which various stakeholders have an interest, resulting in strategic planning, employment security and high-quality production strategies and thus a long-term outlook. In the Anglo-Saxon model or liberal market economy, on the other hand, governments tend to keep companies at arm's length as they see it as their primary task to provide a functioning market in which the different corporations can compete. The corporation's value at the stock market is seen as the decisive indicator of its success and its health measured by returns on invested financial capital.[13] Subsequently, the focus of the corporations is on increasing shareholder value. As corporations in the Anglo-Saxon model depend highly on the stock market as a means to raise finance, this encourages 'firms to be attentive to current earnings and the price of their share on equity markets',[14] which leads to a short-term outlook.

### Corporate governance in the VoC approach

The differences between the two models are reflected in the way in which issues of corporate governance are being addressed. Issues of corporate governance constitute an important and inherent part of the VoC approach because corporate governance deals with some of the issues at the heart of every economy, namely how the control over corporations is organized. Table 3.1 sums up the major differences between the two varieties. According to the VoC approach the different features of a corporate governance system are functionally interconnected. This idea of complementarity is reflected in the argument that dispersed ownership in the Anglo-Saxon model and market capitalization are two sides of the same coin. Because companies must turn to the stock market to raise capital, ownership tends to become dispersed. In this variety it is the Board of Directors, which includes the top of management, that

*Table 3.1*   Major corporate governance features of the Anglo-Saxon and Rhineland varieties of capitalism

|  | Anglo-Saxon model | United Kingdom | United States | Rhineland | Germany |
| --- | --- | --- | --- | --- | --- |
| Ownership | **Dispersed** | Dispersed | Dispersed | **Concentrated** | Concentrated |
| Control | **Outsider** | Outsider | Outsider | **Insider** | Insider |
| Dominance of 1- or 2-tier system | **One-tier** | One-tier | One-tier | **Two-tier** | Two-tier |
| Market capitaliza-tion as proportion of GDP in 2000 | **High** | 0.76 | 0.58 | **Low** | 0.19 |

*Source*:  Hall and Soskice (2001) (see endnote 10); T. Beck and R. Levine, *Stock Markets, Banks and Growth: Panel Evidence*, National Bureau of Economic Research (NBER) Working Paper 9082 (2002).

has to supervise management. In turn, the Board is held accountable to the Annual Shareholders' Meeting, where the shareholders as the bearers of the residual risks and profit rights decide on the composition of the Board. In this one-tier system other stakeholders are hardly represented. The opposite is the case in the Rhineland variety. Here a Supervisory Board is the primary organ to control management. In this Supervisory board large shareholders as well as other stakeholders are represented. 'Hausbanken' and other actors that are closely related to the corporation exercise control over the managerial behaviour, leading to a system that can be labelled as 'insider control'.

## Varieties of capitalism travelling to the east?

During the last years several attempts have been made to categorize the emerging forms of capitalism in ECE into one of these varieties.[15] There has been some discussion on the applicability of the approach to the transition economies, but this criticism is rather superficial and does not challenge the basic assumptions of the VoC approach. Recently, David Lane for instance has called for 'further discussion in the context of the "varieties of capitalism" paradigm,' albeit with a loose interpretation of this approach.[16]

There are also references to concepts of the VoC in the case of the Czech Republic. Here we can observe an interesting shift in the analyses throughout the last decade. In 1992, David Stark predicted a tendency towards Anglo-American capitalism with a strong focus on 'raising investment funds through markets' instead of the more 'European' solution of bank monitoring.[17] The Czech voucher privatization has been the most 'marketized' form of privatization in the region; and in this respect, it comes closest to an Anglo-Saxon form of capitalism. The idea was that popular shareholding would increase the social acceptance of the transition process. However, in practice Investment Privatization Funds (IPFs) played a crucial role in mediating between individual citizens and corporate control over companies, leading to more concentrated ownership than originally planned. Therefore, at the end of the 1990s, Neumann and Egan classified the Czech economy as a combination of the German and the Anglo-Saxon model, with 'cross-ownership among banks, investment funds and firms along the same lines as the German or Rhineland model'.[18] Palda also supports the idea of the development of a hybrid between the Rhineland and Anglo-Saxon models of governance.[19]

During the early 2000s, practices tended to move further towards a Rhineland model. Martin Myant argues that we are witnessing the rise of a European model of capitalism. He argues that the initial attempts to develop a Czech model became stranded in the economic crisis of the late 1990s. Myant substantiates his claim by pointing at four different features: (1) the number of foreign-owned firms steadily increased, (2) banks are largely under Western European ownership, (3) all important policy areas are constrained by the EU, and (4) the way in which the pension reform is being conducted resembles the Swedish model.[20]

If we take a look at some major features of the corporate governance systems that are emerging in ECE (Table 3.2), we come across some surprising findings. Despite different initial institutional choices regarding the mode and speed of the privatization process, the corporate governance practices throughout the region show great similarities. It seems that different starting points and initial policy choices have nevertheless led to more or less similar outcomes. Except for the Hungarian case, where direct sales to foreign investors have led to concentrated ownership, all other ECE countries initially demonstrated dispersed ownership that is now rapidly concentrating. In this respect we see a tendency towards a Rhineland variety. Moreover, if we look at the other three features of the corporate governance systems, insider control, a two-tier system and a relatively low market capitalization, this would lead us to conclude that the emerging systems in important respects resemble Rhineland capitalism. This is also the conclusion that Lane draws as he

*Table 3.2*   Main corporate governance features in ECE

| | Czech Republic | Poland | Hungary | Slovakia | Slovenia |
|---|---|---|---|---|---|
| Ownership | Initially dispersed, now concentrating | Initially dispersed, now concentrating | Concentrated | Initially dispersed, now concentrating | Initially dispersed, now concentrating |
| Control | Insider | Insider | Insider | Insider | Insider |
| Dominance of 1- or 2-tier system | Two-tier | Two-tier | Two-tier | Two-tier | Two-tier |
| Market Capitalization as % of GDP (2003) | 16.5 | 17.2 | 18.7 | 3.5 | 23.3 |

*Source*:  Hungarian National Bank.

argues that the Czech Republic, Hungary, Poland, Slovakia and Slovenia are the 'closest to the continental type of market capitalism'.[21]

Together these developments pose the question whether the states in ECE are indeed throwing off their Anglo-Saxon feathers in exchange for Rhineland ones. For some the idea that ECE is turning into a look-alike of Germany and Austria might seem intuitively correct. The resemblance to the German model of capitalism might not be very surprising if we take into account that 'the spontaneous expansion of German business and the resulting structural dependency of the Czech political economy on Germany are indisputable.'[22]

## The transition as a transnational process: the role of FDI

However, as I will argue in the rest of this section, the correspondence with the Rhineland model is only superficial. Here I agree with Lane's criticism that the traditional VoC approach misses out on some of 'the building blocks of capitalism'.[23] Instead of developing a distinct variety for the ECE, I will argue that the approach misses out the transnational nature of the transformation process that is taking place. The practical functioning of the corporate governance system in ECE is fundamentally different, mostly due to the fact that strategic economic sectors are now under foreign ownership. In a later section I will further illustrate this claim with examples of EU influence on the coming about of corporate governance regulation in the Czech Republic.

In the current institutional setup, the banking sector plays an important role as the facilitator of credit and as supervisor of corporate behaviour. Throughout the 1990s the significance of banks has increased. Initially, Czech banks were 'major actors in the failed voucher privatization programme of the early 1990s... and often seemed to be at least one step ahead of the supervisors'.[24] In this role they have contributed to the concentration of ownership and have turned into the primary guardians of corporate control. Given this important role of the banking sector in the Czech economy, the fact that the banking sector has become increasingly dominated by foreign capital is of special importance. After an explosion in the number of banks during the first three years after the breakdown of the socialist system, we have seen on the one hand a steady but absolute decrease of national banks, and an increase in the influence of foreign banks on the other (Table 3.3). Most of the privatization projects that started in the late 1990s and continued during the early 2000s took the form of direct sales to European foreign investors. In 2000, European banks made up almost 50 per cent of the Czech banking sector, almost six times as much as their American counterparts (see Table 3.4).

*Table 3.3*   Foreign ownership in Czech banks

| Year | Total number of active banks | Number of foreign-dominated banks |
|---|---|---|
| 1990 | 9 | 0 |
| 1991 | 24 | 4 |
| 1992 | 37 | 11 |
| 1993 | 52 | 18 |
| 1994 | 55 | 21 |
| 1995 | 55 | 23 |
| 1996 | 53 | 23 |
| 1997 | 50 | 24 |
| 1998 | 45 | 25 |
| 1999 | 42 | 27 |
| 2000 | 40 | 26 |
| 2001 | 38 | 26 |
| 2002 | 37 | 26 |
| 2003 | 35 | 26 |
| 2004 | 35 | 26 |

*Source*:  Czech National Bank.

*Table 3.4* Ownership structure of Czech banks by share of equity, in per cent

| Year | Total Foreign | Of which EU | Of which US |
| --- | --- | --- | --- |
| 1995 | 22.8 | 13. 3 | Na |
| 1998 | 38.7 | 28.6 | 4.6 |
| 2000 | 54.5 | 43.5 | 7.7 |

*Source*: Hanousek *et al.* (2005) (see endnote 26).

The fact that it is foreign banks that dominate the Czech banking sector undermines the idea of a national variety of capitalism. The VoC approach sees the banking sector as an endogenous product of the national economy. Government intervention into the national banking sector has been at the heart of the distinct national variety. 'Governments have supported and guaranteed both domestic banking systems and, more sporadically, securities markets. These have been shaped by differences in endogenous state capacity, by the structural distinctiveness of particular national economies, and by their relative degree of vulnerability to trans-national market forces.'[25] These conditions however do not apply in the Czech case, nor do they hold in any other ECE country. Whereas the economic systems of Western Europe have developed over more than two centuries and in times in which the state could perform a more autonomous steering role, the Czech state has not had the time to shape its own banking sector due to pressures from transnational actors such as the EU and the IMF.

Advocates of the VoC approach might argue that these last observations are irrelevant for their approach since they concentrate on the question of how different institutions hang together and to what extent they reflect the comparative advantages of different states. In this approach banks are just simply banks, regardless of their ownership structure. However, what they ignore is that the same institutional structures might lead to diverse outcomes in different contexts. In the case of the Czech Republic, due to the dominance of foreign capital in key positions in the Czech economy, the objectives behind the different institutions are not the realization of economic development on a national basis but rather the interest of foreign capital. Hanousek *et al.* have concluded that international and domestic firms in ECE adopt different corporate strategies. Whereas foreign-controlled corporations focus on the increase in sales revenues, domestic firms centre their attention on the reduction of labour cost (employment).[26]

Apart from the fact that origin matters, the newly established institutions are subordinated to the inflow of FDI. The debate on the institutional setup is not centred on the question of which institutions provide the biggest comparative advantage, but rather on which institutions best serve the protection of foreign capital. In an attempt to attract as much FDI as possible, states 'use' their institutional setup to attract as much capital as possible. Of course comparative advantages and the attractiveness to foreign capital to some extent coincide, as economic growth that serves international capital might well stem from distinct national comparative advantages, but the way in which comparative advantages are being defined becomes subordinated under the interests of transnational capital and therefore transcends the boundaries of a distinct nation-state. Moreover, the structural adjustment programmes advocated by transnational actors have impacted the institutional setup in the region. This is not to say that transnational actors have determined the outcome of the process of institutionalization, but rather that the outcomes are the result of a continuous interaction between transnational and domestic forces. The constitutive character of foreign capital as well as other transnational actors is in this respect of vital importance. Their impact on social relations influences the behaviour and position of domestic actors, 'enabling as well as constraining economic exchange',[27] and impacts on the domestic balance of power. However, their interaction with other transnational and domestic actors has influenced the transition process to such an extent that we can no longer speak of independent national trajectories, but rather of national variations on a common transition theme.[28] VoC in ECE does not explain this common transition theme and in order to do so we need an approach that transcends the level of the nation-state, focusing on the transnational influence on and the social function of the newly established institutions.

### The role of the EU in the
### transnationalization of the state

Most of the foreign investments discussed above stem from Western Europe (see Table 3.5). Germany, Austria and the Netherlands dominate these flows and, although many of the MNCs cannot be considered to represent the interests of the specific state or the European Union, nor vice versa, the large European corporations, organized in the European Round Table (ERT), have been among the biggest advocates of opening the ECE markets and the accession of the region in the

EU and their interests in the region have been represented by the Commission on several occasions.[29] The Commission has applauded the inflow of foreign capital into ECE. In its first Regular Report in 1997 it argued forcefully in favour of foreign investors, stating that the 'modernization of industry and the introduction of new technologies through the more widespread involvement of foreign investors, together with continued restructuring of enterprises, should lay the foundations for a more dynamic and competitive industrial sector'.[30] More specifically in the field of corporate governance, the Commission reported that 'foreign ownership has been crucial in enhancing corporate governance and pushing forward business reorientation in the banking sector'.[31]

The EU influence on corporate governance regulation and practices is in this respect of special importance as issues of corporate governance play an important role in the context of the economic transition, namely the institutional protection of changed property rights. This kind of institutional protection resembles what Gill calls 'new constitutionalism', which involves 'a particular set of political and constitutional changes linked to the reconstitution and protection of capital on a world scale'.[32] The influence of the EU can be understood as getting the institutions in place that provide this kind of protection. EU conditionality and influence constitute a part of a hegemonic project that is aimed at securing the interests of predominantly European capital and that is shaped in the interaction between transnational actors and domestic forces in the Czech Republic. Although the EU has not exported blueprints of corporate governance systems, their influence has shaped the development of new institutions in the region.

EU influence has also impacted the power balance within the Czech state. The Commission supported some policy initiatives that were in line with its ideas on institutional development whereas others were criticized, impacting the domestic debate and thus contributing to the so-called internationalization or transnationalization of the state.[33] Those agencies in closest touch with the world economy were strengthened vis-à-vis nationally oriented agencies.[34] This is not to say that those internationally oriented agencies become 'unbeatable', as we shall see in the next section. Nor does it mean that the Czech state has ceased to exist or has become powerless. Rather, it has remained 'the central arena of contestation for the construction of transition order, vital in the transformative process',[35] but decisively influenced and shaped by the pressures of transnational actors and capital.

*Table 3.5*   Origin of foreign stock (2003)

| Country | % of total FDI positions |
| --- | --- |
| Netherlands | 31 |
| Germany | 21 |
| Austria | 12 |
| France | 8 |
| United States | 5 |

*Source*:  Czech National Bank.

## The politics of corporate governance in the Czech Republic in the face of EU enlargement

Many of the developments discussed above can be illustrated with examples from the policy field of corporate governance. Apart from their role in the VoC approach, issues of corporate governance play another important role in the context of the economic transition: the institutional lock-in of changed property rights. During the last years of the communist regimes and the first years of the transition, the liberalization of prices and the imposition of financial discipline were emphasized. After this first step of liberalization, a second phase shifted the focus towards the restructuring of property rights. In the early 1990s, privatization was at the heart of the political and academic debate, or as former Czech minister for Privatization Dusan Triska put it: 'Privatization is not just one of many items on the economic program. It is the transformation itself.'[36] However, when the first two waves of the transition process had passed by, privatization proved not to be the panacea many had hoped for. Although the private share in GDP went up, none of the former communist countries, except for Poland, had reached the 1989 GDP level in 1997. Furthermore, the transformation had been primarily focused on the downsizing of production, assets and employment. This defensive strategy was not accompanied by any deeper restructuring aimed at investments and innovative business strategies, as the World Bank reported.[37]

The literature on the economic transition attributes these developments to the lack of proper institutions to guide the transfer of property and regulate corporate control in the newly privatized companies. Privatization without underlying corporate governance mechanisms does not 'clearly solve the problem of having well-identified private owners who actually control and govern newly privatized enterprises... qualitative privatization could only be achieved by coming to grips with the corporate governance issues'.[38] Acknowledging these problems, governments turned their attention to mechanisms 'to remedy problems identified through the experience of the initial legislation, to improve the quality of law-making and law-enforcement, but also to offer more effective and forward-looking solutions'.[39] Corporate governance issues therefore constitute the *third phase* of the economic transformation in ECE after the initial phases of stabilization and privatization.

The Czech Republic constitutes perhaps the clearest example of this development. The method of voucher privatization led to considerable problems in the field of corporate control and chaos in financial structures. Investment Privatization Funds (IPF) acquired over 50 per cent of the shares and subsequently were alleged to act on behalf of the fund managers instead of the shareholders. With disclosure rules still limited throughout the 1990s, IPFs, banks and firms did not give full accounts of their performance, thus hindering effective shareholder control. As the IPFs and banks did not control the corporations they owned, corporate governance issues were transferred to the level of these institutions without being solved, begging the question of 'who guards the guardians?'[40]

### The neglect of corporate governance issues during the first years of the transition

During the first years of the transition, most corporate governance issues were hardly dealt with. Both transnational actors and the national Czech government did not place the issue on the top of their reform agenda. The right-wing government under the leadership of Klaus therefore hardly addressed the question of financial transparency and focussed predominantly on rapid privatization. The inherent fear behind the reform programme of the Klaus government was that the transition to a market economy would fail because of over-regulation. According to the Klaus government, the transition was best managed by leaving the markets to do their job. As a result of their attempts to depoliticize the economy, 'the Czech government impeded from institutional development to aid firm restructuring and creation'.[41]

Initially the international financial institutions supported this approach. The IMF and the World Bank favoured a clear-cut break between the socialist era and the post-socialist period and focussed primarily upon the opening up of new markets. Their agenda constitutes the breaking up of the traditional trading patterns between the former socialist states in the Comecon, redirecting the trading patterns to the west and introducing liberalization and privatization.

These latter objectives demanded a hands-off approach when it came to government-induced organization of the economy, thus bringing about a process of deregulation.

Although dependence on financial support of international financial institutions, such as the World Bank and the IMF, ceased shortly after 1993, Meaney concludes that, during the first years of the transition, foreign experts have been more influential in shaping the mode and practices of privatization in the Czech Republic than in neighbouring Poland and Hungary, as they enjoyed 'the unqualified support from the head of state'.[42] The outspoken right-wing coalition, clearly committed to market reforms, determined the course of transition until 1998, in contrast to most of the other ECE cases where either the Social Democrats or the Socialists gained office after the second round of post-communist elections. The role of the Washington Consensus organizations was therefore first and foremost 'to help its protagonists overcome the main political opposition to their designs'.[43] Here we see the clear dialectical interaction between transnational actors that strengthen the position of those domestic actors that represent their position on the one hand, and domestic counterparts that support the involvement of trans-national agencies on the other.

However, as the recession hit the Czech Republic in 1997 the call for stable institutional underpinnings was most loudly heard in Prague, and international institutions became aware of the importance of a sound legal foundation. Almost overnight the Czech Republic was no longer the favourite pupil of the Washington Consensus, but a rather weak student. Most critique was aimed at the banking sector that was left 'intentionally non-privatized',[44] which led *The Economist* to con-clude that the Czech banking sector was 'parochial and politicised'.[45] In the 1992 voucher programme the Czech government had only priva-tized parts of the four largest banks of the country, while keeping a significant degree of the shares in those banks during the following years. The European Commission became increasingly critical of Czech performance, highlighting the lack of corporate governance structures and the weakness of the banking and financial system and criticizing the Klaus government for lacking commitment and unimplemented reforms.

This shift coincided with a qualitative shift in the role of the EU as an actor in the region. During these first years, the role of the EU remained rather informal and predominantly took the form of policy advice. Although different European states, with Germany as forerunner,[46] had their own policies towards Central Europe, the EU was rather reluctant to offer the region prospects of EU membership. Only after the Copenhagen summit in 1993 did the EU demonstrate more willingness to offer EU membership to the most advanced post-communist states,[47] and it took until 1995 before the Commission published a first White Paper to lay out a more general framework by which it could address the region. It became clear that the Commission would have to adopt a hands-on approach towards the applicant states, as it stated that EU involvement would go 'beyond a simple listing of relevant legislation' but that the Commission would identify 'the key measures in each sector' and would suggest 'the sequence in which approximation could be tackled'.[48] Furthermore, the Commission explicitly referred to technical assistance in drawing up national laws.[49] With the signing of the Accession Partnerships in 1998 the EU possessed a bigger carrot and therefore also a firmer stick. From then on the EU was in the position to impose conditions upon applicant states, which ended a period of negotiations that had more of a bargaining character.[50] Jacoby speaks in this respect of a shift from voluntary and functional compliance to certain European templates towards less voluntary thresholds.[51] From 1998 onwards, when the Accession Treaties were signed, the EU continuously urged for the creation of new institutions that lock in the newly established economic realities. The Commissioner for Enlargement, Günther Verheugen, stressed this point on several occasions: 'There are weaknesses everywhere – even the so-called frontrunners – in administrative capacity, the judicial system, in some cases, corruption. That is why we have started to concentrate our support to overcome these weaknesses',[52] reflecting the idea in Brussels that 'market making is about the re-making of the state, about re-regulation of relations among economic actors, and about the re-institutionalisation of the economy'.[53]

### After the accession treaties

Domestically, the economic setback – among others – resulted in a power shift on the Czech scene. After two legislature periods, the Klaus government was overthrown in the 1997 elections and replaced by the Social-Democratic minority government of Prime Minister Milos Zeman. Although they had campaigned as strong opponents of letting go of the state's bank shareholdings, the privatization of the banking sector soon got under way. It proved to be able to appease the EU by privatizing the last publicly controlled bank in 2001. In general, the Social-Democratic minority government was far more EU-minded than its centre-right predecessor.

This is not to say that all government members agreed on the pursued strategy. Industry and Trade Minister Miroslav Gregr and Finance Minister Pavel Mertlik, in particular, collided on several occasions. Whereas the latter was able to get things his way during the first years of the Zeman government, he resigned after a struggle over the privatization of publicly controlled power companies. Their biggest controversies concerned an ambitious revitalization programme aimed at the restructuring of some big and highly indebted corporations. Here again we see the role of the EU in influencing the national debate by supporting its domestic counterpart, i.e., the Minister of Finance, who at the same time supports the role of foreign actors at the domestic level.

The Revitalization Agency was set up in 1999 as a political response to deal with the consequences that resulted from the lack of proper corporate governance regulation. The lack of regulation on transparency and bankruptcy had led to severe problems in some of the large Czech corporations. Under 'mounting pressure from foreign investors'[54] the Czech government decided that a new agency was to deal with the restructuring of troubled Czech companies. The US investment bank Lazard Frères and the European consultancy company Latona Associates were invited to manage the new Agency. Managing Director Savage of bank Lazard Frères argued that the revitalization programme would be 'an integral step in preparing the Czech Republic for its admission into the European Union'. The Commission was initially also very positive towards Mertlik's version of the Revitalization Programme. In its 1999 Annual Report it stated that the revitalization programme 'could be a step in the right direction'[55] because the plan that was submitted was 'non-interventionist and market-oriented' and 'will abide by the provisions of the European agreement and the acquis'.[56] Mertlik, on the other hand, supported the idea of foreign advisors to the Revitalization Agency. He continued to support the role of these advisors even after criticizing the functioning of the agency as a whole. At the end of 2000, Mertlik stated that the Agency had become redundant, but at the same time invited the Lazard Frères and Latona Associates 'to continue revitalizing the four companies currently in the RA program'.[57]

However, within his own Social-Democratic Party and within the government, Mertlik lost his political battle for his version of the revitalization programme to his political opponent Greg, who favoured a more hands-on approach for the restructuring of the troubled corporations. After several defeats, including a failed attempt to become deputy chairman, and subsequent government decisions regarding economic policy, Mertlik resigned in April 2001. After Mertlik's resignation, the Commission became more critical of the Revitalization Agency. Although it did not directly refer to Mertlik's resignation, it argued that the 'momentum of restructuring and privatization, which was noted last year, appears to have slowed down as regards major industrial undertaking'.[58]

Mertlik's resignation, however, did not mean a decisive blow to the Czech accession aspirations. On other corporate governance issues the Czech Republic received praise from the Commission. The 2001 report already stated that 'good progress' had been made in 'strengthening protection of creditors and minority shareholders'[59] and called the reforms in the field of accounting and disclosure that allow for the implementation of the International Accounting Standards an improvement of the already solid basis.[60] In 2002, the Commission concluded that 'privatization and consolidation have laid the foundations for a solid financial sector, which is able to fulfil its intermediation role'.[61] It rather seems that the main differences between the EU and the Czech government are more related to the pace and sequencing of the restructuring of the Czech economy than to a differently defined goal. As joining the EU was given priority over control of the pace of the transition process, the Social Democratic Zeman government accepted EU pressures for further and more rapid reforms on several other occasions. Compliance with the Copenhagen criteria and the acquis required substantial reforms that were politically feasible in the light of joining the EU, which was widely regarded as a reward for the successful completion of the reform programme and the end of the transition period.

## Conclusion

'A common perception in CEE is that convergence with West European models is part of economic and social "modernization" and the "return to Europe." '[62] The question is, however, whether this common perception is correct. After a little more than two years of EU membership it is too early to assess the impact of the EU on the corporate governance regulation in the Czech Republic. Nor are we able to fully assess the impact of the EU, but ECE is still far away from full and equal political, social and economic participation with the rest of Europe.[63] Although at first sight it might seem that we have been witnessing a process of convergence on a Rhineland model of corporate governance, a closer look teaches us that the resemblance is only superficial. The new type of capitalism emerging in ECE can best be characterized as based upon foreign investments with some post-socialist characteristics that result from the communist period and the process of privatization. From these features, the penetration of the region by foreign capital will be the most important trait.

The integration of the Czech Republic into the EU is a clear example of the transnationalization of the Czech state. The two examples of the Czech privatization process and the Revitalization Agency might serve as illustrations of how the domestic and transnational level interact in the case of the transition process in ECE. Here, the transnational character of the EU goes beyond the notion of an exogenous force limiting policy options, but instead functions as an actor that impacts more directly on domestic politics.

Yet, the notion of transnationalization of the state does not solve all questions regarding the current developments in the field of corporate governance. With regard to the nature of the corporate governance practices that have evolved in the Czech Republic we can conclude that the current practices resemble those of the old EU-15. However, in the EU-15 Rhineland practices are part of what Rhodes and van Apeldoorn have called 'embedded neoliberalism,' which is 'premised on a strong belief in the free market and supports neo-liberal policies of deregulation and flexibilization, but recognizes that the market must be embedded in a regulatory framework fostering both competitive business and social consensus'.[64] In the context of ECE the same kinds of practices do not lead to a strong welfare state.[65] In this respect ECE is distinctly different from Western Europe. The similarities between the various former Visegrád states, in both regulation and practices, and the profound impact of foreign forces on the transition process, lead to the conclusion that the transition processes and the rise of a specific type of capitalism cannot be explained by looking only at the national level.

## Endnotes

1. S. Estrin, D. M. Nuti and M. Uvalic, 'The Impact of Investment Funds on Corporate Governance in Mass Privatization Schemes: Czech Republic Poland and Slovenia, *Moct-Most*, 10(1), 2000–, 1–26 (p. 1); see also M. Boycko, A. Shleifer and R.W. Vishny, 'Second-best economic policy for a divided government', *European Economic Review* 40(3–5), 1996, 767–74.
2. D. Lipton and J. Sachs, *Privatization in Eastern Europe: the Case of Poland*, Brooking Papers on Economic Activity, 2(2), 1990, 93–342.

3. R. V. Aguilera and G. Jackson, 'The Cross-National Diversity of Corporate Governance: Dimensions and Determinants', *The Academy of Management Review* 28 (3), 2003, 447–65 (p. 450).

4. H. Lasswell, *Politics: Who Gets What, When, How*, New York: McGraw-Hill, 1936.

5. S. Shields, 'Global Restructuring and the Polish State: Transition, Information, or Trans-nationalisation?' *Review of International Political Economy* 11(1), 2004, 132–54 (p. 132).

6. B. Deacon, M. Hulse and P. Stubbs, *Global Social Policy: International organizations and the future of welfare*, London: Sage, 1997, p. 147.

7. R. O. Dragneva and W. B. Simons, 'Corporate Governance revisited: Can the Stakeholder Paradigm Provide a Way out of "Vulture" Capitalism in Eastern Europe', *Review of Central and East European Law* 27(1), 2001, 93–111 (p. 94).

8. Commission, *Regular Report from the Commission on Czech Republic's Progress Towards Accession*, Brussels, 1999, p. 24.

9. Commission, *Regular Report from the Commission on Czech Republic's Progress Towards Accession*, Brussels, 1997, and European Commission, *Regular Report*, Brussels, 1999.

10. P. A. Hall and D. W. Soskice, *Varieties of Capitalism: the Institutional Foundations of Comparative Advantage*, Oxford: Oxford University Press, 2001, p. 1.

11. M. Albert, *Capitalism against Capitalism*, London: Whurr, 1991.

12. Hall and Soskice, op. cit.

13. M. J. Rubach and T. C. Sebora, 'Comparative Corporate Governance: Compe titive Implications of an Emerging Convergence', *Journal of World Business* 33(2), 1998, 167–84.

14. Hall and Soskice, op. cit., p. 27.

15. See for instance D. Lane, 'Emerging Varieties of Capitalism in Former State Socialist Societies', *Competition and Change* 9(3), 2005, 227–47, and L. Cernat, 'Institutions and Economic Growth: Which Model of Capitalism for Central and Eastern Europe?', *Journal for Institutional Innovation, Development and Transition* 6, 2002, 18–34, for ECE; D. Lane, 'What kind of Capitalism for Russia? A comparative analysis', *Communist and Post-Communist Studies* 33(1), 2000, 485–504, for Russia; M. Feldmann, 'Emerging Varieties of Capitalism in Transition Countries: The Case of Wage Bargaining in Estonia and Slovenia', mimeo: C. Buchen, 2004, 'What Kind of Capitalism is Emerging in Eastern Europe? Varieties of Capitalism in Estonia and Slovenia', Paper presented at the 13th Research Seminar on 'Managing the Economic Transition', University of Cambridge, 12 March 2002, for Slovenia and Estonia. http://www.met-network.org.uk/met13_clemensbuchen.pdf (accessed 6 December 2006).

16. Lane, 'Emerging Varieties of Capitalism', p. 246.

17. D. Stark, 'Path Dependence and Privatization. Strategies in East Central Europe', *Eastern European Politics and Societies* 6, 1991, 17–54, p. 36.

18. S. Neumann and M. Egan, 'Between German and Anglo-Saxon Capitalism: the Czech Financial Markets in Transition', *New Political Economy* 4(3), 1999, 173–94, p. 175.

19. K. Palda, 'Czech Privatization and Corporate Governance', *Communist and post-communist Studies* 30(1), 1997, 83–93, p. 93.

20. M. Myant, *Czech Capitalism: Towards a European Model?*, paper presented at the 13th Research Seminar on 'Managing the Economic Transition', University of Cambridge, 12 March 2004.
21. Lane, 'Emerging Varieties of Capitalism', p. 245.
22. H. Jerábek and F. Zich, 'The Czech Republic: Internationalization and Dependency', in P. J. Katzenstein, ed., *Mitteleuropa: Between Europe and Germany*, Oxford: Berghahn Books, 1997, p. 190.
23. Lane, 'Emerging Varieties of Capitalism', p. 228.
24. J. Hawkins and D. Mihaljek, *The banking industry in the emerging market economies: competition, consolidation and systemic stability – an overview*, Bank for International Settlements Working Paper 2004, p. 29.
25. P. G. Cerny, 'International Finance and the Erosion of Capitalist Diversity', in C. Crouch and W. Streeck, eds, *Political Economy of Modern Capitalism: Mapping Convergence and Diversity*, London: Sage, 1997, p. 175.
26. J. Hanousek, E. Kocenda and J. Svejnar, *Origin and Concentration: Corporate Ownership, Control and Performance*, Cerge-EI Working Papers 259, 2005, pp. 23–4.
27. N. Bandelj, 'Embedded Economies: Social Relations as Determinants of Foreign Direct Investment in Central and Eastern Europe', *Social Forces* 81(2), 2002, p. 433.
28. See S. Strange, 'The Future of Global Capitalism; or, will divergence persist forever?' in Crouch and Streeck, eds, 1997, 182–91, for a similar argument.
29. O. Holman, 'The Enlargement of the European Union Towards Central and Eastern Europe: the Role of Supranational and Trans-national Actors', in A. Bieler and A. D. Morton, eds, *Social Forces in the Making of the New Europe. The Restructuring of European Social Relations in the Global Political Economy*, Basingstoke: Palgrave, 2001, 161–84.
30. Commission, *Regular Report*, 1997, p. 19.
31. Commission, *Regular Report from the Commission on Czech Republic's Progress Towards Accession*, Brussels, 2002, p. 42.
32. S. Gill, *New Constitutionalism and the Reconstitution of Capital*, 1998, p. 1, http://www.meijigakuin.ac.jp/~iism/pdf/nenpo_002/Gill.pdf (Last accessed 01 December 2006).
33. R. W. Cox, *Production, Power, and World Order: Social Forces in the Making of History*, New York: Columbia University Press, 1987; L. Panitch, 'Rethinking the Role of the State', in J. Mittelman, ed., *Globalization: Critical Reflections*, Boulder: Lynne Rienner, 1996; N. Poulantzas, *Classes in Contemporary Capitalism*, translated by D. Fernbach, London: New Left Books, 1975 in general; for the context of ECE see Shields, op. cit.
34. Cox, op. cit., p. 253.
35. Shields, op. cit., p. 149.
36. Triska, quoted in J. Nellis, *Privatization in Transition Economies: What Happened? What's Next?*, Washington DC: World Bank, mimeo 2000.
37. World Bank, *World Development Report: From Plan to Market*, New York: Oxford University Press, 1996, p. 47.
38. W. Andreff, 'Corporate Governance of Privatized Enterprises in Transforming Economies: A Theoretical Approach', *MOCT-MOST*, 2, 1996, 59–60.

39. Dragneva and Simons, op. cit., p. 94.
40. J. Stiglitz, 'Quis Custodiet Ipsos Custodes?' (Who guards the guardians?), *Development Economics* 6, 1999, 26–68.
41. G. A. McDermott, 'Institutional Change and Firm Creation in East-Central Europe: An Embedded Politics Approach', *Comparative Political Studies* 2, 2004, p. 189.
42. C. S. Meaney, 'Foreign Experts, Capitalists, and competing agendas: Privatization in Poland, the Czech Republic, and Hungary', *Comparative Political Studies* 28, 1995, p. 303.
43. M. Dangerfield, 'Neoliberalism and the Czech Transformation: Neoliberal Rhetoric or Neoliberal Reality?', *East European Politics and Societies* 3, 1997, p. 440.
44. M. Havrda, 'The Czech Republic: the Case of Delayed Transformation', in M. Federocwicz and R.V. Aguilera, eds, *Corporate Governance in a Changing Economic and Political Environment. Trajectories of Institutional Change*, Basingstoke: Palgrave, 2003, p. 133.
45. *The Economist*, 'Bohemia's fading rhapsody', 31 May 1997, p. 65.
46. K. van der Pijl, *German Reunification and World Politics*, Sheffield Papers in International Studies, No. 7, 1991.
47. D. Bohle, 'Erweiterung und Vertiefung der EU: Neoliberale Restrukturierung und trans-nationales Kapital' (Widening and Deepening of the EU: neoliberal restructuring and trans-national capital), *Prokla* 3, 2002, p. 361.
48. Commission, *White Paper: Preparation of the Associated Countries of Central and Eastern Europe for Integration into the Internal Market of the Union*, Brussels, 1995, p. 4.
49. Commission, *White Paper*, p. 33.
50. H. Grabbe, *A Partnership for Accession? The Implications of EU Conditionality for the Central and East European Applicants*, Robert Schuman Centre Working Paper 12, Florence: European University Institute, 1999.
51. W. Jacoby, 'Tutors and Pupil: International Organizations, Central European Elites, and Western Models', *Governance* 2, 2001, 169–200.
52. Verheugen, as quoted in 'Enthusiasm for a larger Europe starts to wane', *Financial Times*, 6 June 2001, p. 3.
53. L. Bruszt, 'Making Markets and Eastern Enlargement: Diverging Convergence?', *West European Politics* 2, 2002, p. 128.
54. G. Lawson, *The Czech Republic and the Poverty of Transitology*, paper presented at the Fifth Pan European International Relations Conference, The Hague, 9–11 September 2004, p. 34.
55. Commission, *Regular Report*, 1999, p. 26.
56. Commission, *Regular Report*, 1999, p. 39.
57. *The Prague Post*, 'Industrial program packs it in. Revitalization Agency proved too inefficient', 20 December 2000.
58. Commission, *Regular Report from the Commission on Czech Republic's Progress Towards Accession*, Brussels, 2001, p. 79.
59. Commission, *Regular Report*, 2001, p. 51.
60. Commission, *Regular Report*, 2001, p. 48.
61. Commission, *Regular Report*, 2002, p. 43.

62. H. Grabbe, 'European Integration and Corporate Governance in Central Europe: Trajectories of Institutional Change', in M. Federocwicz and R. V. Aguilera, eds, *Corporate Governance in a Changing Economic and Political Environment. Trajectories of Institutional Change*, Basingstoke: Palgrave, 2003, p. 248.
63. D. Bohle and B. Greskovits, 'Ein Sozialmodel an der Grenze' (A social model on the border), *Osteuropa* 5–6, 2004, 372–86.
64. M. Rhodes and B. van Apeldoorn, 'Capital unbound? The transformation of European corporate governance', *Journal of European Public Policy* 5(3), 1998, p. 422.
65. Bohle and Greskovits, op. cit.

# 4
# On the State of the State: The Czech Transformation and the Moment of Convergence in the Visegrád Region

*Jan Drahokoupil*

## Introduction[1]

The emergence of the 'regional tiger under the Tatras', as the financial press called the radical neo-liberal reform program of the former centre-right Slovak government, illustrated an important shift in the policy orientation of many other East-Central Europe governments (ECE). This shift reflected one of the ways in which post-socialist Eastern European governments produced their own forms of post-Fordist global transformation.

Post-socialist states are currently committed to developmental strategies based on supply side management and efforts to attract foreign direct investment. This chapter turns to regulation theory and a state-theoretical analysis to show how the dominant state project in the Visegrád-Four region (V4) has been able to construct a particular form of capitalism. The chapter focuses primarily on the Czech Republic and adopts a regulationist and state-theoretical approach to understanding these transformations. Regulation theory is concerned with the ways in which the state, economy and society influence each other, particularly in ways in which capital and labour-power are reproduced in specific settings.[2] In ECE, the transformation from state socialism to capitalism is recent, and so it is necessary to focus not only on the *re*production but also on the *production* of capitalist relations and forms.[3]

First, I introduce the methodological and analytical dimensions of this inquiry. Second, I focus on the role of the state in introducing generic forms of capitalist relations in ECE. I call this project the neoliberal transformational state. Then, I investigate the transformation of the particular state project and accumulation strategy in the Czech Republic. I provide a model of a state, which I call Klausian welfare national state (KlWNS). In the early 1990s this Klausian project was the form in which a particular kind of state and economy were built in the Czech Republic. However, this project failed to reproduce itself and soon fell into crisis. Finally, I describe the Porterian workfare post-national regime (PWPR) as a description of the kind of state project that is currently emerging as a solution to the crisis of the mid-nineties is sought.

## Analysing the (capitalist) state in post-socialism

The state and other extra-economic institutions have a crucial role in constituting what is conventionally understood as the economy. The capitalist economy cannot produce itself without other essential (not accidental) elements, such as labour, environment, and the thousands of laws and regulations that constitute the state system within which market norms can emerge. Any comprehensive analysis of the economic role of the state must, therefore, include at least four elements.[4] First, the role of state is important in securing the conditions for the *continuation of private business* (this is the realm of economic policy). Second, the state must secure the conditions for the *reproduction of labour-power* from the perspective of both employers and workers (this is the realm of social policy).[5] Third, the state must secure the geographical dimensions of structured and coherent economic and social policy (this is the question of *scalar organization*). Fourth, the state must also secure the *mechanisms of coordination* which supplement market forces in securing socio-economic reproduction and compensate for their failures. There is no guarantee that any of these functions of the state will lead to stable economies, either individually or in combination. Their effects are, as Lipietz has argued, a matter of chance and trial – and error.[6]

Post-socialist regimes introduced capitalist forms only recently and so it is necessary to deal with the role played by the state in relation to capitalist accumulation on at least two levels. First, we must focus on *generic* features of the capital relation, including the ways in which the state and economy are articulated, the legal and institutional forms through which the state exercises its monopoly on violence, and the role of state taxes, administration, rule of law and formal sovereignty.[7] That is, one has to question the extent to which the basic forms of capitalist relation, such as private ownership, rule of law, and separation of the state from the economy, have been institutionalized and whether the capitalist state has emerged in post-socialist societies. Only after considering these issues can we turn to the second level in which we address the *specific concrete* forms of the state and the accumulation regimes that seem to be emerging.

A form-analytical methodology for regulationist, state-theoretical analysis typically identifies dominant social forms (e.g., the commodity form, wage form, price form, legal form, and state form), investigates whether and how they correspond to/contradict each other, and examines how the dominant forms shape possibilities of action. For example, the Fordist economies in the post-war era were characterized by mass production as a dominant form of labour process and by Keynesian policies as dominant form of state economic intervention. The Keynesian welfare national state was the dominant state form of the time and was co-constituted by the Fordist accumulation regime, characterized by a virtuous circle of mass production and mass consumption.[8] However, one cannot expect to identify the same levels of coherent organization of social forms in societies in radical transformation. Moreover, in the case of state-socialist transformations we are dealing with social formations where the basic social forms are only in the process of institutionalization and are thus contested by different social actors and path-dependencies.

There are two solutions to this methodological problem. First, one may use the form analysis by following Robert Boyer's distinction between two ways of understanding social forms' hierarchies. Accordingly, in the periods of transformation, '[a]n institutional form may be said to be hierarchically superior to another if *its development implies a transformation of this other form,* in its configuration and logic.'[9] That is, it may impose its developmental logic on other forms in the process of co-evolution.[10] The second solution is to give up the ambition of considering formal adequacy of state forms and conduct a path-dependent, path-shaping *functional* analysis of state *projects* and the particular dynamics of capitalist accumulation, and thus to focus on the trial-and-error search for an 'appropriate' state project that would co-constitute a relatively stable accumulation regime.[11] Since an object of regulation and its mode of regulation are mutually co-constituted, one cannot presuppose its functionality. Thus, a state project or form would be functional if it co-constitutes with its object of regulation a relative functional coherence that manages to reproduce itself. Therefore, functionality is a descriptive feature of a state project or form, not an explanation of its existence.

In this analysis, I follow mainly the second solution. I try to identify a dominant logic of state intervention (if any) which may co-constitute a growth dynamic. The analysis on the level of generic forms of capital relation and capitalist state form follows the functional logic as well. Thus, it does not provide an ideal type of a formally adequate state for the transition from state socialism to capitalism; instead, it deals with the functionality of the state project that emerged in respect to introducing generic forms of capitalism.

## Introducing capitalism into East Central Europe: the neo-liberal transformational states

The transition of post-communist regimes to capitalism started at a time when the global hegemony of neo-liberalism was at its height.[12] Thus, the neo-liberal premises of the Washington consensus and respective advisors shaped the policies aimed at radical systemic transformation from non-capitalist regimes to capitalist ones.[13] The transition to capitalism was designed to be essentially market-led. The policies were based on the assumption that it is sufficient to introduce the most basic, and narrowly economic, preconditions for a market economy. This would give rise to the invisible hand of market, which would discipline social actors on the way to capitalism. The policies also included the International Monetary Fund's (IMF) one-size-fits-all monetarist panacea of anti-inflationary policy based on fiscal and monetary restraint. Moreover, for various reasons, it was considered crucial to introduce the conditions for emergence of the market at once and as soon as possible. Thus, most of the policies implemented in post-socialist states included anti-inflationary measures of budgetary and monetary restraint, shock price liberalization, privatization, and trade liberalization. Similar policies were implemented in all countries of ECE and in many other post-communist states. However, in the Visegrád countries, the original neo-liberal enthusiasm of reformers for austerity measures was not fully realized. Some form of compensation and compromise soon emerged to preserve social cohesion as an important element of public policy. For instance, Poland experienced huge political backlash against the downturn caused by shock therapy and, already in 1991, the Olszewski government 'forfeited shock therapy' and attempted to create social

*Table 4.1*   Neo-liberal transformational state in ECE

| |
| --- |
| Shock stabilization |
| Shock price liberalization |
| Shock trade liberalization (+ reorientation) |
| Privatization |
| Some form of compensation and compromise to preserve social cohesion |

compromise by a more cohesion-oriented strategy.[14] Thus, in introducing generic conditions for capitalist accumulation, a distinctive state form emerged, which I call the *Neo-liberal transformational state* (see Table 4.1).

The Neoliberal transformational state was relatively functional in the CEE states. Basic forms of capital relation such as money form, wage form, and commodification of labour power were institutionalized in the early nineties. Moreover, CEE states have basic generic features and fulfil basic functions of the capitalist state such as institutional separation between state and economy, monopoly of coercion, tax capacity, and the rule of law. However, elsewhere in the post-Soviet states, the neo-liberal transformational state failed to institutionalize capitalist forms, leading to what Burawoy called 'economic involution' to a non-capitalist social formation.[15] In the ECE states, the basic measures of property-rights provision, wage systems, and tax-raising capacity are broadly comparable to the situation in the advanced capitalist countries: the figures also show that the turnover in barter, which indicates institutionalization of the market and social forms it presupposes, is very low in the ECE states (see Table 4.2). Moreover, as seen in Figure 4.1, the World Bank's indicators of governance, a measure of the formal adequacy of the state, for ECE states have similar levels to those of the advanced capitalist states, in contrast to the post-Soviet states.[16] The relative success in ECE in contrast to the painful failure elsewhere is usually explained by the presence of foreign direct investment in ECE, by ECE's location, by the initial level of development, and by the inherited institutional framework.[17]

## Klausian Welfare National State

The Czech strategy of post-socialist transformation was heavily influenced by ideas articulated by Václav Klaus.[18] However, Klaus' own reform

*Table 4.2*   Some basic measures of institutionalization of capitalist relations

| | Insecure property rights | Untaxed sales (less than 50% taxed) | Tax revenue as a % of GDP (2000) | Barter more than 25% turnover | Overdue wages | Substantial amount overdue to workers |
| --- | --- | --- | --- | --- | --- | --- |
| Germany | 14% | 19% | 26% | NA | NA | NA |
| Italy | 29% | 18% | 39% | NA | NA | NA |
| Spain | 11% | 13% | NA | NA | NA | NA |
| Sweden | 10% | 18% | 35% | NA | NA | NA |
| UK | 13% | 25% | 35% | NA | NA | NA |
| Czech Republic | 23% | 20% | 32% | 3% | 31% | 2% |
| Hungary | 14% | 8% | 33% | 0% | 5% | 1% |
| Poland | 10% | 7% | 28% | 5% | 18% | 4% |
| Slovakia | 14.% | 91% | 31% | 21% | 32% | 3% |
| Lithuania | 29% | 2% | 23% | 3% | | 0% |
| Estonia | 8% | 4% | 27% | 2% | | 0% |
| Romania | 22% | 2% | 27% | 8% | 13% | 0% |
| Bulgaria | 20% | 22% | 29% | 3% | 8% | 2% |
| Kazakhstan | 15% | 10% | 10% | 22% | | 10% |
| Kyrgizstan | 38% | 2% | 12% | 23% | | 10% |
| Uzbekistan | 10% | 12% | NA | 14% | 33% | 7% |
| Russia | 42% | 11% | 22% | 34% | 37% | 10% |
| Ukraine | 44% | 21% | 22% | 32% | 24% | 13% |

*Sources*: *Insecure property rights* is the percentage of World Bank's World Business Environment Survey 1999 (WBES) that reported that they disagreed in most cases or strongly disagreed that the legal system will uphold contract and property rights. *Untaxed sales* is the percentage of WBES that reported typical taxes less than 50 per cent of sales. The source of *tax revenue data* is the World Bank's Development Indicators. *Barter turnover* and overdue wages data are from the Business Environment and Enterprise Performance Survey, developed jointly by the World Bank and the European Bank for Reconstruction and Development, 1999 data.

scenario of economic reform was a product of a strategic compromise.[19] Indeed, in the path-shaping moment of 1990, the group of monetarist economists around Klaus had a relatively weak position in Václav Havel's Civic Forum and especially in the Government of the National Understanding. Klaus had to compromise with social-democratically-leaning 'anti-political' dissidents around Havel and their allies who were brought to power by the 'Velvet Revolution'.[20] Therefore, in spite

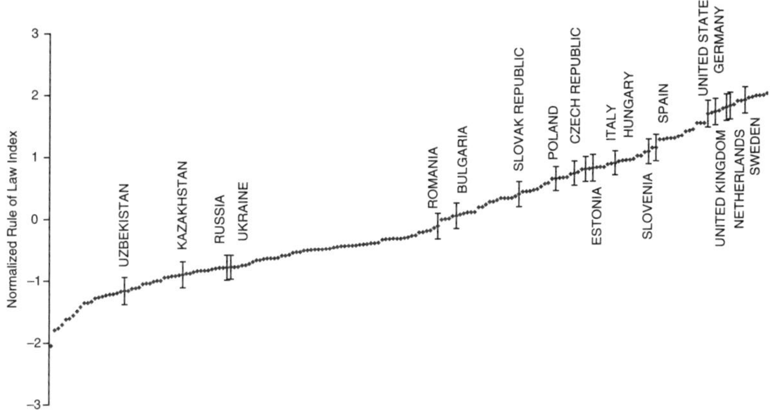


*Figure 4.1*   Rule of law 2002 (1996)

*Source*: 'Governance Matters III: Governance Indicators for 1996-2002' by Daniel Kaufmann, Aart Kraay and Massimo Mastruzzi, 2003.

of the radical neo-liberal rhetoric, the actual reform strategy could by characterized as 'social-liberal'.[21] It was formulated in the governmental document entitled *The Scenario of Economic Reform*, which was approved by federal parliament in September 1990 and launched in January 1991.[22] The scenario included anti-inflationary policy based on monetary restraint (essentially the standard IMF package, indigenously produced however[23]); price liberalization and the freeing of imports; strict wage control, particularly aimed at keeping wages in state-owned enterprises under control;[24] internal currency convertibility; and, finally, it contained what Myant calls an 'incongruous appendage',[25] the social policy section.[26] This contained programs for the reduction in the size and the retraining of the labour force, legalization of collective bargaining, and a comparatively generous and elaborate social and healthcare system. However incongruent this part may be from the viewpoint of the radical neo-liberal rhetoric that it accompanied, it became an important distinguishing feature of Czech reform strategy (see Table 4.3).[27]

I call the state project that became dominant in the early nineties *Klausian* because Czech post-socialist economic reform and economic thinking was dominated by Klaus, who promoted, for various reasons, a very specific mix of economic policies. Klaus' individual agency is not

*Table 4.3*   Klausian welfare national state, 1990–6

| Distinctive set of economic policies | Distinctive set of social policies | Primary scale (if any) | Primary means to compensate market failure |
| --- | --- | --- | --- |
| Creating capitalism (not developmental) | 'Silent' welfare provision in order to keep social | Primacy of national scale (monetarist | Compensating state |
| Promotion of local capital | peace during the transformation | reasoning of national aggregates) | |
| Monetarism | Collective | Centralized | |
| Minimal regulation | bargainingLow-wage | administration | |
| Bank socialism | low-unemployment policy | Economic nationalism in an open economy | |
| *Klausian* | *Welfare* | *National* | *State* |

crucial here; instead, he is important as an emblematic figure whose thinking was very much reflected in policy-making in the early 1990s. As the KlWNS was an integral part of the broader project of the neo-liberal transformatory state, the ultimate mission was to create conditions for capitalist accumulation and to break from the past.[28] Klaus managed to achieve a discursive closure by presenting his specific shock-therapy aid path to capitalism as the only alternative to communism. Thus, on the discursive level, there was no 'third way' – anyone seeking alternatives to his monetarism presented a threat to the democratization process as a whole and would lead the country back to 'before November 1989'. This rationale was that, in order to achieve economic recovery and development, it is enough to introduce the most basic and narrowly economic preconditions for market economy, in particular private ownership, free prices, and macroeconomic equilibrium. The 'invisible hand of the market' would give existing enterprises and new actors signals that would guide them in adapting to the environment.

Klausian strategy was *monetarist* and based on the diagnoses of economic problems and corresponding precepts of the IMF economists.[29] These economists did not fear a fall in output, but were fixated on avoiding inflation and trade deficits.[30] In addition to these neo-classical and monetarist assumptions, Klausian strategy was also based on *economic nationalism*. There was a rather naïve view of the country's economic level compared with the EU. This included an exaggerated notion of the level of industrial development, its prowess, or competitiveness. It built upon the inter-war history and on its legacy of (once) famous brands. The Czechoslovak, subsequently the Czech, economy was approached as a distinct entity and internal solutions, including domestic ownership, were preferred.[31] Economic interventions sought to create local bourgeoisie, which would subsequently provide organic support for the new regime. In sum, the rationale of 'nationalist monetarism' saw no need for a positive industrial policy since the actors were assumed to 'know how' and if they did not they would be taught by the market. Moreover, the economic subjects (though yet to be constructed as capitalist) did have a nationality, which very much mattered.

Policies of the time very much reflected this way of thinking. The therapy started with the macroeconomic shock of price liberalization and fiscal and monetary restraint, resulting in the decline of output.[32] Most medium and large enterprises were included into the process of 'large privatization' (regulated by the privatization act of February 1991) which was centred on the voucher method (launched in February 1992).[33] The idea was not only to denationalize industry (of which more than 80 per cent was state-owned) but also to 'educate' citizens, inculcate in them capitalist reasoning, and gain political support for the transformation strategy. Moreover, it aimed to prevent foreign investors from buying out the disorganized and undervalued Czech economy. Thus, most of the shares of the companies were distributed among the population (of whom 80 per cent participated) virtually for free. However, most of these shares soon ended up in the privatization funds that were led by state-owned banks. This produced a structure of corporate governance involving multiple conflicts of interest. The four largest state-owned banks owned six of the largest investment privatization funds, which in turn owned enterprises which were indebted to the state-owned banks. The ownership structure, bank socialism, guaranteed the environment of soft credit. The state-owned banks would support inefficient firms in their portfolios.[34] The politicians were aware of that and were unwilling to privatize banks, fearing the chain of insolvency.[35] Governed by some strategic considerations and by the belief in the superiority of unhindered market mechanism in identifying particular private owners, Klaus *et al.* vehemently opposed regulating and/or introducing any control mechanisms into the financial market and corporate governance, which enabled the management of enterprises and investment funds to 'tunnel' out the assets for their private gain.[36] Moreover, in spite of rejecting any effort to develop positive policies of industrial development, Klausian strategy included both explicit industrial policy of a weak bankruptcy framework and implicit industrial policies to provide for ad hoc intervention to help strategic enterprises threatened with bankruptcy.[37]

As far as the second dimension of state intervention is concerned, KlWNS was a *welfare* state. An elaborate system of welfare provisions was introduced in order to guarantee social peace during the process of post-socialist transformation. The social protection was introduced into the original strategy as a result of the strategic compromise with the social-democratically-leaning dissidents in the early nineties. This 'unwanted baby' became a distinguishing feature of the Czech reform strategy. The social measures included a universal and unified system of social welfare with universal compulsory health and social insurance, cash unemployment benefits, active unemployment policies, pay-as-you-go pension-security benefits, family allowances, social care benefits, social services system, and a universal healthcare system. The collective bargaining mechanism was established within a tripartite structure in January 1991. On this platform, the government negotiated a wage control system which meant that prices could rise faster than wages, but it was guaranteed that the latter would not fall by more than 12 per cent in real terms per year as a whole. The government also committed itself to various safeguards for the lowest paid, such as a minimum wage. Wage controls were envisioned to end by 1992; however, they actually continued until 1995.[38] Moreover, the social policies included the above-mentioned soft policies to keep large enterprises from failing. There was an implicit soft policy towards loss-making large enterprises. Concerned with demonstrating the success of privatization, the government encouraged the expansion of credit by keeping banks in state hands – state-owned banks. In addition, managers often welcomed protest from employees over social issues as it was a convenient bargaining issue in their quest for help from the government.[39] This helped to maintain very low unemployment during the first half of the 1990s. Together these unemployment and social policies played an important role during the transformation, particularly as they won support of vulnerable classes for the economic reform; as inequalities increased dramatically living minimums were guaranteed.[40]

When he consolidated and acquired full power after the elections in June 1992 and after the splitting up of Czechoslovakia in January 1993, Klaus waged an assault on this welfare system. He began by reducing social benefits, raising eligibility criteria, and moving away from the universal benefits toward targeting. Klaus let the minimum wage devalue and opposed corporatist negotiations in the tripartite councils. His efforts were, however, only partially successful because of the institutional path-dependency of the welfare state introduced by the strategic compromise of the early 1990s.[41] Moreover, his liberalization policies did not attempt to change low-wage low-unemployment policies, housing subsidies or wage controls. Not surprisingly he faced resistance to his attacks on social welfare and this certainly enabled the Social Democratic Party to give support by mobilizing against Klaus's attacks on welfare. The result was that the overall trends in welfare expenditure were surprisingly stable throughout this period.[42]

KlWNS was a *national* state as the national scale was a primary scale of intervention. The monetarist reasoning of national aggregates, combined with some elements of economic nationalism, made the national economy and national society taken-for-granted objects of intervention. It was the national economy with its prized enterprises that competed in the wider environment. Foreigners were generally not welcomed in the privatization. Industrial relations were negotiated on a national tripartite platform. And policy making was highly centralized, with anecdotes that, during the 'large-scale' privatization, Klaus and his colleagues and friends would sit days and nights in the office making enormous decisions about the destiny of all medium and large enterprises in the country.[43]

Even though the market had primary and superior role in the discursive construction of desirable governance mechanism, both direct state intervention and indirect steering through personal networks remained important in economic governance.[44] This compensatory state was actively involved in moderating and compensating for the social cost of economic transformation.[45]

I have described the dominant state project in its economic dimension in the Czech Republic (Czechoslovakia) in the first half of the 1990s. This project co-constituted a specific growth dynamics that Martin Myant named 'Czech capitalism'.[46] After 1993 the Czech Republic experienced accelerating, low-wage, low-inflation growth and an economic boom, which was often interpreted as a 'Czech economic miracle' proving neo-liberal prescriptions right. But this was not the 'non-hyphenated capitalism' that Klaus had sought to construct, but was largely based on particular driving forces produced by KlWNS's policies that can hardly be interpreted as 'laissez-faire'. 'The [...] boom embodied trends several of which soon exhausted themselves, in some cases leaving a legacy that held back recovery. It was linked to activities where the *new private sector* was strong, to some *state-led investment and spending* and to successes in some *established sectors* which soon approached limits.'[47]

KlWNS was only to a very limited extent functionally adequate to the growth logic of the Czech capitalism. It compensated for limited adjustment in some enterprises by securing conditions of soft credit. KlWNS investment projects (such as rebuilding of infrastructure) and social spending also played an important role in stimulating demand. Further, KlWNS secured low-wage, low-currency value, and low-inflation environment. Among other things, this environment enabled quick adaptation of existing enterprises, which was one basis for recovery from the depression.[48] Moreover, KlWNS played a crucial role in securing social reproduction by socializing the costs of transformation.

However, the Klausian project could not institutionalize as a relatively stable mode of regulation. Indeed, in the mid term, Czech capitalism was not able to reproduce itself. The functional adequacy of KlWNS had narrow limits and the factors that caused the downturn were largely produced by the very driving forces of Czech capitalism. In 1996, the Czech Republic experienced an economic downturn which was accompanied by a serious current account deficit. In April 1997, the government reacted by introducing two 'little packages' of restrictive economic measures. These were unable to avert the crisis, and instead, they undermined one of the economic driving forces. 'The downturn reflected partly the exhaustion of specific sources of growth, partly the effects of a changed approach from commercial banks following an over-extension of credit and partly the effects of the "packages" of mid-1997 which had a strong impact on household spending.'[49]

In addition, 1996 and 1997 saw a series of bank failures and frauds in the financial sectors. These failures were clearly caused by lack of regulation in the banking sector and securities market. What is more, some of these transactions were explicitly approved by the government. Klaus's governing party was hit by a stream of finance scandals that revealed corrupt intermingling of the ruling party and the class of people profiting from the frauds and privatisation. The political and economic crisis culminated in Klaus's resignation in November 1997. A search for an alternative has begun.

## Porterian workfare postnational regime

The political and economic crisis of the mid-1990s, which resulted in extraordinary elections in July 1998, brought the Social Democrats to power. 1998 marks a sea change in thinking about economic policy and in the actual orientation of Czech economic policies. It is a shift from an

*Table 4.4*　Porterian workfare postnational regime [accentuation of trends]

| Distinctive set of economic policies | Distinctive set of social policies | Primary scale (if any) | Primary means to compensate market failure |
| --- | --- | --- | --- |
| Manages insertion of the locality to 'global' economy | Subordinates social policy to economic competitiveness | Shift of power upwards, downwards, and sideways | [Shift to governance] |
| Supply-side intervention | Emphasis on employability | New role of the national scale | |
| Emphasis on skill-intensive, technology-rich activities | Downward pressure on the 'social wage' and attack on welfare rights | Equalizing/ compensating spatial project | |
| *Porterian* | *Workfare* | *Postnational* | *Regime* |

internally oriented economic nationalism towards externally oriented competitive policies of supply-side intervention. The government has fundamentally changed attitude to foreign investors, introducing ambitious investment-attracting schemes, and it has generally preferred foreign investors in the remaining privatization decisions. It has sold state shares in banks and has attempted to introduce a positive industrial policy. Social democrats also changed the attitude of government to social policy, putting it back on the political agenda, implementing some workfarist measures and addressing some of the 'post-materialist' issues such as equal opportunities and gender mainstreaming. This transformation of the dominant state project of the Czech economy has been achieved by further embedding the circuits of European and/or global capitalism. This change cannot be understood in pluralist terms as it goes across the political spectrum. Moreover, it actually started in the last days of Klaus's government. Thus, after the Social Democrats took power, the Civic Democratic Party (ODS)[50] has started to frame its economic policy in terms of promoting competitive supply-side intervention.[51] It is to this new state project, Porterian workfare postnational regime (see Table 4.4), that I now turn. I construct a stylized model of the state form based on a one-sided extrapolation of shifts in economic and social policies and in respective discourses.

As far as economic policy is concerned, I call KIWNS's successor *Porterian* as it engages in competitive policies which are very much based on the notion of competitiveness promoted by the emblematic thinker, management guru Michael Porter. PWPR is competitive as it aims to secure economic growth by promoting competitive advantages for capital based in the country. It engages in a supply-side intervention in order to manage the insertion of locality into the 'global' economy. It attempts to manage this insertion by discriminating among investors in terms of their potential contribution to the local economy. This management follows Porterian logic of competitiveness which is achieved from high and rising levels of labour productivity associated with high-tech production processes and highly-qualified-labour-intensive activities.[52] In contrast to Jessop's account of the state transformation in the advanced capitalist states, I do not call PWPR Schumpeterian since it does not engage primarily in promoting permanent innovation and enterprise as SWPR would do.[53] Instead, it focuses mainly on attracting high-quality investment to upgrade existing industrial bases. Thus, PWPR's policies aim at supporting skill-intensive and technology-rich projects. In the Czech case, it actively secures competitive advantages primarily for capital that invests on a larger scale in the country. In addition, the Porterian orientation implies that it emphasizes the importance of clusters, which are groupings of firms and public bodies such as universities or research institutes. Clusters are considered crucial for innovation and long-term development of a locality.[54] Nevertheless, PWPR's characterization as Porterian needs a qualification. The Porterian notion of competitiveness prioritizes indigenous firms[55] or it sees local development in conflict with the foreign capital.[56] The Czech version of Porterian competitiveness is largely foreign-investment-based; thus, PWPR attempts to network foreign investors with local suppliers.

The main instrument that the PWPR uses at the moment is the scheme of incentive packages for potential investors and the emerging project of cluster promotion.[57] The package to attract investors includes tax reliefs, land transfers to the investor (which often means transport of land for free), substantial subsidies for training of the labour force, and monetary bonuses for creating jobs.[58] In comparison with the general trend of neo-liberal restructuring of governance in Europe,[59] a distinctive feature of Czech supply-side intervention is its spatio-social dimension: the policy is aimed at regions with relatively higher unemployment or at regions otherwise 'structurally handicapped'. The extent of support varies accordingly.[60] A closer analysis of actually supported investments reveals that the policy is not able to meet its goals fully as the geography of investment does not seem to be influenced by the spatial dimension of state support. Moreover, as far as the quality of supported investment is concerned, the actual investment support tends to over-emphasize its quantity targets.[61] Thus, PWPR engages largely in promoting a kind of neo-Ricardian static comparative advantage (in contrast to the dynamic competitive one).[62]

As far as social policy is concerned, the Social Democrats actually stopped the retrenchment of Klaus's era. Tending to be more generous in this respect, they brought social policy back on the political agenda.[63] The unions have gained greater access and influence in policy-making.[64] However, the institutional role of tripartite negotiations remains weak.[65] The budgetary and political constraints have prevented substantial expansion of the welfare system. Instead, reforms follow a *workfarist* logic, aimed largely at motivating welfare recipients to actively look for jobs and discourage them from passively consuming benefits.[66] The competitive orientation of economic policy remains a challenge for welfarist and redistributive measures, as policy-makers at all levels remain focussed on the implications of social policies on the country's competitiveness. It is extremely important that the welfarist and redistributive orientation is *perceived* as at odds with the locational preferences of mobile capital. The radical neo-liberal reform in Slovakia by Dzurinda's government is an important reference point in the Czech Republic.[67] The underclass discourse of non-deserving clients of the welfare state has also gained in importance, with the social-democratic minister of labour as one of its vocal proponents.[68] As Potůček, one of the important participants in the discussion on social policy that the government initiated, notes, '[m]ost outcomes of such [...] negotiations resemble the centre-left recommendations well known from the contemporary British Labour Party'.[69] The New-Labour-minded people are currently dominant in the social democracy. The 2006 elections brought back to power ODS, which had been mobilizing for a radically neo-liberal workfarism.[70]

As far as the primary scale of socioeconomic intervention is concerned, recent rescaling trends allow us to characterize the PWPR as *postnational*. Even though the national scale remains dominant, the power of the national state has shifted upwards, downwards, and sideways. The accession of the Czech Republic to the European Union represents a decisive shift of state power upwards. Other international governmental and non-governmental organizations, such as CEE Bankwatch network, play an important role in decision-making and political struggles.[71] As far as the shift downwards is concerned, the government established regional self-governing units in 2000. These units have rather limited power, but in some areas, such as attracting foreign direct investment, their power is significant or about to grow.[72] Further, the workfarist social reform shifts some responsibilities to the municipal scale.

These scalar transformations make the ability of social actors to 'jump scales' an important asset in the social struggle. Moreover, rescaling, along with the shift of power sideways (see below), has changed the role of the personal networks. These networks thus can increasingly be utilized as a mechanism of interscalar steering.[73] And in these cases, the scalar steering becomes clan-like. Clan is a mechanism of governance consisting of informal networks based on mutual trust and confidence, which is upheld by stable, preferential, particularistic, mutually obligated, and legally non-enforceable relationships.[74] '[These relationships] may be kept together by either value consensus or resource dependency – that is, through "culture" and "community" – or through dominant units imposing dependence on others.'[75]

There has been only a limited shift of state power sideways so far. However, some trends and governmental plans indicate that the transformation will probably follow this direction. For instance, in 2003, the government introduced an institutional reform to promote public – private partnership (PPP) 'as known from the countries like the United Kingdom, France, Canada, and Australia...'.[76] 2004 has seen further development of this policy, including the launch of the Centre for Implementation of PPP.[77] Non-governmental agencies and forms of public–private partnership have gained in importance and are about to gain much further. Moreover, the state is seeking to have an active role not only in its promotion but also in its metagovernance.[78] This shift and rescaling are most significant in the process of attracting investment, in which economic, state, and non-state actors operating on different scales meet,[79] and where the governmental agency CzechInvest, a regional self-governing body, a municipality, 'partly-public' regional developmental agency, public-private Partnership for Support of Foreign Direct Investment, and an investor (mostly a multinational corporation) work together.

Can the PWPR secure expanded reproduction in a longer term and provide a social fix to a nascent accumulation regime? The PWPR has resolved some of the problems of Czech capitalism and its intervention addresses key elements of the renewed expansion of 2000 – foreign direct investment. 'The "successful" capitalism in the Czech Republic by 2002 appeared to be foreign rather than Czech-owned.'[80] Thus, it seems that 'foreign capitalism' is the motor of Czech economy after the exhaustion and dissolution of the Czech one.[81]

> The second boom coincided with some renewed growth in personal incomes, following some restoration of government spending. It was also boosted by strengthening growth in branches of manufacturing that depended on inward investment: this was important for its

contribution to GDP and even more important as a factor holding back the balance of payments deficit, thereby enabling the government gradually to relax its restrictive policies.[82]

However, a thorough assessment of the potential of the PWPR to be a part of a mode of regulation would have to leave the national scale. The potential object of regulation of the PWPR would be the Czech economic space as inserted into the globalizing, knowledge-based economy. Thus, PWPR may be functional in securing growth within the national economic space. However, as a mode of regulation, PWPR has to be conceived as a part of the European triadic governance regime. This is the level on which the emergent principal contradiction and dilemma of the globalizing knowledge-based economy can be addressed.[83] Thus, as a potential social fix, the PWPR can be nothing more than a local articulation of a complex European regime of governance. In this context, it is important to note that the shift towards PWPR in the Czech Republic marks a wider moment of convergence in the V4 region. Thus, after a period of distinctive national projects, we can witness a moment of relative convergence towards the PWPR in the region.[84]

## Conclusion

In this chapter, I have provided an account of the transformation of the dominant state project and intervention in the Czech Republic after the dissolution of state socialism. This account has been written from a regulationist, state-theoretical perspective. I was concerned with the effects of the state intervention on the reproduction of capital accumulation. In order to do so, however, I employed a methodology applicable to the social formations in transition. Thus, I analysed the role of the state in post-communist transition on the level of creating generic conditions of capitalism and on the level of mutual constitution of specific state regimes and specific dynamics of accumulation. On the generic level, I have described the neo-liberal transformational state that managed to introduce basic forms of capital relations in the V4. Consequently, I have provided a periodization of dominant state projects and accumulation strategies with respect to their functional adequacy in relation to the dynamics of capitalist accumulation in the Czech Republic. I have described the crystallization of a distinct state project of the early 1990s, which I have called the Klausian welfare national state. This state project constituted, and was presupposed by, a distinctive growth dynamic, Czech capitalism. However, Czech capitalism failed to reproduce itself.

The crisis of Czech capitalism in the mid-nineties gave rise to a search for an alternative. The Porterian workfare postnational regime, which is currently emerging not only in the Czech Republic, but also in the wider region of the V4 as a part of broader European governance regime, may provide a social fix to an emergent accumulation regime. It is a question to what extent the Porterian orientation of the V4 'necessarily' reflects the position of the region in the international division of labour and to what extent it is an effect of other factors having important consequences for the position of the respective states.[85] The emergence of PWPR is not a matter of automatic steering; on the contrary, it must be perceived as one of the possible and contingent outcomes of the search for a solution to the problems of post-socialist capitalisms in the V4. Thus, the PWPR is a political project with social forces and structural conditions underlying it. It is a challenge for future research to illuminate the conditions of its existence.

## Endnotes

1. I have extremely benefited from Bob Jessop's and Colin Hay's feedback on the earlier version of this paper. I am also grateful to Nitsan Chorev, Neil Brenner, and Dorothee Bohle for their comments. Needless to say, the full responsibility for the argument of this paper remains with me.
2. See B. Jessop, *The Future of the Capitalist State*, Cambridge, UK and Malden, MA: Polity Press, 2002; R. Boyer, *The Regulation School: A Critical Introduction*, New York: Columbia University Press, 1990.
3. For a detailed discussion of the concepts of state project and accumulation strategy, see B. Jessop, *State Theory: Putting the Capitalist State in Its Place*, University Park, PA: Pennsylvania State University Press, 1990.
4. Jessop, *The Future of the Capitalist State*.
5. Social policy is analysed here primarily in the context of reproduction of labour power, which implies that some aspects of welfare are ignored.
6. A. Lipietz, *Mirage or Miracles*, p. 15.
7. See Jessop, *The Future of the Capitalist State*, pp. 36–48.
8. See B. Jessop, *The Capitalist State*, Oxford: Oxford University Press, 1982; Jessop, *State Theory*; Jessop, *The Future of the Capitalist State*.
9. R. Boyer, 'The Political in the Era of Globalization and Finance: Focus on Some *Régulation* School Research', *International Journal of Urban and Regional Research*, 24, 2, 2000, 274–322, p. 291.
10. Cf. B. Jessop, 'The Crisis of the National Spatio-Temporal Fix and the Tendential Ecological Dominance of Globalizing Capitalism', *International Journal of Urban and Regional Research*, 24, 2, 2000, 323–60.
11. State projects are attempts to give a given contradictory complexity of state institutions relative internal unity to guide its action. They may give rise to state forms. Accumulation strategies are attempts to give a certain substantive unity and direction to the circuit of capital. See Chapters 11 and 12 in Jessop, *State Theory*.

12. Cf. C. G. A. Bryant and E. Mokrzycki, 'Introduction. Theorizing the Changes in East-Central Europe', in C. G. A. Bryant and E. Mokrzycki, eds, *The New Great Transformation? Change and Continuity in East-Central Europe*, London: Routledge, 1994.
13. Cf. J. Williamson, 'Democracy and The "Washington Consensus"', *World Development*, 21, 8, 1993, 1329–36.
14. Chapter 2 in M. A. Orenstein, *Out of the Red: Building Capitalism and Democracy in Postcommunist Europe*, Ann Arbor: The University of Michigan Press, 2001.
15. M. Burawoy, 'The State and Economic Involution: Russia through a China Lens', *World Development*, 24, 6, 1996, 1105–17. See also L. P. King, 'Does Neoliberalism Work? Comparing Economic and Sociological Explanations', *New Political Economy*, 2006 [under review].
16. D. Kaufmann, A. Kraay, and M. Mastruzzi, *Governance Matters III: Governance Indicators for 1996–2002*, Washington: World Bank, 2003.
17. L. P. King, 'Does Neoliberalism Work? Comparing Economic and Sociological Explanations', *American Journal of Sociology*, 2004 [under review]; M. Myant, 'Czech Capitalism – Towards a European Model?' (Paper presented at the Managing the Economic Transition, 13th Research Seminar 'What Type of Capitalism in the Post-Communist Economies?' Cambridge University, Cambridge, 2004).
18. A former research economist born in 1941, admirer of Margaret Thatcher, Klaus would describe himself as a follower of Milton Friedman. He experienced minor repression after 1968; however, he was able to retain his job in the state bank. During the 1980s, Klaus took part in the activities of a group of economists around the Institute of Forecasting who were able to relatively freely access and discuss western economic theories. In the position of Minister of Finance and later prime minister, he was a principal designer of Czech reforms. Following a period in opposition after his resignation in the crisis of 1997, he was elected president in 2003.
19. Orenstein, *Out of the Red*; J. Gould, 'Beyond Creating Owners: Privatization and Democratization in the Slovak and Czech Republics, 1990–1998' (PhD, Columbia University, 2001).
20. On the discursive production of the monetarist and anti-political subjectivities, see G. Eyal, 'Anti-Politics and the Spirit of Capitalism: Dissidents, Monetarists, and the Czech Transition to Capitalism', *Theory and Society* 29, 2000, 49–92; G. Eyal, *The Origins of Postcommunist Elites: From Prague Spring to the Breakup of Czechoslovakia*, Minneapolis and London: University of Minnesota Press, 2003.
21. Orenstein, *Out of the Red*. cf. M. Dangerfield, 'Ideology and the Czech Transformation: Neoliberal Rhetoric or Neoliberal Reality?', *East European Politics and Societies*, 11(3), 1997, 436–69.
22. Klaus originally wanted to follow Balzerowicz's strategy of 'revolutionary legitimacy' and to launch the reform without electoral approval; however, the leading members of the government were reluctant to do so; M. Myant, *Transforming Socialist Economies: The Case of Poland and Czechoslovakia*, Aldershot: Edward Elgar, 1993, p. 173; Orenstein, *Out of the Red*. The plan was thus put to the electoral test in June 1990, Klaus eventually stressing winning popular support for the reform; V. Klaus, *Rok Málo Či Mnoho V Dějinách*

*Země? [a Year a Lot or a Little in the History of a Country?]*, Prague: Repro-Media, 1993). This also explains the 'delay' in comparison with Poland.

23. On a 'complete meeting of minds' between the reformers on the one hand and the IMF and the IBRD on the other, see former GATT official Drábek; Z. Drábek, 'IMF and IBRD Policies in the Former Czechoslovakia', *Journal of Comparative Economics*, 20, 2, 1995, 235–64. However, it seems that the influence of the IMF and the World Bank importantly contributed to the success of the monetarists in imposing their philosophy on economic reform; J. Adam, 'Transformation to a Market Economy in Czechoslovakia', *Europe-Asia Studies*, 45, 4, 1993; J. Bockman and G. Eyal, 'Eastern Europe as a Laboratory for Economic Knowledge: The Transnational Roots of Neoliberalism', *American Journal of Sociology*, 108, 2, 2002, 310–52.

24. D. Lipton and J. Sachs, 'Creating a Market Economy in Eastern Europe: The Case of Poland', *Brookings Papers on Economic Activity*, 1, 1990, 75–133, p. 101.

25. M. Myant, *The Rise and Fall of Czech Capitalism: Economic Development in the Czech Republic since 1989*, Cheltenham, UK and Northampton, MA: Edward Elgar, 2003, p. 18.

26. The economic part of the scenario was drafted by Klaus and Vladimir Dlouhý, the social part by the labour minister Petr Miller.

27. Orenstein, *Out of the Red*.

28. From today's perspective, it is interesting to note that the aim of introducing capitalism was highly contested at the beginning of the transformation. Petr Uhl of the dissent fraction of Civic Forum provocatively proposed to include introducing capitalism to the programme of the Civic Forum (without agreeing with it) in 1991 – the proposal was rejected; P. Uhl, 'KSČM zatím jen nadbíhá nostalgii [KSČM Only Make up to the Nostalgia So Far]', *Právo*, 2004.

29. Such as Lipton and Sachs, 'Creating a Market Economy in Eastern Europe: The Case of Poland'.

30. Myant, *Rise and Fall of Czech Capitalism*, pp. 22–6.

31. Ibid., pp. 13–15; Orenstein, *Out of the Red: Building Capitalism and Democracy in Postcommunist Europe*, pp. 76–9.

32. Myant, *Rise and Fall of Czech Capitalism*.

33. See N. Shafik, 'Making a Market: Mass Privatization in the Czech and Slovak Republics', *World Development*, 23, 7, 1995, 1143–56. Before the large privatization act was passed, a few large foreign takeovers/mergers and joint ventures of state-owned enterprises had occurred involving state-owned enterprises. The most important was the takeover of Škoda by Volkswagen; P. Pavlínek, 'Transformation of the Central and East European Passenger Car Industry: Selective Peripheral Integration through Foreign Direct Investment', *Environment and Planning A*, 34, 2002, 1685–709.

34. See Z. Kudrna *et al.*, *Vzestup a Pád Investiční a Poštovní Banky [The Rise and Fall of Investiční a Poštovní Banka]*, Prague: e-Merit, 2002, available at http:// www.historieipb.cz/.

35. Gould, 'Beyond Creating Owners'.

36. E.g., R. Cull, J. Matesová, and M. Shirley, 'Ownership and the Temptation to Loot: Evidence from Privatized Firms in the Czech Republic', *Journal of Comparative Economics*, 30, 2002, 1–24.

37. Myant, *Rise and Fall of Czech Capitalism*, pp. 188–93.
38. M. Myant and S. Smith, 'Czech Trade Unions in Comparative Perspective', *European Journal of Industrial Relations*, 5, 3, 1999, 265–85.
39. M. Myant, 'Employers' Interest Representation in the Czech Republic', *Journal of Communist Studies and Transition Politics*, 16, 4, 2000, 1–21.
40. J. Veerník, ed., *Zpráva O Vývoji České Společnosti 1989–1998 [Social Report of the Czech Republic in 1989–1998]*, Prague: Academia, 1998.
41. Cf. P. Pierson, *Dismantling the Welfare State? Reagan, Thatcher, and the Politics of Retrenchment*, Cambridge: Cambridge University Press, 1994.
42. M. Potůček, 'Accession and Social Policy: The Case of the Czech Republic', *Journal of European Social Policy*, 14, 3, 2004, 253–66.
43. P. Husák, *Budování Kapitalismu V Čechách: Rozhovory S Tomášem Ježkem [Building Capitalism in Bohemia: Interviews with Tomáš Ježek]*, Prague: Volvox Globator, 1997.
44. In contrast, Poland constructed 'deliberative governance structures' that helped public and private actors learn from and monitor one another. See G. A. McDermott, *Embedded Politics: Industrial Networks and Institutional Change in Postcommunism*, Ann Arbor: The University of Michigan Press, 2002.
45. B. Greskovits, *The Political Economy of Protest and Patience: East European and Latin American Transformations Compared*, Budapest: Central European University Press, 1998.
46. Myant, *Rise and Fall of Czech Capitalism*.
47. Ibid., p. 52, emphasis mine.
48. This often happened, however, by regressing to exporting products associated with a lower level of development, ibid., p. 42.
49. Ibid., p. 52.
50. In Czech, Občansko demokratická strana.
51. ODS opposes governmental policy by promoting different, market-based, means of competitiveness promotion. See M. Říman, *Nový růst: Modrá šance pro podnikání [New Growth: Blue Chance for Entrepreneurship]*, Prague: Civic Democratic Party, 2003.
52. M. E. Porter, *The Competitive Advantage of Nations*, London: Macmillan, 1990.
53. Jessop, *The Future of the Capitalist State*.
54. Cf. P. Benneworth and N. Henry, 'Where Is the Value Added in the Cluster Approach? Hermeneutic Theorising, Economic Geography and Clusters as a Multiperspectival Approach', *Urban Studies*, 41, 5/6, 2004, 1011–23.
55. Cf. Myant, *Rise and Fall of Czech Capitalism*, pp. 245–62.
56. A. M. Rugman and A. Verbeke, 'Multinational Enterprises and Public Policy', *Journal of International Business Studies*, 29, 1, 1998, 115–36.
57. See CzechInvest, *Clusters: Programme Approved by Government Resolution No. 414/2004 on 28 April, 2004*, Prague: CzechInvest/Ministry of Industry and Trade, 2004.
58. The Czech Republic, along with other ECE states, such as Slovakia, provides the maximum subsidies that the EU regulations allow.
59. Cf. N. Brenner, *New State Spaces: Urban Governance and the Rescaling of Statehood*, Oxford and New York: Oxford University Press, 2004.
60. However, investment projects even in the capital of Prague can be and are supported by the state.

61. Cf. T. J. S. Mallya, Z. Kukulka, and C. Jensen, 'Are Incentives a Good Investment for the Host Country? An Empirical Evaluation of the Czech National Incentive Scheme', *Transnational Corporations*, 13, 1, 2004, 109–48.
62. Static comparative advantage refers to 'natural' factor endowments (e.g. raw materials, cheap labour power). Dynamic competitive advantage relates to 'social' factors – basically, to the overall efficiency of resource allocation. Long-term competitiveness would be based on developing competitive advantage. Jessop, *The Future of the Capitalist State*, pp. 119–23.
63. Cf. Potůček, 'Accession and Social Policy'.
64. Interview with Martin Fassmann of Czech-Moravian Confederation of Trade Unions, 26 October 2005.
65. See M. Fassmann and H. Čornějová, *Czech Republic: National Social Dialogue on the Formulation, Implementation and Monitoring of Employment Policies*, Geneva: International Labour Office, 2003.
66. Cf. J. A. Peck, *Workfare States*, New York: Guilford Press, 2001.
67. See, for instance, Ministry of Finance, *Rozpočtový výhled 2003–2006: Koncepce reformy veřejných rozpočtů [Budgetary Prospect 2003–2006: Concept of the Public Budgets Reform]*, Prague: Ministry of Finance of the Czech Republic, 2003; B. Sobotka, 'Chceme podpořit růst a prosperitu [We Want to Support Growth and Prosperity],' *Hospodářské noviny*, 2004; 'Slovenská reforma daní je mnohem hlubší než česká [Slovak Tax Reform Is Much Deeper Than the Czech One],' *Hospodářské noviny*, 2004.
68. A. Kramer, 'Nemůžeme si dovolit štědrost k těm, kteří nechtějí pracovat, says Zdeněk Škromach [We Cannot Afford to Be Generous to Those Who Do Not Work (Interview with Zdeněk Škromach)],' *Právo*, 2004.
69. Potůček, 'Accession and Social Policy'.
70. E.g., A. Páralová, *Více svobody, méně regulace [More Freedom, Less Regulation]*, Prague: Civic Democratic Party, 2004.
71. E.g., J. Drahokoupil, 'From Collectivization to Globalization: Putting Populism in Its Place', *Slovak Foreign Policy Affairs*, Spring, 2005, 65–74.
72. Interview with Pavel Mertlík, 24 October 2005.
73. See Drahokoupil, 'From Collectivization to Globalization: Putting Populism in Its Place'.
74. J. R. Hollingsworth and L. N. Lindberg, 'The Governance of the American Economy: The Role of Markets, Clans, Hierarchies, and Associative Behaviour', in W. Streeck and P. C. Schmitter, eds, *Private Interest Government: Beyond Market and State*, London: Sage, 1985; L. N. Lindberg, J. L. Campbell, and J. R. Hollingsworth, 'Economic Governance and the Analysis of Structural Change in the American Economy', in J. L. Campbell, J. R. Hollingsworth, and L. N. Lindberg, eds, *Governance of the American Economy*, Cambridge: Cambridge University Press, 1991; W. G. Ouchi, 'Markets, Bureaucracies, and Clans', *Administrative Science Quarterly*, 25, 1, 1980, 129–41; W. Streeck and P. C. Schmitter, 'Community, Market, State – and Associations? The Prospective Contribution of Interest Governance to Social Order', in W. Streeck and P. C. Schmitter, eds, *Private Interest Government: Beyond Market and State*, London: Sage, 1985.
75. J. R. Hollingsworth, P. C. Schmitter, and W. Streeck, 'Capitalism, Sectors, Institutions, and Performance', in J. R. Hollingsworth, P. C. Schmitter, and

W. Streeck, eds, *Governing Capitalist Economies: Performance and Control of Economic Sectors*, Oxford and New York: Oxford University Press, 1994, p. 6.

76. MF, *Rozpočtový výhled 2003–2006: Koncepce reformy veřejných rozpočtů [Budgetary Prospect 2003–2006: Concept of the Public Budgets Reform]*, p. 132.

77. MF, *Informace O Stavu Systémové Implementace Partnerství Veřejného a Soukromého Sektoru [Information on the State of Systemic Implementation of Public-Private Partnership]*, Ministry of Finance of the Czech Republic, 2004.

78. Metagovernance refers to organization of the conditions of governance in a broad sense. Jessop, *The Future of the Capitalist State*.

79. J. Drahokoupil, 'Post-Fordist Capitalism in the Czech Republic: The Investment of Flextronics in Brno', *Czech Sociological Review*, 40, 3, 2004, 343–62.

80. Myant, *Rise and Fall of Czech Capitalism*, p. 3.

81. Cf. A. Zemplinerová, 'The Importance of Foreign-Owned Enterprises in the Catching-up Process', in K. Liebscher *et al.*, eds, *The Economic Potential of a Larger Europe*, Cheltenham, UK and Northampton, MA: Edward Elgar, 2004.

82. Myant, *Rise and Fall of Czech Capitalism*, p. 52.

83. On the new contradictions and dilemma of the knowledge-based economy, see B. Jessop, 'The State and the Contradictions of the Knowledge-Driven Economy', in J. R. Bryson *et al.*, eds, *Knowledge, Space, Economy*, London: Routledge, 2000; Jessop, *The Future of the Capitalist State*, pp. 138–40, 271–75.

84. J. Drahokoupil, 'The state of the Capitalist State in East-Central Europe: Towards the Porterian Workfare Post-National Regime?', in B. S. Sergi, W. T. Bagatelas and J. Kubicová, eds., *Industries and Markets in Central and Eastern Europe*, Aldershot, UK: Ashgate, 2007.

85. In this context, it is important to note that the Baltic states have developed a distinct model of competition states relying more on market forces and provision of a flexible, low-cost environment. Slovenia has developed another, balanced neo-corporatist, type of competition state. See D. Bohle and B. Greskovits, 'Europeanization and the Variety of Competition States in Central-Eastern Europe', 2006, unpublished manuscript.

# 5
# Corporate Control Models in Russian Companies and Business Integration

*Tatiana G. Dolgopyatova*

## Introduction[1]

Following the completion of Russian voucher privatization in the 1990s, issues of corporate governance became increasingly important. Initially, the main focus of attention was on the dominant role played by employee stock ownership, the power of managers to control firms and the limited role played by outside investors and owners. Foreign investors, in particular, were often shocked by the forms of Russian corporate governance that emerged as privatization and property redistribution were shaped by political compromises between the government and employees.

The economic uprising that followed the 1998 financial crisis triggered a further round of property redistribution and revealed problems in Russian companies caused by loopholes in corporate legislation and enforcement. The result was an increase in academic and policy interest in Russian corporate governance and much greater attention to the relationship between structures of ownership and the role of specific actors in corporate governance. This chapter focuses on the development of stock ownership, the establishment of micro-level forms of corporate control, and the different roles and motivations of key actors in these emerging forms of corporate governance. The chapter shows how concentrated insider ownership and consolidated corporate control are emerging in Russian companies following a period of intensive transformation of stock ownership.

The chapter is based primarily on empirical surveys of enterprises carried out in 1999–2005 and in-depth interviews conducted with directors or/and owners of Russian joint-stock companies (JSCs), including 19 interviews in industry in five regions of Russia carried out in Autumn 1999;[2] 20 interviews at open JSCs in industry and other sectors in six regions carried out between Summer and Autumn 2003;[3] and 33 interviews with industrial JSCs in eight Russian regions carried out in Autumn 2003.[4]

## Evolution of corporate ownership and type of corporate governance during the 1990s

In the late 1980s, state-owned enterprises fell under the *de facto* control of coalitions forged between managers and employees, coalitions that were initially strengthened by the distribution of share ownership resulting from voucher privatization. After privatization, the Russian corporate sector was characterized by forms of dispersed employee share ownership[5] and insider corporate governance models with weak shareholders and strong managers.[6] As shareholders themselves, managers were able to use a wide range of tools for exercising control over companies and expropriating their value from other owners: asset stripping and violation of general shareholder rights were common.[7] Throughout the 1990s, general shareholders benefited little from holding an interest in property that did not provide any tangible benefits. Enterprises were generally loss-making, actually or formally, and so it was rarely possible to profit by selling shares or earning dividends. Even the owners of large shareholdings could not exercise their legal rights over managers effectively given the limited *de facto* legal protections. Ownership could generate revenue only if it gained control over the cash-flows of an enterprise. Consequently, buying shares typically resulted in a struggle to control the day-to-day activities and accounts of a company.

Since this time major changes have occurred and incentives for corporate property redistribution have now been in place for more than 12 years:

i. Continuing privatization has reduced the role of state authorities at all levels.
ii. Managers have increased their equity holdings at the expense of the equity share held by employees.
iii. External non-state actors have become larger equity owners, particularly with vertical and horizontal integration and the emergence of conglomerates in the Russian economy. In particular,

successful Russian exporters of oil, gas, and minerals have now acquired large stockholdings across the economy.

iv. Individual shareholders and coalitions of shareholders have emerged as substantial stockholders, now accounting for about 40–50 per cent of total stock.

After the financial crisis of 1998, economic growth resulted in private sector expansion, the transfer of ownership from company managers to outside private businesses, and further property redistribution and concentration. Powerful business groups emerged, not all of them national 'oligarch' groups, but also groups of companies operating at regional and local scales.[8] Large privatized companies were restructured into several interlinked company groups and these in turn expanded through mergers and acquisitions.[9] The result has been that private sector firm organization in Russia has become more diversified, while the development of market structures and the emergence of national corporate governance systems have become more tightly linked processes.

There is some evidence to suggest that this process of business integration may be having positive effects on enterprise performance. For example, enterprises that are members of 'oligarch' groups demonstrated better use of labour and capital in the 2000s and accelerated growth of total factor productivity in comparison with enterprises not involved in company groups.[10] Indeed, surveys carried out between 1999 and 2002 have shown that enterprises that were members of company groups made twice the level of investments as non-group companies, and were one and a half times more likely to have invested in new projects or management systems, introduced new products or attracted new suppliers compared with 'independent' enterprises.[11]

In many companies, business integration was followed by takeovers and mergers, a process that sharply curtailed the rights of those who had acquired shares in the mid-1990s. The result has been an increase in corporate battles in recent years. But when stock ownership and control were consolidated and groups of companies were created, property relations within groups became more stable and predictable. The control of a powerful group thus seems to have insured shareholders and member companies against further threats of capture.[12] One consequence is that dispersed employee ownership has declined and its place has been taken by highly concentrated corporate ownership by managers and/or external investors representing domestic private capital. In these cases, external powerful owners and groups increasingly shape management practices and exercise control over individual managers.[13] This form of stock consolidation and control over management has become increasingly common across the Russian corporate sector.

Consolidated insider ownership, often under the leadership of a dominant owner or manager, was a 'second best' option when institutional and legal protections were underdeveloped, but this often led to asset stripping instead of business restructuring and development.[14] Interviews have shown that these incentives for both 'old' insiders (i.e., 'red directors', consolidated large stock) and 'new' insiders (large external shareholders who took the CEO position) have gradually converged.[15] Both types of insider groups expressed interests in business modernization, but 'old' insiders were inevitably faced with much more limited capacities for developing these investments. Moreover, interviews suggest that when a Board of Directors is created under insider management there is a tendency for the number of board members to decrease. This reduction in the size of the Board seems to be limited only by the need to comply with specific legal requirements governing JSCs of more than 1000 and more than 10,000 shareholders. As a rule the average number of members does not exceed seven persons and, as a result, large shareholder representatives and executive managers play leading roles on the Board.

The Boards of Directors at several enterprises interviewed included representatives of work collectives (usually medium-level managers or trade union leaders), especially if there are employee shareholders in the collective. In some cases these representatives pursue a relatively independent policy, but more often they are closely affiliated with management. At the end of the 1990s, it also became more common to include representatives of regional or local authorities who are not shareholders on the Boards of Directors. In this way the authorities were able to 'add' to administrative regulation and informal relationships some more direct (and legitimate) methods of corporate control over the activity of JSCs operating within their jurisdictions, a process that also led to the emergence of 'independent directors' in Russian companies.

These trends in composition of stock ownership and Boards of Directors have been the focus of a number of quantitative and qualitative surveys (Table 5.1). The results demonstrate a growing concentration of equity capital beginning in the mid-1990s and resulting in a situation where many industrial JSCs have a controlling or blocking shareholder. In a survey of 304 open JSCs in different sectors of the economy conducted in Autumn 2002,[16] over 70 per cent of the respondents (76 per cent in industry) thought that their enterprise already had an owner who is able to control activities of the enterprise. A joint survey conducted by the Centre for Economic and Financial Research (CEFIR) and the Institute for the Economy in Transition (IET) in 2002, which covered more than 600 industrial JSCs, showed that the average share of the biggest external shareholder at all companies was about 24 per cent of the equity capital, while that of the company's administration was more than 19 per cent.[17]

*Table 5.1*   Stock property concentration in industry according to survey data of expert organizations

| Concentration indicators | SU HSE -1 | | BEA | | IET | | REB | | | SU HSE -2 | |
|---|---|---|---|---|---|---|---|---|---|---|---|
| | End 1995 | End 1998 | Privati-zation | Jan. 2000 | End 1999 | Feb. 2003 | Feb. 1999 | Feb. 2001 | Feb. 2003 | End 1998 | End of 2001 |
| Share of the biggest shareholder, % | 26.3 | 27.8 | ... | ... | ... | 29.7 | 32.9 | 34.5 | 37.2 | 36.7 | 42.2 |
| Share of three biggest shareholders, % | 40.5 | 45.1 | ... | ... | 38.1* | 48.9 | ... | ... | ... | 48.9 | 57.6 |
| Share of enterprises (%) having a shareholder with interest over 25% | 44.5 | 46.8 | 13.4 | 25.8 | 31.6 | ... | 51 | 51 | 56 | 55.2 | 67.1 |
| Share of enterprises (%) having a shareholder with interest over 50% | 14.8 | 19.6 | 5.5 | 10.3 | 12.8 | ... | 25 | 25 | 26 | 32.0 | 39.5 |

* data for five shareholders

*Source*: author's calculations based on surveys' primary data or published data.

SU HSE -1, survey of 360 enterprises (318 JSCs) conducted in 1999; about 220 JSC responded.

BEA, survey of 437 enterprises conducted by Bureau of Economic Analysis in 2000; about 390 JSC responded.

REB regular surveys; about 100–150 companies responded (Kapelyushnikov, Dyomina, 2005, p. 58).

SU HSE-2, survey of about 520 enterprises (350 JSC); 220 responded.

IET, survey of 201 JSC at the end of 1999; about 190 responded (Radygin, Entov, 2001, pp. 190, 194), and survey at the beginning of 2003; over 280 responded (Drobyshevskii *et al.*, 2003).

Other in-depth interviews have shown that the real concentration of property may be much higher than that reflected in these formal surveys. In the majority of cases, top-managers are the dominating owners. Thus, in two sets of interviews in 2003 with about 50 JSCs, 70 per cent have an owner that controls more than 50 per cent of the shares, and block holders (controlling more than 25 per cent of shares) were represented in about 90 per cent of the companies.

Capital consolidation in the hands of the largest owners is also occurring. A quantitative survey of 822 JSCs conducted in March–June 2005 by a joint project of SU HSE and Hitotsubashi University (Tokyo)[18] has shown that 81 per cent of JSCs surveyed have a block holder and about 70 per cent have a single shareholder with more then 50 per cent of ordinary shares. More than 82 per cent of those surveyed indicated that their JSCs have a stockholder (or consolidated group of stockholders) controlling their company.

## Specifics of national corporate governance

In the past decade, the Russian corporate economy has been characterized by a process of constant property redistribution, which was usually accompanied by the takeover or stabilization of corporate control exercised by 'red' directors. Empirical studies of SU HSE and Russian Economic Barometer (REB) have found that since the mid-1990s, on average, the principal owners of six to eight per cent of industrial enterprises change every year. The earlier survey (above) of 822 companies similarly showed that about 30 per cent of the firms changed their core owners between 2001 and 2004. Redistribution processes annually affect up to one-sixth of stock capital with transactions generally occurring outside organized markets, usually through bankruptcy hostile acquisitions or stock manipulation.[19]

### Non-transparency of JSCs

In most cases, the ownership of Russian companies is not transparent and the principal owners are not necessarily known. Corporate property may be integrated across five to seven levels of affiliated individuals and companies, offshore firms, or nominal holders, as well as multistage company management systems, sometimes using cross-ownership. This complexity has not diminished with tighter regulations, except in companies that have disclosed their beneficiaries in order to enter the stock markets or to buy assets in Western countries. Today, large shareholders maintain a lack of ownership transparency in order to protect their companies (which have historically used illegal financing and other illegitimate methods to acquire such properties) from state authorities or other private businesses.[20]

Not only do ownership structures and business organization operate without transparency, but so too does business performance. Not all public JSCs comply with even formal legislative requirements in regard to the reporting and publication of company information. Existing accounting practices are oriented to tax authorities' needs, but the quality of reporting remains low and, as a result, provides inadequate information to shareholders, creditors and business partners. Again, particularly those companies that deal with foreign investors or place securities in financial markets are more likely to have adopted international financial accounting standards (surveys show that between eight and fifteen per cent of respondents use international standards).[21]

## Business closeness and self-financing

An important feature of insider corporate control is protection from new shareholders. Dividends are often not paid and business development is frequently self-financed, resulting in the dominating owner typically receiving profits in non-dividend forms. However, in recent years, large companies with consolidated ownership and weak minority shareholders have begun to pay dividends. In these cases, dividends serve as a legal source of high incomes for the companies' owners and can be openly used for acquisition of new assets. Large JSCs with significant state shares (such as energy and communication companies) also pay dividends because of pressure from the government. Nonetheless, the majority of public companies fail to pay dividends or they do so irregularly. The above-mentioned survey of 304 open JSCs shows that about 60 per cent of the participants did not pay any dividends in 2000–2.[22] Only one-quarter of the participants paid dividends every year, and one-third of the participants paid dividends twice during these years. The survey of 822 JSCs also found that 63 per cent of companies did not pay dividends for 2001–3 financial years, while only a quarter paid dividends every year.

Investments in the Russian economy are characterized not only by low rates of return, but also by a focus on private sources of investment using company funds or financing from partners with which the company is connected. For many years, the share of external sources of investments invested in fixed assets has not exceeded 50–55 per cent.[23] Bank loans account for only about five to seven per cent of business investments in most years and the stock market remains an undeveloped investment tool. Shares deliver about 0.2–0.5 per cent of investments and bonds about 0.2–0.3 per cent. Only a few Russian companies raise investments in the form of debt or through share offerings in domestic or foreign markets, preferring instead to draw on loans from other enterprises and partners. As a result, the share of foreign investment in the economy remains low at about five to six per cent. In industrial investments the share of own funds is, as a result, much higher (above 68–70 per cent in the early 2000s), although it has been declining steadily since 1998.

Institutional investors have no incentives to acquire majority shares in Russian companies. In fact, up to the time of writing only up to ten JSCs have issued public offerings and the first of these occurred only in 2002. By contrast, the corporate bond market is more dynamic with about 150 companies having issued bonds to raise investment capital, restructure business groups or establish a credit history to enable future borrowing. In practice, because banks have limited resources and enterprises are seen as high-risk borrowers, they are not currently a significant source of industrial credit.

## Models of corporate control at the micro-level

Along with discussions of an emerging national model of corporate governance in Russia, various models or types of corporate control at the micro-level have also been observed. In Affanasiev,[24] three main types and a number of mixed types of corporate control were defined based on the relative roles of managers, employee teams and outside shareholders. This typology reflected mass privatization up to the mid-1990s. Since then stock ownership and corporate control in JSCs have changed dramatically as a result of intense redistribution of property and management turnover, especially since 1997–8. Today a model is emerging that is characterized by more stable forms of control over a joint-stock company between owners and managers. The domination of insider control does not exclude variety in the degree of ownership consolidation and the type of dominating shareholder. Based on these two parameters in our earlier work we identified four distinct types of control models in *privatized* industrial JSCs.[25]

### 1. Model I – private enterprise

This model combines the functions of owners and managers. The major owner is the director and smaller shareholders include other managers, ordinary employees and/or state authorities. The model is characterized by internal stability and, in the future, is likely to be transformed into a family business.

### 2. Model II – collective managers' ownership

This model also combines the functions of owners and managers. In such a 'managers' cooperative' the top managers (normally four to five people) hold the controlling interest. Usually, none of the leading shareholders has a blocking stake but the director's stake exceeds that of any individual member of the team. The model is not free from risk because its important feature may be a deferred conflict between the owners. Disintegration of their coalition is quite possible, and this often results in a revival of painful and costly struggles over ownership redistribution. There are also other risks related to the functioning of the management system such as the difficulties involved in replacing manager-owners with management teams that can work with both shareholders and employees. In small and medium enterprises this model is most likely to be gradually transformed into the private enterprises (or Model I).

### 3. Model III – concentrated outside interest

This model exists where the outside owner holds a controlling stake in the company and managers are hired employees or small stakeholders (three to five per cent). This model was mainly created during the secondary redistribution of privatized stock ownership. Over the past few years bankruptcy procedures have also produced this form. The model is internally stable. Changes are possible where enterprise restructuring occurs as a result of a decision by the major owner (such as where the owners may close the enterprise or reorganize it by merger or spin-off). A typical risk of the model is opportunistic behaviour on the part of top managers.

### 4. Model IV – dispersed ownership

In this model, the management team actually controls the enterprise. It is typical of this model that the manager or management team is normally the owner of a medium-sized block of shares (from five to fifteen per cent). The other shares are dispersed among the smaller shareholders, both employees and outside individuals (some shares may belong to the authorities, institutional investors, or other owners). At first sight, the model is similar to the type of corporate governance common in Western (especially Anglo-Saxon) economies, where efficiency is supported by a number of internal and external mechanisms (the well developed stock market and the transparent and strongly regulated corporate control market). However, under Russian conditions, it may be premature to talk about the availability of such markets. Shareholder control over management is largely absent and, because managers feel insecure, they tend to be unable or unwilling to increase their own shareholdings in the company. The model is particularly common in large and very large enterprises in weak sectors burdened with substantial social costs. Provided there are no long-term shifts in the economic situation to change how the profitability of these businesses is evaluated or to create a demand for the shares, this model is also quite stable.

All other things being equal, the emergence of various micro-models has been affected by the quality of management, individual qualifications of top managers and the interests of other stakeholders as much as it has by such objective parameters as enterprise size and sector. In the first three models, there is a correlation between the structures of corporate control or power and corporate ownership. Significant misalignment of structures of ownership and control is characteristic of the dispersed ownership model. The costs of opportunistic behaviour of managers are markedly lower here than in the case of the concentrated outsider ownership model while the owners incur immeasurably higher costs for maintaining control over managers.

Elsewhere, we have also shown that – with the exception of Model IV (generated by the peculiar nature of the Russian mass privatization in the conditions of deep transformational crisis) – these models have also been observed in new joint-stock companies.[26]

Intensive equity redistribution processes against the background of integration and economic recovery of the 2000s transformed control structures at the micro-level. In the existing institutional environment, the models of control with dispersed and moderately concentrated ownership (IV and II) could not compete with models based on strong equity concentration (I and III) and were gradually pushed out. Many Russian JSCs, for instance, were taken over by large Russian business groups, bought by outside owners or became the general director's property. Today, Model I not only involves the consolidation of shares with the director but also direct involvement of the dominating outside owner in the management process (start-up JSCs or purchase of privatized enterprises and replacement of the 'red' directors). The boundary between Models I and III is mobile. The choice is made by the dominating shareholder, who is free to sell the business, reorganize it and change the management system. It is interesting that, at the same time, the model

*Table 5.2* Models of corporate control on micro-level* (based on in-depth interviews with top managers of open JSCs conducted in 2003)

| NN | Type of business | Origin of business | Integration activities in 1997–2003 | Size (employees) | Concentration of stock property** | Dominating owners | Model of corporate control | Separation of property and control |
|---|---|---|---|---|---|---|---|---|
| 1 | Group of companies | Privatized | Restructuring and creation of the group | 501–1000 | Highly concentrated | Managers | I (possible it will move to III) | Non-separated |
| 2 | Independent enterprise | Privatized | No | 501–1000 | Highly concentrated | Director | I (from II) | Non-separated |
| 3 | Independent enterprise | Privatized | No | 1001–5000 | Concentrated | Managers | II | Non-separated |
| 4 | Independent enterprise | Privatized | No | 200–500 | Moderately concentrated | Managers, the company – partner | II (with elements of III) | Non-separated |
| 5 | Group of companies | Privatized | Bankruptcy, and creation of the group | 1001–5000 | Concentrated | Managers | I or II (from I) | Non-separated |
| 6 | Independent enterprise | Privatized | No | 200–500 | Highly concentrated | Director | I | Non-separated |
| 7 | Member of the group | Privatized | Joining vertical holding, mergers | More than 5000 | Concentrated | Group | III | Separated |
| 8 | Independent enterprise | Privatized | No | 200–500 | Moderately concentrated | Managers | II | Non-separated |
| 9 | Independent enterprise | Privatized | No | 501–1000 | Concentrated | Managers | II | Non-separated |
| 10 | Member of the group | Privatized | Joining vertical holding | More than 5000 | Highly concentrated | Group | III | Separated |

| # | Type | Origin | Restructuring | Size (employees) | Property concentration** | Director | Stage | Property/management |
|---|---|---|---|---|---|---|---|---|
| 11 | Independent enterprise (joining the group) | Privatized | Takeover (friendly) is in progress | 1001–5000 | Concentrated | Director | I (now it goes to III) | Non-separated |
| 12 | Member of the group | Privatized | Joining vertical holding | More than 5000 | Highly concentrated | State-owned holding | III (from IV) | Separated |
| 13 | Member of the group | Privatized | Takeover by the group | More than 5000 | Highly concentrated | Group | III (from IV or II) | Separated |
| 14 | Independent enterprise | Privatized | Takeover | 501–1000 | Highly concentrated | Investment company | III (from I or II) | Separated |
| 15 | Group of companies | Privatized | Restructuring, creation of the group | 1001–5000 | Highly concentrated | Managers | I (from II) | Non-separated |
| 16 | Independent enterprise | Privatized | No | 200–500 | Dispersed | N/A | IV | N/A |
| 17 | Group of companies | Privatized | Reorganization of the group | More than 5000 | Highly concentrated | Group | I (from III) | Non-separated |
| 18 | Group of companies | De novo | Mergers | More than 5000 | Concentrated | Group | I | Non-separated |
| 19 | Joint venture/ subsidiary | De novo | No | 200–500 | Concentrated (as 50:50) | Two firms – Russian and foreign | III | Separated |
| 20 | Member of the group | De novo | Joining the vertical holding | 501–1000 | Concentrated (as 50:50) | Group (two main owners) | III (in long run will probably move to I) | Separated |

* We marked out by grey colour the companies with separation of property and management.

** Property concentration was defined as: dispersed (nobody owns more than 10% of shares); moderate (the largest shareholder has more then 10% but less than or equal to 25% of shares); concentrated (the largest shareholder has more than 25% but less than or equal to 50% of stock); highly concentrated (the largest shareholder owns more than 50% of stock).

of collective managerial property is being preserved by *de novo* Russian businesses.[27] Table 5.2 contains the main characteristics of the open JSCs surveyed in 2003; these characteristics can be used to categorize companies into different micro-models. Our small sample is dominated by Models I and III. Models II and IV are still used in some medium-sized independent enterprises which are in a poor condition.

Today it is rare to see examples of decreasing concentration of ownership regulated by the dominating shareholders, although there are some examples, such as Wimm-Bill'-Dann Food company and about 35–40 other private and public companies that have made public stock offering in 2004–6. These new phenomena may be the first steps towards a new 'regulated dispersed ownership model', but this is likely to be a model available only to a small number of companies and which, in the short and medium term, will be dominated by a large stockholder rather than by the managers.

## Separation of ownership and control and the demand for corporate governance

Using separation of ownership and control as a criterion, we can distinguish two types of companies exhibiting a model of insider domination. This separation of ownership and control is not necessarily connected with the origin of a business as a start-up or by privatization, but is more likely to occur as large integrated business groups or holding companies begin to experience the gradual withdrawal of 'red' director-owners and the hiring of new managers to run their subsidiaries. The result is a situation where ownership and control are formally separated; the director of the enterprises is not a shareholder, while the other top managers are either hired employees or minority shareholders. Of course, even in companies where ownership and executive management are separated in this way, the operations of the enterprise can still be dominated by the owner through creation of and participation in the Board of Directors, direct participation of the owner in the management of the higher-level holding company, or other largely informal ways of directing the decisions of the company.

In the sample of firms, seven had separated ownership and control, of which one is a company where the controlling stake belongs to a holding company with 100 per cent government participation, and two exhibited no separation of ownership and control (one of them, at the time of the interview, was actually on the verge of a friendly takeover by a business group who kept the old management team which had sold its shares). There are clear differences between the types of business in the two clusters (Table 5.3). Separation of ownership and operational control is also characteristic of enterprises which are business group members (there is only one case where the outside owner is an investment company and it is unknown whether or not it belongs to a group).

Combined ownership and control is a feature of independent enterprises and small groups of companies. If the company group is big, the owners of the holding company are executives themselves and they control the business as a whole. Operational control over enterprises in a large group is given to hired managers. Their loyalty is ensured by high salaries and by imposing special rules for corporate behaviour.

Separation of ownership and control correlates with a higher degree of ownership concentration and also with the replacement of 'old' top and medium-level managers by modern management teams. The Boards of Directors of these companies are strictly controlled by the dominating owner or business group. Sometimes the executive management is not even represented on the Board. It is in these companies, the biggest business groups, that the Boards perform the decision-making and monitor performance of the executive management. It is obvious, however, that there are also formal (so-called 'phoney') Boards. These Boards operate by signing off on decisions worked out outside the framework of

*Table 5.3*  Comparison of the main types of corporate control (based on in-depth interviews with top managers of open JSCs conducted in 2003)

| Indicators of business state and activities | Clusters of companies divided by corporate control features: | |
|---|---|---|
| | **TYPE 1: Separation of property and control – 7** | **TYPE 2: Non-separated property and control – 12** |
| Type of business interviewed | Independent enterprises – 1 Members of groups/subsidiaries – 6 Groups of companies – 0 | Independent enterprises – 7 Members of groups/ subsidiaries – 0 Groups of companies – 5 |
| Size of business interviewed | From 200 up to 1000 employees – 3 More than 1000 employees – 4 | From 200 up to 1000 employees – 6 More than 1000 employees – 6 |
| Strategic horizon of decision-making | Short-term – 0 Mid-term – 2 Long-term – 5 | Short-term – 4 Mid-term – 4 Long-term – 4 |

Continued

Table 5.3 Continued

| Investments | Regular – 7<br>Irregular or no investments – 0 | Regular – 8<br>Irregular or no investments – 4 |
|---|---|---|
| Investments funds | Own funds – 6<br>Bank credits – 5<br>State subsidies or credits – 1 | Own funds – 10<br>Bank credits – 5<br>State subsidies or credits – 2 |
| Level of equity concentration | High concentration – 4<br>Medium concentration – 3 (incl. two JSCs with 50:50 stock)<br>Moderate concentration – 0 | High concentration – 5<br>Medium concentration – 5<br>Moderate concentration – 2 |
| Need for further concentration | Need – 3<br>No need – 4 | Need – 3<br>No need – 6<br>No data – 3 |
| Management team type | New – 4<br>Mixed – 3<br>Old – 0 | New – 1<br>Mixed – 4<br>Old – 7 |
| Replacement of topmanagers | Yes – 5 | Yes – 1 |
| Threat of capture | Yes – 2 | Yes – 3 |
| Divergence of interests among large and minor shareholders | Yes – 3<br>N/A – 2 | Yes – 3<br>No data – 1 |
| Divergence of interests among managers and owners | Yes – 2 | Yes – 0<br>N/A – 8 |
| Regular dividends policy | Yes – 1 | Yes – 3 |
| Dominating opinion in a Board of Directors | Groups' or owners' – 7 | Managers' – 9<br>Groups' or owners' – 2<br>No data – 1 |
| Role of a Board of Directors in a company | Nominal – 2<br>Monitoring, decision-making – 5 | Nominal – 8<br>Monitoring, decision-making – 0<br>Expert – 4 |
| Facts of corporate conflicts | Yes – 2 | Yes – 3 |
| Preferable ways of settlement of corporate conflicts | Negotiations – 5<br>Courts – 5<br>Business associations – 0<br>Authorities – 0 | Negotiations – 11<br>Courts – 4<br>Business associations – 2<br>Authorities – 0<br>No data – 1 |

the formal corporate procedures or made directly by the owner(s). By contrast, where a combination of ownership and control turns the Boards over to the managers, it is then difficult to distinguish between shareholders, directors and executive managers.

Corporate conflicts and differences in the interests of many corporate governance stakeholders appear to be pushing some companies to press for more effective legal mechanisms. In our qualitative survey there is no mention of differences in the interests of major owners and managers (in most cases they coincide). But there are differences in the interests of minor and big shareholders, a problem that was observed relatively more often where ownership and control were separated. Corporate conflicts or corporate blackmailing was observed rarely in both clusters, but where there was a separation of ownership and control the court was more highly valued as a corporate conflict resolution mechanism.

## Concluding remarks

The prevailing feature of Russian corporate ownership today is property concentration by insiders and large external shareholders. Formally, the dominating owners were company managers and non-financial enterprises. Sometimes these include the large, well known 'oligarch' groups and sometimes they include regional groups founded by domestic business, often with latent support from and participation of regional and municipal administrations.

Consolidated ownership and the control of a dominating shareholder (be they 'red' directors or new external stockholders) against the background of strong incentives for business integration have become the most important feature of corporate governance in Russian companies. The prevailing type of corporate control is that exercised by owners who play a direct role in management or who tightly control the decisions made by hired managers. At the micro-level, corporate governance procedures are based on internal mechanisms, such as Boards of Directors or shareholders meetings, and these tend to be dominated or 'captured' by the large shareholders.

All of these forms of corporate governance exist in a situation where the stock market is weak. The main property redistribution processes and corporate control acquisition transactions are going on outside organized markets. With a larger number of companies with attractive assets (for example, oil and gas sector, metallurgy, etc.), ownership consolidation has proceeded at a faster rate than in other Eastern

European countries and has been, for the most part, completed.[28] Consolidation of property serves as a substitute for the market and as a tool for stabilizing businesses. As a result, in recent years models of firm organization based on dispersed property ownership have been replaced by models with more concentrated property forms.

At the present time, separation of ownership and corporate management is rare in Russian companies, but business integration is gradually promoting a separation of control in some companies. On the whole, two main types of company management are emerging: one in which day-by-day management is concentrated in the hands of the owners and a second in which ownership and day-by-day control are separated. A logical consequence of this tendency will be the normalization and regulation of relations within the chain of 'dominant shareholder – board of directors – executive bodies of a joint-stock company', in which a growing demand emerges for legitimate institutions used to exercise shareholders' corporate control over executive managers through Boards of Directors, civil contracts, and the courts.

At the moment, three types of joint-stock company dominate the Russian corporate sector: (a) private, family firms with joined ownership and control using self-financing or bank loans; (b) integrated (in fact closed) companies with separated management and control primarily based on internal financing; and (c) public JSCs attracting small and medium-sized investors (including foreign investors) and in which large shareholders exercise control.

## Endnotes

1. The paper was prepared within the project 'Business Integration in the Corporate Sector: Incentives, Patterns and Economic Effects' granted by Moscow Public Scientific Foundation from funds presented by the US Agency on International Development (US AID). The author's opinion reflected in this paper may not coincide with points of view of the US AID or Moscow Public Scientific Foundation. The author thanks the other members of the project team, S. Avdasheva, V. Golikova and A. Yakovlev, for mutual work and comments.
2. T. Dolgopyatova, 'Modeli i mekhanizmy korporativnogo kontrolya v rossiiskoi promyshlennosti' ['Models and Mechanisms of Corporate Control in the Russian Industry'], *Voprosy Economiki* 5, 2001, 46–60.
3. TTPP, *Insiders, Outsiders and Good Corporate Governance in Transitional Economies: Cases of Russia and Bulgaria*, Regional Think Tank Partnership Program Working Papers Series, WP No. 2–5, 2004 (available at www.ttpp.info/library/library_.asp).
4. E. Yasin, ed., *Structural Changes in the Russian Industry*, Moscow: Publishing House of SU HSE, 2004.

5. J. Blasi, M. Kroumova and D. Kruse, *Kremlin Capitalism: the Privatization of the Russian Economy*, Ithaca: Cornell University Press, 1997; T. Dolgopyatova, *Rossiiskie predpriyatiya v perekhodnoi ekonomike: ekonomicheskie problemy i povedeni* [*Russian Enterprises in Transition Economy: Economic Problems and Behaviour*], Moscow: DELO Ltd, 1995.

6. E. Berglof and E-L. von Thadden, *The Changing Corporate Governance Paradigm: Implications for Transition and Developing Countries*, Centre for Economic Policy Research Working Paper No. 263, London: CEPR, 1999.

7. B. Black, R. Kraakman and A. Tarassova, 'Russian Privatization and Corporate Governance: What Went Wrong?', *Stanford Law Review* 52, 2000, 1731–1808; T. Dolgopiatova, *Corporate Control in Russian Companies: Models and Mechanisms*. Working paper WP1/2002/05, Moscow: SU HSE, 2002 (also available at http://www.hse.ru/science/preprint/default.html#wp1).

8. M. Deryabina, 'Restrukturizatsiya rossiiskoi economiki cherez peredel sobstvennosti i kontrolya' ['Restructuring of the Russian Economy Based on Redistribution of Ownership and Control'], *Voprosy Ekonomiki* 10, 2000, 5–69; Ya. Pappe, 'Rossiiskii krupnyi biznes kak ekonomicheskii fenomen: osobennosti stanovleniya i sovremennogo etapa razvitiya' ['Russian Big Business as Economic Phenomenon: Specifics of Emergence and Development'], *Problemy Prognozirovaniya* 1, 2002, 29–46.

9. S. Avdasheva, 'Biznes gruppy kak forma restrukturizatsii predpriyatii: dvizhenie vpered ili shag nazad?' ['Business Groups as a Tool for Enterprises' Restructuring: Move Forward or Backward?'], *Rossiiskii zhurnal menedzhmenta* 3, 1, 2005, 3–26; T. Dolgopyatova, 'Sobstvennost' i korporativnyi kontrol' v rossiiskikh kompaniyakh v usloviyakh aktivizatsii integratsionnykh protsessov' ['Corporate Ownership and Control in the Russian Companies in the Context of Integration'], *Rossiiskii Zhurnal Menedgmenta*, 2, 2, 2004, 3–26.

10. S. Guriev and A. Rachinsky, 'The Role of Oligarchs in Russian Capitalism', *Journal of Economic Perspectives* 19, 1, 2005, 131–50.

11. Yasin, op. cit.

12. *Russian Industry: Institutional Development*, T. Dolgopyatova, ed., Moscow: Publishing House of SU HSE, 2003; TTPP, *Insiders, Outsiders*, 2004.

13. *Russian Industry*, 2003, chapter 2.

14. J. Stiglitz, 'Quis custodiet ipsos custodes? Corporate Governance Failures in the Transition', the paper presented at the World Bank's Annual Conference on Development Economics (ABCDE), Paris, June 1999, *Challenge* 42, 6 (available at www.findarticles.com/p/articles/mi_m1093/is_6_42/).

15. TTPP, *Insiders, Outsiders*, 2004, Part 4.

16. V. Golikova, T. Dolgopyatova, B. Kuznetsov and Yu. Simachev, 'Spros na pravo v oblasti korporativnogo upravleniya: empiricheskie svidetel'stva,' in *Razvitie Sprosa na Pravovoe Regulirovanie Korporativnogo Upravleniya v Chastnom Sektore. Seriya 'Nauchnye doklady: nezavisimyi economicheskii analiz'* ['Demand for Corporate Law: Empirical Evidence' in *Evolution of Private Sector Demand for Regulation of Corporate Governance. Series 'Academic Reports: Independent Economic Analysis'*], No. 148, Moscow: Moskovskii obshestvennyi nauchnyi fond, Necommercheskaya organizactiya ' Proecty dlya budushego', 2003, 229–339 (also available at http://www.mpsf.org/lib.html).

17. S. Guriev, O. Lazareva, A Rachinskii, S. Tsukhlo, *Korporativnoe upravlenie v rossiiskoi promyshlennosti. Seriya '«Nauchnye doklady: nezavisimyi economicheskii analiz' [Corporate Governance in the Russian Industry. Series 'Academic Reports: Independent Economic Analysis'],* No. 149. (Moscow: Moskovskii obshestvennyi nauchnyi fond, CEFIR, 2003) (also available at http://www.mpsf.org/lib.html).

18. The random stratified sample in industry and communications was constructed and the field-work was implemented by the well-known Russian sociological organization 'Analytical Centre of Yurii Levada' in 64 Russian regions. Funds for implementation of the survey were granted by Moscow Public Scientific Foundation and the Ministry of Education of Japan. It is possible to find the survey results in T. Dolgopyatova and I. Iwasaki, *Exploring Russian Corporations: Interim Report on the Japan-Russia Joint Research Project on Corporate Governance and Integration Processes in the Russian Economy.* IER Discussion Paper Series B No. 35. (Tokyo: Hitotsubashi University, Institute of Economic Research., 2006) (also availible at http://www.ier.hit-ac.jp/).

19. R. Kapelyushnikov and N. Dyomina, 'Vliyanie kharakteristik sobstvennosti na rezul'taty eckonomicheskoi deyatel'nosti rossiiskikh promyshlennykh predpriyatii' ['Effects of Property Features on Economic Performance of Russian Industrial Enterprises'], *Voprosy Ekonomiki* 2, 2005, 53–68.

20. Ya Pappe, 'Rossiiskii krupnyi biznes kak ekonomicheskii fenomen: spetsificheskie cherty modeli ego organizatsii' ['Russian Big Business as Economic Phenomenon: Specific Model of its Organization'], *Problemy Prognozirovaniya* 2, 2002, 89–90.

21. Yasin,op. cit.; Golikova *et al.*, op. cit.

22. Golikova *et al.*, op. cit.

23. All the figures in this paragraph are based on official statistical data.

24. M. Affanasiev, *Korporativnoye upravleniye na rossiiskikh predpriyatiyakh [Corporate Governance in the Russian Enterprises].* Moscow: Interekspert, 2000.

25. See details in Dolgopyatova, *Models and Mechanisms of Corporate Control,* 2001, or Dolgopyatova, *Corporate Control,* 2002.

26. Dolgopyatova, 'Corporate Ownership and Control', 2004.

27. It should be stressed that the situation is defined by the phenomenon of 'team' organization of the private sector in Russia vs. 'family' organization in European and Asian countries. This organization is typical for both large businesses and SMEs. Detailed discussion of determinants of this phenomenon is outside the scope of this paper.

28. See the comparison of Russia and Poland in D. Woodruff, *Property Rights in Context: Privatization's Legacy for Corporate Legality in Poland and Russia,* Working paper WP1/2003/01, Moscow: SU HSE, 2003 (also available at http://www.hse.ru/science/preprint/default.html#wp1); and Russia and Bulgaria in TTPP, *Insiders, Outsiders,* 2004.

# 6
# Diverging and Harmonizing Corporate Governance in Russia[*]

*Satoshi Mizobata*

## Introduction

Russian enterprises have experienced drastic changes since the financial crisis of 1998. Big businesses, including oligarchic groups, are the most dominant and influential forms. They include independent companies, corporate forms that integrate production and sales companies (specialized integrated business groups) and integrated business groups (the entire business belonging to specific industrial/non-industrial branches). These large groups emerged in the late 1990s when ownership and control were taken on by core companies (the holding companies) while government preserved its influence. With the economic recovery following the financial crisis, changes in ownership and control have occurred. While the integrated business groups continue to exist, their form has changed and the main industrial (energy) companies now occupy the core of the economy and power in it.[1]

Two factors – globalization and nationalization – have been important in this process. On the one hand, big business has transnationalized itself and now is well connected to the international market. As a result, the private sector has recorded an increase in financial debts. On the other hand, while the government has maintained a commitment to liberal reforms, after 2003 the Russian government seems to have changed economic strategy towards being much more interventionist. The state has become active in controlling strategic sectors and the oligarchy–state corporations have been reorganized to adapt to global markets.

In Russia, as in many developed countries, joint-stock companies (JSCs) have become the main form of enterprise, with its legal system modelled on European and American models. The adoption of these legal practices has normalized business structures and practices, particularly after the revision of the Law on JSCs in 2001. In February 2006, the government Council on Competitiveness and Entrepreneurship approved the new regulations: '*The Development Concept for Corporate Legislation in the Period to 2008*' (hereinafter 2006 *Concept*). This *Concept* provides guidelines for the development of corporate legislation and harmonization with European norms.[2] For example, corporate social responsibility (CSR) legislation has been introduced in Russia based on the European Commission's development and adoption of strategic documents such as the Green Paper in 2001 and Communication from the Commission in 2002.

However, normalization and harmonization must not be overemphasized. The rules governing the Russian market are considerably different from those of the west. Legal enforcement is inadequate and corporate behaviour has not necessarily been transformed as much as have the official rules. As the Yukos affair in October 2003 illustrates, political influence over corporations remains strong and the interests of the stakeholders in decision-making remain complex. The interventionist role of the government has been especially strong in strategic sectors of the economy. Although normalization and harmonization with the west have often been by whom?, the behaviour of the large-scale integrated business groups and the volatile investment environment have produced corporate structures and governance models that are unique to Russia and that differ in significant ways from those in the west.

The normalization and the preservation of Russia's corporate structure are occurring simultaneously; this dual trend has resulted in Russia diverging from the traditional corporate governance model of the developed countries. This chapter draws on survey research conducted in August 2004 in cooperation with the Institute for Socioeconomic Problems of Population, Academy of Sciences, Russian Federation.[3] It analyses the present situation and the changes in corporate governance and the mechanisms of governance in Russian enterprises. It further considers which stakeholders influence the decision-making of companies. The chapter concludes with an assessment of the impact of EU enlargement on Russian corporate models.

## Russian corporations and management principles

### Companies in Russia

In the past 10 years, the number of Russian commercial establishments has increased by more than two times and the number of companies in Russia

*Table 6.1*  Number of companies in Russia and Japan (thousand)

| Types of enterprises | Russia | | | Japan | |
|---|---|---|---|---|---|
| | 1995 | 2000 | 2006 | 1996 | 2004 |
| Establishment (total) | NA | 6872.2 | 7216.2 | 6717.0 | 5920.4 |
| Establishment (enterprises) | 1946.3 | 3107.2 | 4767.3 | 3227.8 | 3061.1 |
| Company | 1601.3 | 2471.5 | 3872.3 | 2701.5 | 2527.9 |
| Joint stock company | 546.7 | 416.3 | 459.4 | 1643.0 | 1507.2 |

*Note*: Establishment (total) includes both individual (entrepreneurship) and enterprises. Company includes various kinds of economic corporations. Joint-stock company in 1995 Russia included the number of limited liability company. In 2004 Japan, the number of limited liability company is 986.2.

*Source*: Federal Service of Government Statistics, *Russian Statistic Annual 1996, Socioeconomic situation in Russia*, January, 2001, January, 2006, *Small Entrepreneurs in Russia*, 2005 (in Russian), Statistics Bureau of Ministry of Internal Affairs and Communications, Japan, 1996 *Establishment and Enterprise Census of Japan*, 1999, 2004 *Establishment and Enterprise Census of Japan*, 2005 (in Japanese).

now exceeds Japan's. Joint-stock companies also increased their number, and the private sector increased its share (Table 6.1).

In June 1995, the Law on JSCs was adopted making juridical persons (especially JSCs)[4] the central component of Russian enterprises, allowing the number of shareholders to increase and expanding securities markets. JSCs can be divided into two categories: *open JSCs*, which sell shares on the securities markets, and *closed JSCs*, with a limited number of shareholders. In the open JSCs the minimum capital is 1,000 times the official minimum monthly wage and the number of shareholders is not restricted. Open JSCs have equity and preferred shares (under 25 per cent of capitalization), and reports such as annual financial statements must be publicly announced. The minimum capital for closed JSCs is 100 times the official minimum monthly wage, the number of shareholders is less than 50 and shares are not traded publicly. Shares are owned by the specific incorporated companies and individuals and their transfer to a third party is restricted. As a result, it is difficult to 'buy up' control of closed JSCs without the consent of the majority of shareholders. People's enterprises based on self-management are a variation of this kind of JSC, and in this case more than 75 per cent of the shares are owned by the employee shareholders, with an additional restriction that the number of the company's employees must be greater than 50 and should not exceed 5,000. Corporations that were established in the process of privatization, where shares were owned by insiders, are able to choose this type. With the passage of time, enterprises that belong to employees have become more of an exception.[5]

The Law on JSCs is based on the open JSC.[6] First, the open JSC is legally established for the purpose of acquiring investments. However, many Russian open JSCs are only 'semi-open' because they do not attempt to acquire investment capital externally. Indeed, most JSCs are closed and accumulation of investment capital occurs from within the company itself, a factor of importance to the governance models that are emerging. Second, because open JSCs can be reorganized into closed JSCs or limited companies there was an initial advantage to the open JSC form, particularly because even open JSCs can avoid having to sell stock publicly. Third, free circulation of shares creates dispersed forms of ownership whose impacts on company efficiency remain highly contingent (see previous chapter). Indeed, share dispersal in Russia has its own peculiarities. It is unusual in its scale, in that it occurs across all departments and corporations, and it is unusual in its methods, in that it includes illegal and irregular practices. As a result, open JSCs have increasingly strengthened their concentration of shares.

There have been several attempts to redistribute shares and hence control in these open JSCs through increased capitalization, mergers and reorganization, and through bankruptcy procedures (legally, the bankruptcy system does not concern business management, but it can change the structure of companies). However, these efforts have been complicated by illegal measures that redistributed control without providing compensation to the shareholders and the application of bankruptcy measures for companies that were solvent.

## Management and control structure

The control mechanism of Russian corporations comprises the shareholders' general meeting, the board of directors, the executive committees and the internal auditors (Figure 6.1).[7]

From the legal viewpoint, the central control mechanism is the shareholders' general meeting, which reflects the decisions of the shareholders who have voting rights.[8] The Competencies of in the shareholders' general meeting includes decisions that may affect the continuance of the company and shareholders' status, such as changes in capitalization, reorganization, liquidation, election of the board of directors and auditors, and capital increase. Although the Law on JSCs regulated the authority of the shareholders' general meeting, it could transfer these exclusive authorities to the board of directors. Therefore, in Russia,

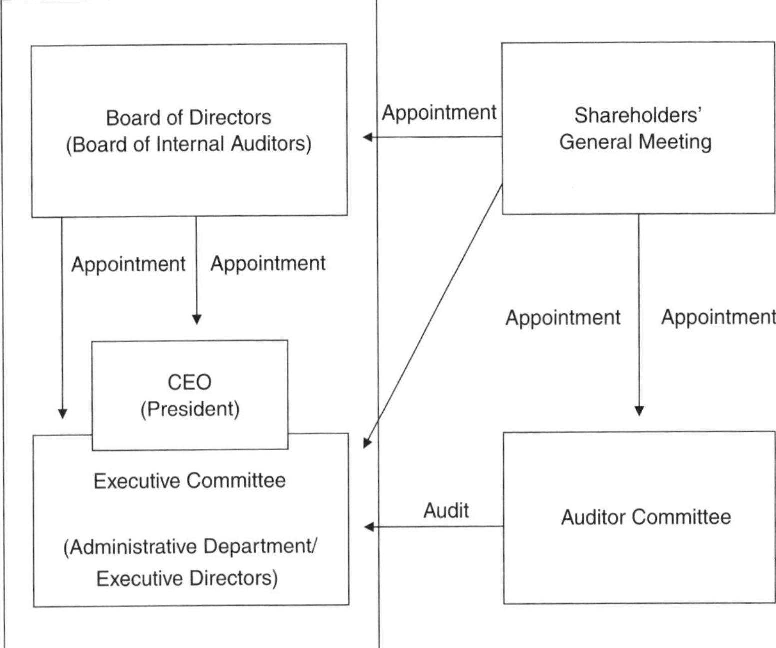



*Figure 6.1*   Main administrative organization of companies in Russia

investors who owned (or managed) a controlling block of shares could make all the decisions while small shareholders' rights were often ignored. In 2001, the Law on JSCs was revised to address these problems of capital expansion and shareholder rights with the implementation of the following regulations: 1) At the time of corporate reorganization, when shares were sold in the securities markets, shareholders were given preferential rights for purchasing shares. These rights had to be in proportion to the shares; 2) In cases where more than 25 per cent additional shares were issued, this had to be carried out as a public open offering (not a closed one); 3) Limits were placed on changes in capitalization to limit the authority of preferred stock owners (now a 75 per cent vote is needed at the shareholders' general meeting); 4) JSCs with more than 50 employees were required to register before the beginning of July 2002. At the very least, these revisions had the potential for avoiding ownership disputes between shareholders and managers through increasing capital concentration and they also had the function of stabilizing the securities markets and protecting individual investors.

The second control mechanism is the board of directors (the board of internal auditors). The board of directors is elected for a specific period of time and is an organization of enforcement and supervision. In incorporated companies, authority tends to shift from the shareholders' general meeting to the board of directors. The board of directors manages and directs a company and, as a result, it is possible for it to turn into a reactionary force against the majority of shareholders. The authority of the board of directors includes the selection of business priorities, convening of the shareholders' general meeting, capital increase (following decisions by the shareholders' general meeting) and the formation of the executive committee. At the beginning of 2002, to redress the use of arbitrary authority by the board of directors, company reorganization, capitalization, stock division and integration, approval of large transactions and buy-back of its own shares by the company all had to be approved at the shareholders' general meeting. The board of directors is elected at the shareholders' general meeting by cumulative voting.[9] This voting method may be regarded as a positive way for minority shareholders' participation.[10] The number of executive committee members cannot exceed a quarter of the members of the board of directors. By organizing the executive committee, the administrative supervisor (board member) and the management are nominally separated; however, the board of directors is controlled by the head of the executive committee (president).[11] Conventionally, more than two-thirds of the board members are chosen from the shareholders and the representative of the directors must be a shareholder.

A company's operational management is carried out through the executive committee, which is either a collective or a single organ. The executive committee is responsible for reporting the information to the board of directors as well as at the shareholders' general meeting. In fact, the main management staff of a company organizes the executive committee and prepares a contract with the board of directors. The representative director may not at the same time be the chief executive officer (CEO); however, in reality, these two posts are often held by one person, resulting in centralization of authority. The CEO controls the board of directors. The executive committee system is similar to the 'work meeting', which traditionally formed the basis of Russian enterprises, and its organization is determined by the shareholders' general meeting or the board of directors.[12] One consequence is that the authority for ownership, supervision and management can – in practice – easily be concentrated in a single individual.

The third control system is the labour group (employees). In a people's enterprise, where more than 75 per cent of the shares belong to employee shareholders, the decisions of the shareholders' general meeting and the chief of internal auditors overlap with the decisions of the workers. The authority of the labour group is considerable in unitary enterprises and in companies in which there is more than 50 per cent state ownership.[13] In addition, employees have been able to influence decision-making as shareholders since the employee holdings were given priority in privatization.[14]

## Ownership and control in the company

### Evolution of ownership and control

The separation of company ownership and management has resulted in a controversy about the appropriate model of corporate governance for Russian business. Legally, ownership is the basis of corporate control. Tables 6.2 indicate the evolution of the ownership structure in

*Table 6.2*   Shareholdings in Russian industrial companies

| Shareholders | 1995 | 1997 | 1999 | 2001 | 2003 | 2005 |
|---|---|---|---|---|---|---|
| **Insiders, total** | 54 | 52 | 50 | 50 | 50 | 48 |
| employees | 43 | 37 | 34 | 28 | 22 | 16 |
| managers | 11 | 15 | 15 | 19 | 25 | 31 |
| **Outsiders, total** | 37 | 42 | 42 | 42 | 45 | 45 |
| Non-financial outsiders | 27 | 31 | 33 | 34 | 36 | 38 |
| Outside individuals | 11 | 15 | 20 | 22 | 21 | 20 |
| Other enterprises | 16 | 16 | 13 | 12 | 15 | 18 |
| Financial outsiders | 9 | 9 | 7 | 8 | 8 | 5 |
| **Government** | 9 | 7 | 7 | 7 | 4 | 7 |
| The number of sample companies | 136 | 135 | 156 | 154 | 102 | 101 |

*Note*: Questionnaires by the Russian Economic Barometer in Industrial Enterprises (%). Financial outsiders are commercial banks, investment funds, and holding companies.

*Source*: S. Aukutsionek, N. Dyomina and R. Kapelyushnikov, Ownership structure of Russian industrial enterprises in 2005, Institute of World Economy and International Relations, *The Russian Economic Barometer*, XIV, 3, 2005, 4.

Russia.[15] While there is great variation in the research results/data and organizations differ greatly, there are common trends after 1992.

During the initial period of privatization, ownership structure did change in an evolutionary manner, but through the revolutionary political decision to privatize.[16] The result was that insiders – mostly the employees – gained a certain amount of influence in almost all the enterprises, on average owning two-thirds of all shares in the first half of the 1990s. Privatization policy, the underdeveloped securities markets and the legacy of the Soviet Union had a decisive effect on these ownership patterns. At the same time, state ownership remained at approximately 20 per cent and the role of outsiders was restricted.

From 1995 to 1999, insider ownership decreased while outsider ownership increased, and there was a shift from state to non-state shareholders (corporations and individuals). Among the insiders, there was also a transfer of shares from employees to managers and shareholdings became more centralized rather than dispersed. The absence of measures for protecting minority shareholders' rights, arbitrary administration of the shareholders' general meeting, directors' arrogance, losses suffered by companies and uncertain information further stimulated centralization of authority into the hands of a few people.[17]

This changing structure of ownership from insiders to outsiders continued after 1998. According to research on the ownership structure of medium-large incorporated Russian companies carried out by the Ministry of Economy, insider ownership declined significantly after 1998 and outsider ownership increased in 2000, inverting the prior ownership structures. Among outsiders, financial and non-financial companies have become increasingly important actors. Although the financial outsiders expanded their ownership in order to gain a greater level of control over the more promising privatized companies, cornered shares for large-scale inside and outside investors, and handled charges and speculative profits, after the 1998 financial crisis large-scale industrial companies also expanded their ownership. However, as Table 6.2 shows, insiders have maintained their ownership following the crisis, and managers in particular have enlarged and now stabilized their share of control.

A central feature of Russian industry is the concentration of ownership and control, particularly the concentration in the hands of nominal owners, irrespective of whether they are insiders or outsiders. Foreign companies have also extended their ownership. Simultaneously, bankruptcies and the poor performance in the commercial banking sector have reduced the ownership role of financial companies in industry, and these assets have been transferred to the large-scale industrial holding companies.

Concentration has given rise to big business groups and these groups have not necessarily adopted the single JSC form. Instead, they are composed of a complicated ownership structure, which includes offshore companies and concentration in the hands of influential individuals.[18] As the business group expands, its structure of ownership and control tends to become more complicated. However, because regulation of these large groups and the mutual relations of companies within the group remain inadequate, company structure remains opaque and is rife with practices such as mutual shareholding, absence of consolidated accounts, and transfer pricing.[19]

## Main features of ownership and control

The evolution of shareholding patterns after the financial crisis of 1998 has had important impacts on the main features of ownership and control. First, as we have just seen, despite their relative decline, insider ownership and control have been maintained. During the first period of privatization, which ended around 1995, the 'insiders', i.e., the employees and managers of companies, tried to control the company in the face of opposition from the outsiders. However, as ownership was formally established, those owners who understood the company, had access to information and were involved in the decision-making process came to be regarded as insiders in the company. They were able to concentrate their control, particularly as managers turned into large-scale outsiders or lawful owners.[20]

Second, concentration of capital has deepened. According to Dolgopyatova, 60–70 per cent of ownership in large-scale privatized companies is now concentrated in the hands of managers. The average shareholding of the three major shareholders in Russian companies is approximately 75 per cent. According to the World Bank,[21] 22 executives now control Russian industrial enterprises of more than 20,000 employees and an annual sale of over 700 million dollars. Stock ownership has also become highly concentrated (Table 6.3).[22]

Third, regardless of the ownership type, managers' control is generally strong, especially where they have been able to convert themselves into owners. Such a process of conversion implies a change from a situation in which there is a separation of ownership and control to one where ownership and control coincide.[23] In industrial sectors, 3.7 per cent of the shares belong to the board of directors (managerial group), 4 per cent are held by the JSC itself and even this part is under the control of the

*Table 6.3*  Concentration of ownership

| | | % in equity capital | | | | | |
| | Number of respondents | 1995 | | 1998 | | 2000 (estimate) | |
| | | Average | Median | Average | Median | Average | Median |
|---|---|---|---|---|---|---|---|
| Biggest shareholders | 213 | 26.2 | 22.0 | 27.6 | 23.0 | 28.8 | 24.2 |
| Three biggest shareholders | 213 | 40.4 | 40.0 | 44.5 | 44.4 | 46.5 | 46.3 |

*Source*: A.V. Buzgalin and A.I.Kolganov, *Theory of Socio-economic Transformation*, Moscow (in Russian), 2003, p. 246.

managerial group. While the state owns 12.8 per cent and the employees possess 20.4 per cent, most of the shares are entrusted to the managerial group through either a voluntary or an involuntary process. As a result, the managerial group possesses more than 40 per cent of all shares while no individual shareholder possesses more than 17 per cent. Not surprisingly, the managerial group does not feel a strong responsibility towards shareholders and the general meeting, and it also does not have a strong sense of responsibility for its labour force or even to its major markets.

Fourth, the corrosion of insider ownership and the concentration of outsider ownership have resulted in different types of ownership depending upon the type of industry.[24] Employee holdings remain high in light industry while holding companies are emerging more in construction and national defence sectors. Manager ownership is high in the food industry. State holdings are high in the machine-building and electric power sectors, and the non-financial company holdings are extremely high in the metal sector. Overall, ownership by incorporated companies is high in dynamic industrial sectors, whereas ownership by insiders is high in stagnating industries.

Fifth, employees exert their influence as stakeholders. Employees possess more of a quiet control as stable insiders. Unlike outside minority shareholders, they do not push for the payment of dividends because they see these as being paid from their wage bill. Instead, they have an interest in the maintenance of workplace welfare programmes and the provision of social services, and they try to influence corporate management to supply these welfare goods. Many companies continue to offer employees both temporary and regular assistance, including housing, meals, and leisure facilities. Such 'public' goods are also provided by the local governments and so local governments and employees together press corporate management to invest in these kinds of social services (Table 6.4). Table 6.5 also depicts the ratio of payments in kind in the total wage. Although company welfare provision becomes a means of garnering quiet support for management from labour, if this quiet power of the employees is ignored labour conflicts arise and

*Table 6.4*  Assistance to employees (% of Yes respondent enterprises)

| Type of assistance | 1994 | 2000 |
| --- | --- | --- |
| *Regular assistance* | | |
| Commuter allowance | 26.6 | 16.3 |
| Food expense assistance | 49.2 | 21.1 |
| Manufactured goods price subsidies | 6.6 | 2.0 |
| Housing allowance | 12.7 | 7.8 |
| Baby and child care assistance | 43.9 | 16.9 |
| Added pension | 7.4 | 5.9 |
| *Temporary assistance* | | |
| Physical support | 79.7 | 70.7 |
| Charges/Payments | 45.5 | 54.7 |
| Medical service payments | 48.4 | 28.3 |
| Retirement payments | 73.8 | 62.9 |

*Source*: *Ekonomika i Zhizn'*, 38, September 2002, 2.

*Table 6.5*  Social service provided to employees (% of Yes respondent enterprises)

| Type of social service | 1990 | 1994 | 1998 |
| --- | --- | --- | --- |
| Meals | 55 | 50 | 41 |
| Health care | 64 | 63 | 56 |
| Leisure facilities | 62 | 56 | 44 |
| Vocational education | 78 | 71 | 59 |
| New housing construction | 45 | 34 | 18 |
| Kindergarten | 66 | 54 | 32 |

*Source*: S. M. Guriev and B. Ikes, Microeconomic obstacles for the economic growth of Russia and the former Soviet countries, E. G. Yasin, ed., *Modernization of the Russian Economy*, 1, GU-VShE, Moscow. (in Russian), 2002, p. 223.

quiet shareholders may quickly turn into a counterforce against management. Therefore, while employees as stakeholders have limited direct effect on decision-making, company managers must work carefully with their employees. However, there are signs that since the financial crisis the influence of employees has substantially declined, as other forms of 'spontaneous restructuring' have emerged.[25] Although employees can influence their wages and employment through workers' contracts, managers[26] have discretionary power, while governments and trade unions continue to have only limited power over wages.[27] The result is a form of corporate managerialism in which the ability of employees to influence wage decisions is weaker than it might otherwise appear.

Sixth, the huge integrated business groups continue to exist. Within such groups, ownership and control of industrial companies are further expanding. The powerful enterprises in these groups have stabilized earnings in export businesses and, as a result, foreign investors are becoming more interested in investing. In turn, these investments and the need to have a good international reputation have encouraged Russian enterprises to observe the law and to adopt stable corporate governance practices.[28]

The evolution of ownership and management has, in turn, meant that companies have become more responsive to market mechanisms with the result that there has been an increase in the turnover in management. Between 1992 and 1999, 71 per cent of enterprises received new top executives, although 24 per cent of these maintained their position even after privatization.[29] Even the red managers of former socialist enterprises seem to have adopted improved business and management practices:[30]

> Approximately 40 per cent of the CEOs were the same as those appointed in the Soviet times, and 60 per cent were 'new' directors who came to power after the implementation of market reform. There exist two polar segments in the population of Russian industrial firms–the 'unstable' segment, where CEOs were replaced repeatedly within the span of rather short intervals and the 'stable' segment, where no renewal of CEOs had been made for a long time.'[31]

That is, corporate governance in Russia is not merely a conflict of insiders and outsiders, but is a more complex process, and a product of the conflict over and harmonization of interests among various stakeholders, markets and the learning process of corporate managers.

# Characteristics of Russian corporate governance

## A comparison between models of corporate governance

Russian corporate governance has been compared in various ways with the three standard models of corporate governance: the Anglo-American model, the German model and the Japanese models.[32] The phrase 'corporate governance' itself has become a standard way of thinking about economic practices the US, the UK, Europe and Japan, and so in this section I turn to the question of whether, and if so to what extent, there is any practical international and ideological convergence between the Russian and these other standard models.

In the Anglo-American model (Figure 6.2), shareholders' authority and the institutional investors usually have a strong influence and managerial power is concentrated in the hands of the CEO. At the same time, particularly in the US, several changes are taking place: ' appointment of a larger number of independent directors to boards of directors, reduction in overall board size, development of powerful board committees dominated by outsiders, closer links between management compensation and the value of the firm's equity securities, and a strong communication between board members and institutional shareholders'.[33]

In the case of the German model (Figure 6.3), management and supervision are separated and shareholders and employees jointly select the board of auditors and 'co-determination now tends to be defended'.[34] The Japanese model (Figure 6.4) is similar to the Anglo-American model,

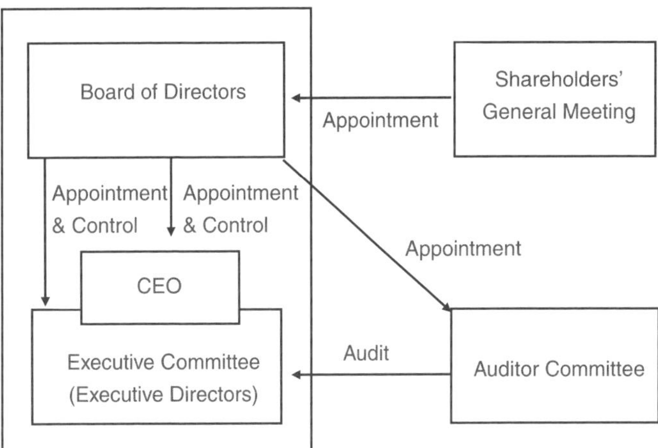


*Figure 6.2*   Main administrative organization of companies in America

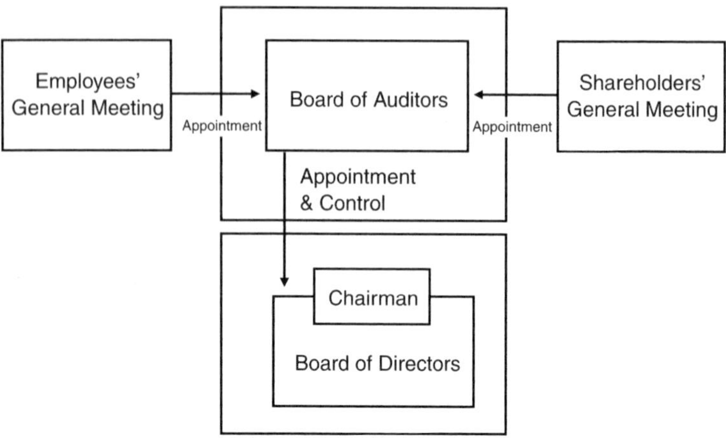


*Figure 6.3*   Main administrative organization of companies in Germany

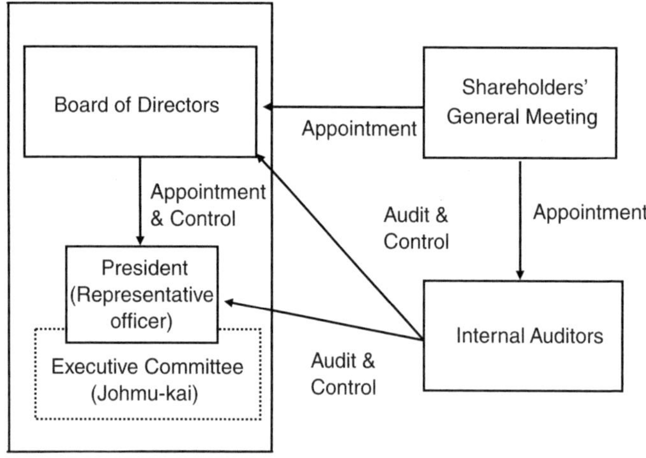


*Figure 6.4*   Main administrative organization of companies in Japan

both superficially and legally (after the amendment in 2003). Here, insiders have a strong influence and a type of harmonious interest is sustained among insiders (managers and employees) within the enterprise or the group. The shareholder-oriented model of the corporation has recently become more influential, although in Japan it has also been strongly criticized.[35]

The Russian model (Figure 6.1) has legal and practice-based similarities with the Anglo-American model, particularly in terms of a strong CEO with strong authority in the organization. However, while 'Russia could well progress towards a German–Japanese network-based model reflecting a stakeholder approach,'[36] it is important to understand the special characteristics of the Russian model. In particular, the ways in which ownership and control are aligned are specific to this model, as are the embedded historical and cultural values, such as a mistrust of outsiders and worker representation.

From a legal perspective, corporate governance in Russian enterprises also has quite distinct features. In general: 1) they have an extraordinarily high degree of ownership concentration; 2) major enterprises operate with closed governance systems (although they are formally open JSCs); 3) companies have been combined into large business groups; 4) ownership and management are conjoined; 5) they operate through internal financing; 6) the role of the boards of directors has been informalized; 7) they operate without external mechanisms; and 8) the state has remained a central actor in corporate governance.[37]

## Conditions for governance

Four conditions sustain these characteristics of corporate governance. First, enterprises operate in undeveloped capital markets. Privatization has not created wide-ranging and highly fluid securities markets, and, furthermore, the development of corporate bond markets is limited. JSCs do not sufficiently disclose their financial information and, as a result, investors are unable to receive credible information on profits and/or deficits. Arrears, barter payments and complex financial relations with subsidiaries compound this lack of financial transparency. Moreover, strategic shares are often traded in closed negotiations, and the immature securities markets and conflicts over corporate control operate informally, restricting opportunities to implement competitive mechanisms and shareholder control over managers.

Second, stakeholders have, in turn, responded to these incomplete institutions. Enforcement of the law on ownership protection (protection of the shareholders' rights) has been inadequate and, as a result, ownership remains opaque. Shareholder rights, particularly those of the minority shareholders, are not well protected either formally or informally. Employees have unexpectedly become shareholders of their companies, but they do not recognize themselves as joint owners or as investors. In such cases, systems of governance that guarantee dividends and strive to maximize profit are difficult to implement. The abuse of power on the part of the managers undermines the development of responsible and efficient management. The acquisition of strategic shares by means of 'shares-for-loans', the close ties of government organizations and enterprises that guarantee these acquisitions, the collusion between municipal authorities and municipal judicial bodies in order to exclude outside investors, particularly foreigners, administrative warnings or physical sanctions against employees who have sold their own shares to 'outsiders' and manipulation of the shareholder register are all common. In addition, by not issuing corporate bonds and by avoiding bank credits, enterprises limit themselves to internal financing mechanisms. But, even if enterprises form huge integrated business groups, they remain little more than 'segmented capital markets that exist in each group'. These financial methods are, in large part, a product of the underdevelopment of Russian capital markets and the poor service provided by banks. As a result, clear institutional norms and market relations are compensated for by informal mechanisms and profits are laundered through offshore institutions.

Fourth, relations between enterprises and the government, political interference in enterprises and the accessibility of enterprises to political influence remain significant. Regardless of the type of ownership, the management of the enterprises is highly dependent on the central and the local governments and their economic policies.[38] In order to enhance their own political role and to reinforce the position of their own local authorities' candidates for election, enterprises often acquire the strategic shares of local leading companies, a situation that has been particularly common in Siberia, the Far East and Southern Russia. As a result, future prospects for corporate governance reforms in Russia lie not only in the strategic policies implemented by the legislative and executive bodies but also in the de-politicization of the enterprises. Despite legal system reform, federal legal institutions find it difficult to maintain their neutrality and judicial objectivity, particularly because their legal staff are often lacking in competence and experience. One of the consequences of the weak legal system is that, anti-monopolistic and anti-oligopolistic regulations do not function effectively.[39]

These four conditions imply that, to be successful, corporate governance reforms require more than reform of the legal system and enforcement mechanisms. Although Russian rules of governance are formally a hybrid of Russian and US/European rules, practical forms of governance have created a distinct national model. First, characteristics of this model, such as underdeveloped capital markets, incomplete market institutions, informal institutional norms, and inertial relations and networks, might be path-dependent, in the sense that initial rules and institutions affect the choices of the subsequent path and policies. When the transplanted formal institutions were seen to be ineffective, informal institutions and personal networks formed their own norms. Second, in parallel with these path-dependent factors, decision-makers and stakeholders opted for this Russia-specific regime and the opportunities it offered.[40]

## Normalization of corporate governance

### Normalizing legal acts

The 1998 financial crisis, the institution-building after the crisis and the corporate governance reform that began in 2000–2, all advanced the normalization of corporate governance in ways that have meant that 'management has undergone qualitative changes–not only with the coming of new people, but also with the learning of the old directors by adapting to a new environment'.[41]

First, the legal institutions have been improved. Several problems of corporate governance were improved between 2000 and 2002. The improvements of the new legislation include capital dilution, the protection of shareholders' rights, particularly the freeze-out of minority shareholders, overseas capital transfer (capital flight) and the enforcement of disclosure requirements. The results can be observed in the amendments to the Law on JSCs, offshore regulations,[42] the information disclosure law and the development of administrative sanctions. In the case of minority shareholders, the risk of losing influence has decreased. Russian corporate reform may also soon incorporate elements of EU company law, particularly measures to strengthen shareholders' rights and third party protection, and foster the efficiency and competitiveness of business. In particular, Russian governance systems would benefit from the creation of European standards for the separation of supervision (the board of internal auditors) and management (the executive committee) (2006 *Concept*).

In 2001, based on the 'OECD Principles of Corporate Governance', the 'Code of Corporate Conduct' was formulated. The final version, formulated by the FCSM and approved by the government in November 2001, had an advisory character and is regarded as the best practical standard of corporate governance for JSCs with over 1,000 shareholders. Reactions to this code from the business community have varied from complete approval to complete negation, with those opposing the code seeing in it a tendency to strengthen bureaucratic forms of economic management.[43] The code does indeed specify the authority of the board of directors and it charges the board with responsibility for the creation of a financial risk management system and the establishment of specific committees.[44]

EU enlargement has served as a positive incentive for the formal harmonization of Russian company law with those of the EU (Europeanization). Indeed, some are convinced that 'the model of European company adopted in 2001 after a 30-year discussion would not present a problem for the corporate law of Russia' because the Russian legislation has many similar standards.[45] However, in contrast to such a positive outlook, the harmonization of corporate governance rules in Russia and in the EU still poses significant challenges, such as transparency, enforcement, and inadequate judicial systems.[46]

## Normalizing corporate behaviour

The business communities themselves are preparing a directive for corporate governance. 'The Charter of Corporate Business Ethics' by the Russian Union of Industrialists and Entrepreneurs urges the need for protection of ownership, compliance with the legal system and dispute settlement through negotiation.[47] The charter presents eight guidelines: 1) business should be carried out based on the principle of fairness; 2) property rights should be inviolate; 3) the law should be complied with; 4) social tension should not be encouraged; 5) no pressure should be put on judicial bodies; 6) enterprises should not compete illegally; 7) false information and the manipulation of information should be avoided and 8) resolution of corporate conflicts should be sought through negotiations. However, the Charter also suggests that arbiters are to be selected by the business community itself and decisions that they make are not to be legally binding. The National Council of Corporate Governance was established in March 2003,[48] and since then the business community has displayed a positive attitude towards corporate governance reforms. In particular, there seems to have been marked improvement in the transparency of enterprises.[49]

Corporate social responsibility (CSR) has also become a popular topic. The Yukos affair, in particular, raised grave issues about compliance with the legal system, social justice and transparency. As a result, managers seem to have intensified social programmes and improved labour conditions and worker training in order to raise the company's reputation and establish a positive corporate identity. Employees and regional residents have benefited directly. Regional governments have actively supported these improvements, in part because they reduce their own expenditures.

In order to realize CSR, managers have taken considerable interest in social investment and policy. According to the Managers' Association, in 2003, the average social investment per employee was 28,300 rubles, its ratio in the total sale was 1.96 per cent and its total profits were 11.25 per cent. The main targets of social investment were the creation of new jobs, corporate in-service training and a healthy corporate system. While intra-firm programmes were dominant with respect to social investment in 2003, investments for the local community such as environmental protection showed an increase in 2004.[50] In the enterprise town, in particular, CSR has been particularly valuable for local residents. A comparison of CSRs in Russia and Europe clarifies the Russian case. In contrast to CSR in Europe, where companies and the local community play a central role in pushing for CSR, in Russia, the central and local governments have been the primary motivators for the adoption of CSR. However, because CSR is not yet a familiar concept among all stakeholders in Russia, not all businesses, communities and the government have been equally enthusiastic or supportive of implementation.[51] In part, this results from the fact that Russian enterprises have evolved from a Socialist system in which social benefits of the kind enshrined in CSR programs have long been regarded as an important sphere of insider corporate control and negotiation between business and the government. Normalization and harmonization of the standard corporate enterprise model occurred gradually after the financial crisis, particularly as enterprises became aware of the need to be more competitive, a process that 'had little to do with government policy and was rather related to the stronger competitive pressure in the course of Russia's integration into the global market'.[52] Investment, bank borrowing and the ratio of long-term commercial loans have all increased.[53] The volume of shares and corporate bonds is increasing.[54] The stock price of some companies (oil, telecommunication, food, etc.) has increased rapidly, as have the dividends that are paid. For example, dividends in oil companies are estimated to be approximately 20 per cent of the net profits.[55]

## Divergence of corporate governance

### Diverging corporate reform

According to research by the Managers' Association and the Russian Directors' Institute in 2002, despite gradual changes in quality, major changes in corporate governance still have not occurred.[56] Most managers have retained their former positions. At that time, only 37 per cent of companies practiced active management, and such companies have concentrated in large cities and in the financial sector. Dividends were not paid by 60 per cent of companies. Although almost all the companies were aware of the Law on JSCs and had their own legal department, most of the small enterprises were ignorant of the legal system. According to *Ekonomika i Zhizn'*, 17 April 2006, only one-third of respondent companies had implemented reporting requirements, only 12 per cent regarded the Code of Corporate Conduct as important, although 67 per cent indicated that they did plan to change their rules and practices to meet the requirements of the Code. Perhaps most significant was the fact that in 26 per cent of respondent enterprises directors indicated that they did not usually represent the interests of their companies.

Patterns of Russian corporate governance seem to be highly fragmented. Companies have either adapted to the new legal requirements, and operate with market-oriented management principles, or adopted a more passive attitude to legal reform and management. Processes of normalization are still uncertain and contested, with pressure to retain existing forms of Russian corporate governance still being strong; undeveloped capital markets, informal mechanisms and close ties between the government and the enterprises (involving interference by the governments and bureaucrats) have all persisted. Since 1999, there have been many executive scandals with the Yukos affair being perhaps only the most visible.[57] The government has continued to pressure enterprises and not always in obvious ways. For example, Yukos is regarded as a company that places importance on disclosure to its shareholders, but it appears that government pressure has been applied to stop any further implementation of corporate governance procedures that would lead to further levels of transparency and openness.

Legal reforms alone did not completely resolve the problems of corporate governance. There are still many areas in which the legal system is undeveloped. For example, the legal system has not been fully reformed in areas such as the management structure of a closed JSC whose shares are owned by one person, the legal system for information disclosure and the restructuring of JSCs and disputes among shareholders.[58] Several other issues still need to be addressed: 1) a law on limited liability companies must be developed as an option for small companies; 2) the restructuring mechanism of JSCs needs to be improved; 3) the merger and takeover mechanisms of JSCs need to be improved; 4) the illegal ownership structure in many JSCs (such as incomplete shares registration) established before 1996 need to be normalized and 5) measures need to be implemented to guarantee the enforcement of court decisions.

In addition, almost all Russian companies have resisted moves to increase transparency and decentralize some of the power of managers. Since auditors are selected from inside the company by managers, managers can easily create moral hazard. While article 71 of the Law on JSCs determines the responsibility of directors and executives, including forms of compensation for any damage done to them, in practice there are no effective judicial institutions and the supporting legal reform is incomplete. There have been some improvements in the litigation system, but these have been limited and partial; for example, Radaev found that 24 per cent of respondents would, if needed, undertake breach of contract actions, but he also found that 11 per cent would resort to violence to ensure the implementation of their contract.[59] Enterprises are also not well protected against illegal intrusions by the state. In recent years, legal protections for enterprises that are in dispute with the state have not significantly improved and, as a result, state organizations infringe on enterprise rights with impunity.

Although corporate control markets are developing at a rate comparable to that of those in developed economies, the legal institutions remain inadequate. On the one hand, since many companies are reluctant to pay dividends, the rights of shareholders are not met. On the other hand, the Law on JSCs in Russia is thought by some to provide too many rights to minority shareholders who, as a result, are thought to abuse their rights, serving as the source of the vast majority of legal actions and takeover moves against companies. By using the shareholders' list and company information it is relatively easy to instigate a court action and, under the Law on JSCs, it is also relatively easy for minority shareholder groups to effectively steal the company.[60] The extraordinary shareholders' general meeting enables a minority of shareholders with more than 10 per cent of shares to take over an enterprise, and these actions account for many of the actual takeovers. As a result, minority shareholders are not only neglected stakeholders but also dangerous ones. The number of these corporate raids is increasing and has generated a growing opposition to corporate reforms and strong efforts to impose restrictions on the shareholder minority, providing rights to shareholders who control a majority of shares to purchase the remaining shares.

## Diverging corporate governance

Changes in patterns of investment are particularly important. The securities markets do not have any practical effect on the actual economy. In interviews in 2004, no respondent enterprises had registered themselves in the financial markets for fear of losing ownership and approximately 70 per cent of all investment came from internal funds.[61] Although bank credits have increased, the banks have not been interested in long-term investment in enterprises and they cannot monitor corporate governance as stakeholders. As a result, the issue of securities, particularly in the Russian capital markets, is concentrated only in a small number of large enterprises.[62]

In our empirical survey of management performance we compared insiders' (i.e., managers') control and outsiders' control, and found that the latter's business efficiency was not always better than that of the former.[63] The research data by TsEMI (Central Econometrical Institute) in 2004 also raised questions about the performance of ownership and control. The Anglo-American type enterprises (where shareholders are dominant) do not always become success enterprises in Russia. The successful Russian enterprises have largely been based on a balancing of stakeholders' interests, with particular attention being paid to the interests of employees. Insider models have exhibited particularly positive attitudes towards foreign enterprises and investors.[64]

Although CSR is part of a process of harmonization with the west, the stakeholders' influence on the specifics of CSR implementation has shaped a particular form of Russian corporate governance. The government is the largest influence on CSR strategy, followed by the company itself (i.e., the main shareholders and the managers). Some regional governments have concluded socioeconomic agreements with large enterprises and many such regional enterprises regard their relation with the regional authority as a deciding factor in their ability to survive.[65] In contrast to the European model, both the employees and the local community have important effects on Russian CSR, while NPOs and NGOs have no effective role.[66]

### Perspective of evolution

In Russia, corporate governance reform is only possible by maintaining trust. Since the financial crisis in 1998, two favourable factors for trust-building have been in play.

The first is that, under the Putin government with its goals of a strong state, economic recovery has been sustained and competition has forced both dominant managers and other stakeholders to adapt to the market environment. Corporate behaviour and the promotion of business efficiency (restructuring) have been recognized as indispensable for the further development of companies. The ability to adapt to the market environment with investment resources and accumulation of internal funds has been improved. Second, since 2001, the legal system has been comprehensively reformed, although there still exist areas where the reforms are inadequate. In the longer term the EU and Russia have agreed to cooperate in creating four Common Spaces, which will in turn require further changes in company law.

At the present time, actual practices of corporate governance are not favourable to further reform because: 1) the foundation of trust lies in the personal networks between the government and the corporate managers, and among managers, and 2) the informal institutions still play an important role in reducing transaction costs. Although many managers have been replaced due to a lack of formal trust after only short periods in the enterprise, many have also been retained in their positions because of the way in which traditional networks operate.[67]

The financial infrastructure is inefficient and banks cannot play the role of a stakeholder in corporate governance. Large-scale commercial banks are limited to a handful of group (oligarchic) banks. They have close ties with energy enterprises and political authorities, and their loan capability remains inadequate and is concentrated in the group. Outside monitoring is carried out by staff with low levels of training and the financial market is fragmented among the groups. At the same time, many top banks are not always transparent because they are controlled by unknown shareholders, such as limited liability companies, or they operate as closed JSCs.[68]

## Conclusion

Russian economic institutions seem to have been reformed and normalized after the financial crisis, and in some sectors Europeanization has occurred. The Law on JSCs is a typical example. In addition, formation of Common European Economic Space with the EU and the WTO negotiation with the EU foreshadow important changes in Russian enterprise practice. In particular, 'Russia can adopt some principles of the *acquis communautaire* of the EU in those fields where Russian economic legislation is still too weak. Success of both initiatives can raise Russia to a position of important integrating actor in a wider Euro-Asian economic space.'[69] However, the institutional changes are often more virtual than real. The opposite of these reforms is also occurring, particularly in cases where state intervention is increasing. Opaqueness of corporate information has had negative effects despite the emergence of IPO markets.[70] Moreover, while the EU plays an important role in institutional reforms in Eastern European countries, this is not the case in Russia, where the benefits of economic integration have been much smaller and the conditionalities of accession have not been present.[71]

The Russian government seems to be aiming to create a European model through its legal and social reforms. The corporate institutions, however, cannot be completely replaced by the imported institutions. Moreover, in the Putin period, Russian peculiarity has been stressed and Russian stakeholders have adapted imported institutions to their own style and the uniqueness of Russia and the interests of its stakeholders are strongly reflected in actual governance practices.[72] Russian corporate governance has been strongly influenced by the privatization process, personal networks and the government, and – consequently – it has been a model that fluctuates among the interest politics of its stakeholders.

## Endnotes

* This chapter is part of a research project on the 'Comparative Analysis of Corporate Governance in Transition Economies', supported by the Grant-Aid for Science Research, the Ministry of Education and Science (project number C, 14530008) in 2002–6 and by the Grant-Aid of the Matsushita International Foundation in 2004. The earlier draft 'Corporate Governance in Russia' was presented at the symposium on the Natural Monopoly Reform and Corporate Governance in Russia, which was held on 23 March 2004 by the Cabinet Office of the Government of Japan and the Nihonsougou Institute. The second draft 'Diverging and Normalizing of Corporate Governance in Russia' was presented at the seminar of CEMI (EHESS) and GERME (Paris 7), held on 21 April 2005, in France. The final draft was presented at the ICCEES VII Congress, July 2005. The author is indebted to Andrei E. Shastitko, Tatiyana G. Dolgopyatova, Bernard Chavance, Jacques Sapir, Eric Brunat, Bruno Dallago and others for their helpful comments. They are not responsible for the possible limitations of this paper.

1. At the end of 2004, there were 12 groups including Gazprom, Lukoil, Alfa, Milhouse Capital, Tatnefti, MDM, Systema and others. These groups have functioned as investment funds (Ya. Pappe, *Ekspert*, 12, 28 March–3 April 2005, 26–31).

2. The term 'harmonization' or 'harmonizing' is often used as a measure of the EU integration, which implies mutual approval of institutions and 'an effort to avoid the standard model than to further it' (H. Hansmann and R. Kraakman, 'The end of history for corporate law', J. N. Gordon and M. J. Roe, eds, *Convergence and Persistence in Corporate Governance*, Cambridge, 2004, p. 62).

3. See S. Mizobata, 'Investigation on the Russian corporate structure and behaviour', *Shimane Journal of North East Asian Research*, Vol. 14 (Forthcoming, in Japanese).

4. See S. D. Mogilevskii, *Legal Bases of Joint Stock Companies' Activity*, Moscow (in Russian), 2004; O. A. Makarova, *Legal Reference-Book for Entrepreneurs*, St. Petersburg (in Russian), 2003; T. G. Dolgopyatova, *Russian Industry*, Moscow (in Russian), 2002, pp. 53–6. Limited companies can be established as major Russian incorporated companies by individuals, juridical persons or state organizations. The Law on Limited Company took effect on 1 March 1998. In many cases, limited companies frequently establish small to medium companies and subsidiaries, and their functions closely resemble those of closed JSCs. Limited companies do not have

restrictions such as those in the case of JSCs (compulsory reserve funds, etc.), and they do not receive special tax benefits. The minimum capital of limited companies is 100 times that of the official minimum monthly wage, and if net assets become less than the minimum capital it is liquidated.

5. See A. A. Semenov, *People's Enterprise*, Moscow (in Russian), 'People's enterprises were used to maintain inter-business ties and prevent takeovers'; S. B. Avdasheva, *Economic Connections in the Russian Industry*, Moscow (in Russian), 2000, p. 103.
6. T. Medvedeva and A. Timofeev, 'Legal research aspects of demand for institutions of corporate governance', Moscow Social Science Fund, *Development of Demand for Legal Regulation of Corporate Governance in the Private Sector*, Moscow (in Russian), 2003, pp. 88–93.
7. For the control mechanism see S. D. Mogilevskii, op. cit.; S. E. Zhilinskii, *Entrepreneurs' Rights*, Moscow (in Russian), 2002; I.V. Doinikov, *Entrepreneurs' Rights*, Moscow (in Russian), 2002; M. G. Iontsev, *Joint Stock Companies*, Moscow (in Russian), 2002; L. S. Blyakhman, *Economics of Firm*, SPb. (in Russian), 1999; A. P. Slivko, L. I. Kotieva and I. L. Borova, *Regulations of Joint Stock Company*, Moscow (in Russian), 2002; I. Iwasaki, 'The governance mechanism of Russian firms', *Post-Communist Economies*, 15(4), 2003, pp. 503–531, p. 136.
8. The shareholders' general meeting is held annually. Since the fiscal year ends on 31 December, the meeting is held between the beginning of March and the end of June (most are held in April and May due to the tax payment period). In addition, a special shareholders' meeting is held upon request by the board of directors/supervisory board and shareholders who own more than 10 per cent of shares. In reality, the general meeting cannot be held without approval from the board of directors (G. Kleiner, *Nezavisimaya*, 8 May 2001).
9. The number of directors is seven or more if the number of shareholders exceeds 1000, and nine or more are elected if the number of shareholders exceeds 10,000. However, in 2004, amendments to the Law set the minimum number of directors at five, regardless of the number of shareholders, and mandated that the election of board members must take place only through cumulative voting. Any shareholder who owns at least two per cent of voting shares has the right to propose candidates (*Russian Business Watch*, 13, 1, January–March 2005, 22–3).
10. In Japan, cumulative voting was introduced in 1950, in imitation of the US law. After that it was thought that this measure caused fractional disputes among directors, and in 1974 cumulative voting was abolished. However, in the process of revision of corporate law in Japan, cumulative voting has been positively regarded for the democratic management and activation of internal corporate organizations. For example, Japan Business Federation published the draft of the corporate laws' modernization, and the draft admitted cumulative voting.
11. See G. Kleiner, *Nezavisimaya*, 8 May 2001.
12. See M. G. Iontsev, op. cit., p. 196.
13. See S. E. Zhilinskii, op. cit., p. 108.
14. With respect to employees, while negotiations through social partnership were acknowledged, real influence on management was limited (OECD, *White Paper on Corporate Governance in Russia*, 15 March 2002, p. 18). The

general meeting of the labour group exists only in name; it is not prescribed in corporate laws. It may appear in the form of strikes in a protest situation; however, in reality, there exist only a few cases.

15. Apart from full ownership (100 per cent), perfect control is regarded as a case wherein ownership exceeds 75 per cent. The decision-making power with respect to the most important issues, such as amendment of the articles, liquidation and reorganization, belongs to the owners. Moreover, 51 per cent or more ownership can secure effective control, and the owners can influence the election of directors and 'major transactions'. Generally, an amount of 51 per cent or more is required for the 'control shares'. The 'block shares' or the 'sub-control shares' (25 per cent or more) are those by which owners can prevent undesirable decisions of the general shareholders' meeting. Moreover, 20 per cent or more implies that the company is subordinate and responsible for disclosure of the official date. The smallest influence is 10 per cent or more, whereby the temporary shareholders' meetings can be summoned.

16. See T. G. Dolgopyatova, op. cit., p. 18.

17. See R. Kapelyushnikov, 'Biggest and dominant owners in the Russian industry', *Voprosui ekonomiki*, 1 (in Russian), 2000.

18. The oil company, Yukos, can be cited as an example. Yukos was located at the centre of the Menatep group, which was led by Mr Khodorkovsky. Yukos's shares were held through the subsidiaries, grandchild companies and the associated companies that were located offshore. Although the influence of the Menatep group was strong, Mr Khodorkovsky and his individual networks were stronger.

19. *Concept*, 2006.

20. T. G. Dolgopyatova, op. cit., pp. 38–40.

21. See the World Bank, 'Ownership and control of enterprises', *Voprosui ekonomiki*, 8 (in Russian), 2004, 10–13.

22. A. V. Buzgalin and A. I. Kolganov, *Theory of Socio-economic Transformation*, Moscow (in Russian), 2003.

23. G. Kleiner, *Nezavisimaya*, 8 May 2001.

24. See R. Kapelyushnikov, 'Ownership and control in the Russian industry', *Voprosui ekonomiki*, 12 (in Russian), 2001.

25. L. Ia. Kosals, 'Technological innovation in Post-Soviet Russia', mimeo (in Russian), p. 2.

26. The most influential body on wages decision is the board of directors, followed by the shareholders.

27. R. Kapelyushnikov, 'Policy of wages in Russian enterprises', L. M. Grigoriev *et al.*, eds, *1000 Best Enterprises in Russia*, Moscow (in Russian), 2003; 'Russian model of labour market', E. Mokhova, ed., *What Kind of Labour Market is necessary in the Russian Economy?* Moscow (in Russian), 2003.

28. A. Yakovlev, *Ekspert*, 3, 26 January–1 February 2004.

29. A. Radygin and S. Arkhipov, 'Ownership, corporate conflicts and efficiency', *Voprosui ekonomiki*, 11 (in Russian), 2000, 121.

30. See A. Yakovlev, 'Competitive environment and corporate governance', Russian Academy of Sciences, Institute of World Economy and International Relations, *The Russian Economic Barometer*, XIII, 3, 2004, pp. 19–24, p. 137.

31. R. Kapelyushnikov and N. Demina, 'Concentrated ownership and management turnover: The case of Russia, Institute of World Economy and International Relations', *The Russian Economic Barometer*, XIV, 1, 2005, 14.

32. Through a comparison with the Russian model, this paper addresses three typical corporate models. Pryor divides corporate models into four models – Anglo-Saxon plus, Nordic Economic System, Western Economic System and South European Economic System – based on the role of the government and the institutions (F. Pryor, Market economic systems, *Journal of Comparative Economics*, 33, 1). Amable (2005) divides capitalism into five types on the basis of competition, labour relations, the financial sector, social protection and education – market capitalism, socio-democratic economies, Asian capitalism, European continental capitalism and Mediterranean capitalism (B. Amable, Les Cing Capitalisms, *Coll. economie humaine*, ed. du. Senil, 2005).

33. H. Hansmann and R. Kraakman, op. cit., p. 51.

34. Ibid., p. 39. In the German reform, the enforcement of management by the board of directors becomes strong, while the supervisory function of the board of auditors is clearly separated (*Nihonkeizaishibun*, 17 June 2003).

35. Although some big businesses adopted the American management model, approximately 60 per cent of the large firms have preserved the traditional model (*Nihonkeizaishinbun*, 6 January 2003). On 29 June 2005, the new corporate law was adopted, and the enterprise groups could be easily reorganized.

36. S. M. Puffer and D. J. McCarthy, 'The emergence of corporate governance in Russia', D. J. McCarthy, S. M. Puffer, S. V. Shekshnia, *Corporate Governance in Russia*, Edward Elgar, 2004, p. 23. The Russian governance is similar to the Japanese, as far as the board of internal auditors is organized.

37. A. D. Radygin, R. M. Entov, E. V. Mezheraups, 'The specifics of formation of a national corporate governance model. Moscow', *IEPP*, 2003, 55 (in Russian), 59.

38. Yukos certainly influenced political affairs. It was estimated that Yukos paid between 270–350 million dollars for lobbying and sent 130 Members of an Assembly as maximum. (*Profil'*, 21 November 2004).

39. See Ya. Pappe, *Ekspert*, 41, 1–7 November 2004.

40. V. Gel'man, 'The unrule of law in the making', *Europe-Asia Studies*, 56(7), 2004, pp. 1021–1040.

41. A. Yakovlev, op. cit., 2004, p. 23.

42. See *Kommersant, Vedomosti*, 10 December 2002. There are those who express critical views on offshore companies (*Vedomosti*, 20 December 2002) and, moreover, regulations imposed on them have been tightened under the Putin Government. The central bank has revised the bank law, which prohibits offshore companies from owning more than 10 per cent of Russian banks' shares (for the purpose of enhancing the banks' transparency). Until then, this condition had been applied only to banks seeking bank deposit guarantees, but whether it should be applied to all banks is being deliberated. Likewise, whether the regulations should target the effectively controlling companies, in addition to the nominal owners, is also being deliberated. This is particularly because offshore companies never directly own shares and comprise the chain of control through limited companies regulated by Russian domestic laws; the impact this regulation will have on offshore companies is significant (*Kommersant, Vedomosti*, 10 December 2002).

43. While many of the big corporations such as Yukos, Sibneft and the United Energy System of Russia that had adopted their own rules in order to improve their investment reputation welcomed the code, many top executives who expected the code to provide the mechanisms for protection from

the shareholders' pressure or the lobbying of other stakeholders expressed disappointment.

44. A corporate secretary system for the company's information policy, the drawing up of the documents for the shareholders' general meeting and an auditor system, which supervises the company's financial and management plan, were proposed (T. G. Dolgopyatova, op. cit., pp. 58–60). The Code of Corporate Conduct was adopted in 2001. With regard to this, a survey conducted on top managers in 100 large firms indicates that 49.5 per cent believe that the provision of the code should be normal ordinance, and 29.5 per cent believe it should be the law. This Code reflects not only the US system (shareholder-rights-oriented) but also the German system (the OECD principles) (D. J. McCarthy and S. M. Puffer, 'Corporate governance in Russia: Towards a European, US, or Russia Model?', D. J. McCarthy, S. M. Puffer and S. V. Shekshnia, *Corporate Governance in Russia*, Edward Elgar, 2004, p. 394).

45. Radygin, Entov, and Mezheraups, op. cit., p. 59.

46. http://www.iet.ru , 23 February 2005.

47. *Vedomosti*, 21 October 2002.

48. *Nezavisimaya*, 22 December 2003.

49. See The Russian Institute of Directors, *Annual Research on Practice of Corporate Governance in Russia*, 2005 (in Russian).

50. In the industrial branch, in the case of companies involved in electricity, fuel, chemical, nonferrous metal and steel, the share of social investment for external purposes is high (more than 40 per cent) (*Ekonomika i Zhizn'*, 1 January 2005).

51. *Ekonomika i Zhizn'*, 1 January 2005.

52. A. Yakovlev, op. cit., p. 24.

53. *Ekonomika i Zhizn'*, 11 March 2005.

54. See A. Abramov, 'Evolution of demand and supply in legal regulation of corporate bond market', *Development of Demand for Legal Regulation of Corporate Governance in the Private Sector*, Moscow (in Russian), 2003. In 2003, financing by shares and bonds was estimated to reach 11 billion dollars in sum total, including 3 billion dollars that had been domestically procured (*Ekspert* 2, 19–25 January 2004, 34).

55. *Vedomosti*, 12 November 2003; I. Kostikov, 'Governance in an emerging financial market', P. K. Cornelius and B. Kogut, eds, *Corporate Governance and Capital Flows in a Global Economy*, Oxford, 2003, p. 449. The 2004 amendment of the Law on JSCs stipulates the source of dividends (net profit).

56. See V. Golikova, T. Dolgopyatova, B. Kuznetsov and Yu. Simachev, 'Demand for rights in corporate governance', *Development of Demand for Legal Regulation of Corporate Governance in the Private Sector*, Moscow (in Russian), 2003.

57. These scandals include conflicts in the Vyborg cellulose and paper factory in 1999, the arrest of the managers in the petrochemical holding company 'Sibur', the subsidiary company of Gazprom and other affairs such as those involving Mr Khodorkovsky and other entrepreneurs.

58. See A. D. Radygin, R. M. Entov and E. V. Mezheraups, op. cit.

59. J. Kornai, 'Honesty and trust in the light of the post-Soviet transition', *Voprosui ekonomiki*, 9 (in Russian), 2003.

60. V. Volkov, *Izvestiya*, 15 July 2004.

61. See S. Mizobata, op.cit.

62. *Ekspert*, 2, 19–25 January 2004.
63. R. Kapelyushnikov, 'Biggest and dominant owners in the Russian industry', *Voprosui ekonomiki*, 1 (in Russian), 2000.
64. See G. Kleiner, R. Kachalov and E. Sushko, 'Economic State and institutional environment of Russian industrial enterprises', *Voprosui ekonomiki*, 9 (in Russian), 2005, 77–9.
65. See M. V. Kurbatova and S. N. Levin, 'Social responsibility of Russian business', *EKO*, 4 (in Russian), 2005, 68–9.
66. *Ekonomika i Zhizn'*, 1 January 2005.
67. *Profil'*, 21, 6 June 2005.
68. The Russian banking sector displays features that are similar to those in other petrostates, i.e., informal pocket banks with unidentified shareholders and state giants like Sberbank (A. Gnezditskaia, '"Unidentified shareholders": the impact of oil companies on the banking sector in Russia', *Europe-Asia Studies*, 57(1), 2005, 476).
69. See S. A. Afontsev, 'Economic agreements and regional cooperation', paper for Symposium on the Russian Economy by Cabinet Office, Japan, 30 March 2005.
70. *Vedmosti*, 22 September 2005.
71. 'For the EU accession countries, the European Union looks like an anchor, peer, and savior, providing their dominant export market, as well as a source of institutions and financing. ... Russia continues to play a key role for other CIS countries as their main export market and as a peer.' (A. Åslund, *Building Capitalism*, Cambridge University Press, 2002, pp. 454–5).
72. V. Mau, 'Economic policy in 2004', *Voprosui ekonomiki*, 1 (in Russian), 2005, 8.

# Part 2

# Social Mobilization and Economic Transformation

# 7
# State–Society Relations in Belarus: A 'labour dimension'

*Kiryl Haiduk*

## Introduction

For many commentators, the survival of authoritarianism and an illiberal economy in Belarus in the midst of emerging democratic and market societies across East–Central Europe and the more recent 'coloured revolutions' in neighbouring states remains an enigma. This chapter focuses on the consequences of these dynamics in Belarus and argues that an understanding of these specific configurations of state and society depends on an analysis of social relations, particularly those related to labour. By focusing on labour, however, I do not mean to imply that all contemporary social phenomena have their roots in the social relations surrounding work and production. Rather, my point is that labour and production remain key terrains where state and society interact and from which, in this case, important trajectories of socioeconomic development are emerging. Understanding how the power relations between the layers of hierarchy in production are organized, including such instances as employment practices and wage-setting procedures, helps to clarify important aspects of social and political organisation more generally.

## Theorizing transition and the 'Belarusian' path of transformation

Belarus is an outlier among the transition economies of East–Central Europe which have opted for a democratic polity, a market economy, and EU membership. It also deviates from the experience of Ukraine and Russia, which have progressed much more in building a market economy and corresponding private sector, despite their lack of democratic reform.[1] In institutional terms, the preference for authoritarian policy in Belarus can be explained by an inheritance from state socialist rule, which has led to rigidities in adopting new more efficient market mechanisms.[2] Divergent development such as this emerges precisely because of the distinctiveness of specific historical experiences, while these divergent paths also tend to converge over time as societies adopt the most efficient common institutions and practices of the market (of which property rights are the most important).[3] In this view, countries learn slowly through trial and error, in part because elites resist external advice. In this view, change might occur, but only over a generation or more. The Polish 'Bathory Foundation' report makes a similar point when it claims that Belarus is divided on important issues of public life not only by the geographical schism between the Eastern (orthodox Christian with closer ties to Russia) and Western (catholic Christian populated by the Polish minority) parts of the country, but also by differences between generations.[4]

For others, differences in political attitude and orientation can be explained by issues related to identity. In this view, 'a return to Europe' by East–Central European states has been possible because of the 'common thrust' of transition foreign policy seeking full access to global markets and Western security regimes.[5] Such a transition has been driven by the desire to obtain 'full recognition as being Europeans in the liberal tradition',[6] a reorientation that was helped by the fact that dissident intellectuals who entered the first post-socialist governments were exposed to liberal thinking in the 1970s.[7] At that time, the ideas of monetarism started to penetrate state socialist societies, particularly through Hayek's *Road to Serfdom*, as well as through the circulation of monetarist pamphlets, which even then were serving as guides for dissidents feeling deep discontent with, and distrust of, authoritarian rule.[8] These influences and the strong orientation towards the European Union by the East–Central European members of the 'fraternal socialist camp' were, however, shaped in important ways by their prior experience with 'bourgeois' democracy, particularly in inter-war Czechoslovakia and the pre-war Baltic states. Thus, Tsygankov explains the difference in trade policy orientations of Belarus and Lithuania not by considerations of comparative advantage, but by 'substantial variations in the strength of the new republics' national identities'.[9] Such influences of national identity on policy outcomes are not direct, but are mediated by 'domestic structures and coalition-building processes', particularly in situations in which 'a well-developed national identity increases the power of nationalist-oriented groups and their ability to influence the foreign policy decision-making processes'.[10]

The Belarusian political system is one of 'authoritarian populism' of the kind also found in other parts of the second and developing worlds. Eke and Kuzio[11] point to the lack of 'ruling ideology', except 'a vague pan-eastern Slavic nationalism that is at odds with the Soviet Belarusian patriotism of the Belarusian ruling elites'.[12] Indeed, policy statements of Belarusian officials often look as if they had been borrowed from the speeches of the communist leaders of the Soviet Union, who seemed to constantly stress that the chief goal of state socialism was 'the near-complete satisfaction of material and spiritual needs of the Soviet people'. In Belarus these speeches often also emphasize the need to build a socially oriented state, where the bureaucracy is serving the people; low unemployment and steadily growing real wages are presented as achievements of the kind of 'gradualist' model of transformation selected for Belarus. Indeed, despite all the criticisms of inefficient economic policies that keep unprofitable, non-privatized enterprises afloat and suppress economic freedom, the Belarusian economy demonstrates relatively high growth rates and sustained real wage increases (Table 7.1).

These indicators tend to support the view that authoritarian policies have been able to generate welfare increases and popular support for government policies has been 'bought' by persistently delivering wage increases. Such economic growth has not been achieved without some kind of state-guided developmental policy, perhaps of the type initiated in the East Asian 'developmental states',[13] for which David Collier's notion of the 'bureaucratic authoritarian state' as a product of import substitution policies that, in turn, lead to the emergence of industry-guiding apparatuses might be useful.[14] Industrial capacity utilization rates in the early 2000s (60 per cent) have yet to return to the high rates of 1990 (96 per cent);[15] nonetheless, the first presidential elections in Belarus (held in 1994) were won under the populist slogan of 'making factories and plants work again', a direct invocation of a state development and full employment model from Soviet Union times.

If we accept the argument that authoritarianism in Belarus was born out of claims to improve social welfare, then was the establishment of the authoritarian state 'inevitable'? Did the Belarusian state have other options in negotiating its past legacies, the populist reaction to the chaos of the early 1990s and the lack of 'pro-European' identity in the country at large? Certainly, cases like Columbia, Venezuela and Chile suggest that problems of industrial stagnation can be resolved by democratic means (including the policy of export promotion supported by limited devaluation),[16] a view that is also supported by the experience of the post-war European societies.[17]

*Table 7.1* Major macroeconomic indicators, 1994–2005

| | 1994 | 1995 | 1996 | 1997 | 1998 | 1999 | 2000 | 2001 | 2002 | 2003 | 2004 | 2005 |
|---|---|---|---|---|---|---|---|---|---|---|---|---|
| GDP growth, per cent | −12.6 | −10.4 | 2.8 | 11.4 | 8.4 | 3.4 | 5.8 | 4.7 | 5.0 | 7.0 | 11.4 | 9.2 |
| Capital investment, per cent of GDP | 25.3 | 18.4 | 15.6 | 18.6 | 22.6 | 20.6 | 19.8 | 17.8 | 17.2 | 19.5 | 21.6 | 23.3 |
| Profit, per cent of GDP | 39.5 | 14.3 | 12.6 | 15.4 | 16.4 | 21.8 | 16.9 | 10.1 | 9.9 | 10.3 | 7.6 | 10.1 |
| The share of loss-making enterprises, per cent | 7.3 | 17.9 | 18.4 | 12.3 | 16.2 | 16.9 | 22.3 | 33.4 | 32.0 | 27.2 | 19.2 | 3.5 |
| Inflation (CPI), per cent | 2220.9 | 709.3 | 52.7 | 63.8 | 73.0 | 293.7 | 168.6 | 61.1 | 42.6 | 28.4 | 18.1 | 10.3 |
| Dollarisation (Currency deposits to M3 ratio), per cent | 47.1 | 38.3 | 31.1 | 39.9 | 61.3 | 70.1 | 64.5 | 57.3 | 51.4 | 46.9 | 41.6 | 32.1 |
| Employment dynamics (change to preceding year) per cent | −2.6 | −6.2 | −1.0 | 0.1 | 1.1 | 0.6 | 0.0 | −0.5 | −0.8 | −0.9 | −0.5 | −0.03 |
| Registered employment, per cent | 1.8 | 2.5 | 3.8 | 3.5 | 2.5 | 2.2 | 2.1 | 2.3 | 2.7 | 3.1 | 1.9 | 1.5 |
| Wages to GDP, per cent | – | 30.2 | 30.0 | 29.7 | 32.2 | 31.6 | 31.2 | 34.1 | 33.3 | 31.0 | 31.7 | 31.8 |

*Source*: Ministry of Statistics and Analysis; The National Bank of Belarus.

Modernization of industry in post-war Western Europe depended on the assistance of the state, but intervention was of a different scale and nature, built on the specific social compromise of the 'Keynesian welfare state',[18] which responded to the historical circumstances of post-war economic crisis, the strength of employers vis-à-vis workers, and the defeat of fascism and fear of communism. The existence of a well-organized labour movement, institutionalized in strong trade union and political parties, operating at the political level in order to obtain their goals, was a 'reflection of a particular level of economic and socio-political development' in Western Europe, conditioned in part by histories of previous rounds of industrialization that combined with strong colonial–national economies to underwrite successful social democracy plus Keynesianism.[19]

By contrast, in Southern Europe (Spain, Portugal, and Greece), domestic 'late' modernization occurred within an environment in which authoritarian state power and corporate interests forged a different relationship with civil society.[20] As a result, macroeconomic policy – as a reflection of a particular, but constantly changing, balance of power – had been neither Keynesian nor counter-Keynesian. If post-war Keynesianism in Western Europe did not depend on the use of government to direct decisions made in the private sector, but was based on social democracy as a medium of such policies, in Southern Europe the state did act to direct public and private investments in specific ways. Consequently, prior to becoming EU members, the Southern European states were characterized by less established mechanisms of social compromise and intense inequality in the distribution of wealth and incomes, characteristics that meant that social confrontation was an always present threat.[21] This confrontation might cause social upheavals and strikes in a climate of social unrest. The latter could be 'cooled down' by various means, from populist–authoritarian ones of a Latin American type to social–democratic ones of a Western European type. However, in the Southern European authoritarian states it was the absence of a considerable middle class, on the basis of which social democracy could be mobilized politically, that prevented alternatives to authoritarian orders emerging in Southern Europe. Here, macroeconomic regulation of demand had been embodied in a system of state-corporatism that functioned by interest mediation and manipulation. Any 'genuine', Western European type of social compromise was very difficult under these circumstances.

In many ways, Belarus replicates the essential features of this Southern European model, including the attempt to impose a certain vision of the world on society to foster authoritarian forms of organization with some elements of social protection such as employment guarantees and real, albeit slow, growth in real incomes. Antagonisms that arise in the course of such policies are not resolved in a negotiated, consensual fashion,[22] but instead are dealt with through channels that are tightly controlled by the state, including trade union organizations.

A dominant theme in contemporary comparative political economy[23] and its 'varieties of capitalism' approach[24] is a focus on the implications of labour organization for macroeconomic performance and political stability in different societies. In these approaches, macroeconomic policies, state, and society are linked by systems of labour control and motivation that 'tend to produce different wage levels, different productivities, and from there different histories, societies, and politics'.[25] These organizational forms vary from the 'minimalist' Anglo–American model to the strong 'social partnership' of the Continental European model,[26] and thus researchers distinguish between liberal market economies, such as the United States and the United Kingdom, and coordinated market economies, such as Germany and Sweden. The former coordinate economic activity through markets and corporate hierarchies and therefore perform successfully on the basis of low costs and major, radical product and technological innovations. The latter coordinate economic activity more through non-market mechanisms, such as informal networks and corporatist bargaining, and therefore perform successfully on the basis of high quality products and innovations in production processes.[27]

Such approaches to institutional diversity and incorporating labour as a key social actor are an attractive approach for the study of transition economies, including Belarus, where non-market mechanisms have prevailed over the past decade. However, there are some essential underlying assumptions in varieties of capitalism literature that make the application to Belarus (and other transition economies) problematic. In particular, these approaches tend to assume a democratic organization of the political process, the role of interest mediation and the developed status of the economy. Moreover, because of their focus on specific markets, such as labour or financial markets, the debate tends to resemble the one between New Keynesian and New Classical economists, a focus that tends to stress the economic over the social.

## State, society, and labour

Conceptually, the system of interest mediation is not simply the channel through which particular macroeconomic policies can be implemented, but a social process that occurs through a 'combination of a number of forms of social relations of production'.[28] In this reading, the state is understood as a site where particular forces are concentrated and directed either towards maintaining the existing order or towards bringing about a new order. The order that does emerge is thus based on the ways in which civil society and the state interact. Following Gramsci,[29] these modes can be based either on the use of force or coercion (authoritarianism) or the use of agreement and compromise, or consent (democracy). The interaction of state and society in the labour sphere could then take several forms, including so-called 'state corporatism', where the state intervenes to control conflict by legitimizing workers' and employers' organisations but controlling both of them to different degrees. Power relations are organized between the official worker organizations, employers, and state agencies in which the state is almost always, in the last resort, dominant. Historically, this form of state corporatism has been notable in Spain under Franco and Chile under the Pinochet regime as well as in the Philippines since 1972.[30]

The Soviet system of labour relations in Belarus had some specific elements that make it distinct from state corporatist systems. Workers had few formal political rights,[31] while economic struggles were inherently political.[32] Any form of independent worker representation was subordinated to politico-ideological constraint. The collapse of the Soviet Union has made the de-politicization of labour relations possible; indeed, some representatives of the state and employers have insisted on the economic necessity of labour market restructuring, thus leading to drastic cuts in the 'social costs' of labour overcoming the 'lumpen mentality' of 'state-dependent' workers, and attacking the 'excessive job security' in the market economy.[33]

In Belarus these claims have not materialized in any significant way. Instead, the articulation of interests of labour as well as the implementation of reforms have occurred within an institutional framework only slightly modified from that existing before the collapse of the Soviet Union. Under late socialism, enterprise-based labour collectives headed by the patron-director had become the core unit of institutionally organized labour and socio-economic struggles tended to be restricted to these concrete production units. Often, an implicit enterprise-based worker–management alliance was motivated to artificially increase the costs of production in order to get more resources at the expense of other units.[34] As a result, workers' solidarity did not normally extend beyond the immediate work group because 'the principal levers of production management were based on fomenting and exploiting divisions within the between work-groups'.[35] Accordingly, there was no basis of

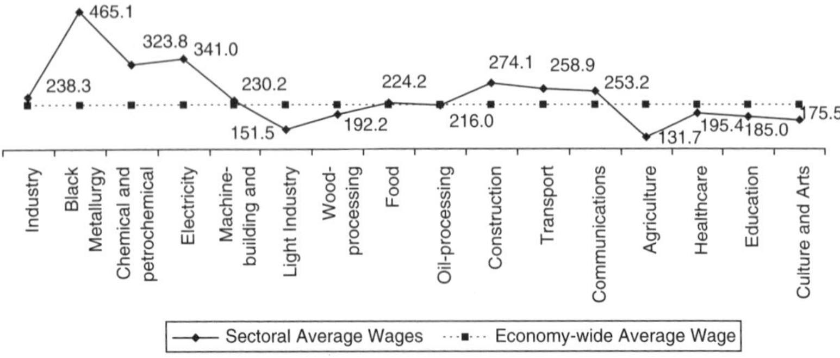


*Figure 7.1* Wage differentiation (in USD) in the Belarusian economy in 2005 (Economy-Wide Average Monthly Wage is equal to 218 USD)

*Source*: Based on data from the Ministry of Statistics and Analysis.

collective organization on which workers could grow. The destruction of the centralized apparatus of the state destroyed the structures of support for hierarchical internal structures of trade unions. As a result, they were able to decentralize and each level (national, regional, and local) acquired a degree of autonomy and independence.

In Belarus, by 1998–9, trade unions gained autonomy at the enterprise level at the expense of industry and national levels. In particular, they have been able to negotiate enterprise-based first-grade wages, which remained the cornerstone of the wage-setting system in Belarus. As a result, wage differentiation started to occur and export-oriented sectors (such as black metallurgy and chemical industry) and monopolistic suppliers of energy and services (energy and communication sectors) became wage leaders, while light and agricultural industry and some branches of manufacturing have lagged behind (Figure 7.1).

The government has been increasingly concerned by this growing polarization of incomes and has begun to take steps to reduce wage inequalities (see below).[36] Some of the sectors are still able to set wages above the average trend along with the provision of higher benefits for workers, but these collective agreements are now backed by performance agreements and occur mainly in export-oriented and semi-monopolistic enterprises.

As in other countries of the region, Belarus has also suffered from wage delays and non-payments, especially in the first half of the 1990s, although the scale of the problem was somewhat less than in Russia or Ukraine. However, the lack of productive jobs in the 'official' economy has stimulated the development of 'exit' strategies.[37] These have mainly occurred at the individual level and, as a result, have removed political pressure for reform of the current transition strategy (a process that has been similarly registered in other economies of East–Central Europe).[38] Individual 'exit' strategies have ranged from search for a second or third job usually in the informal sector[39] to collective forms of living (redistribution of resources within families and groups of friends) to subsistence small-scale agricultural production which helps some part of the population to maintain their living standards. The IMF has estimated the incomes from 'unregistered business activity' are about one-third of all incomes earned by households in 2001 in Belarus.[40] Although independent and democratic trade union organizations have tried to advocate alternative, more solidarity-based forms of organization, including the conduct of collective bargaining at the industry level, their influence in this context has remained limited.[41]

## Labour market policies and state–society relations in Belarus

The lack of labour organization and the coexistence of national, regional, and local levels of bargaining (where the latter has gradually become the most important site) have caused wage differentiation and segmented labour markets. Export-oriented enterprises and state-owned providers of essential services have acquired stronger sustainable positions in the economy, while loss-makers in agriculture and manufacturing have been facing lower pay and lack of investment. Instead of restructuring, the government has adopted a paternalistic attitude towards 'problematic' enterprises by financing them with 'soft credits', usually indirectly, through banks.[42] Moreover, enterprises have been granted various concessions like tax deferrals. All these measures have allowed enterprises to stay afloat, but not to become profitable and competitive on the domestic market, let alone internationally. Competition from abroad has been artificially restricted by increasing tax duties so that currently up to one-third of revenues come from the collection of VAT and other import taxes. Moreover, the state has recently decided to implement a policy of economy-wide average wage increases, often disregarding whether they are backed up by adequate improvements in productivity (Figure 7.2).

Since 2001, real wages have grown faster than productivity, in contrast to trends in East–Central Europe, where the opposite has occurred.[43] Considerations of competitiveness were ceded to what some have termed the 'political business cycle'.[44] The latter is a shorthand

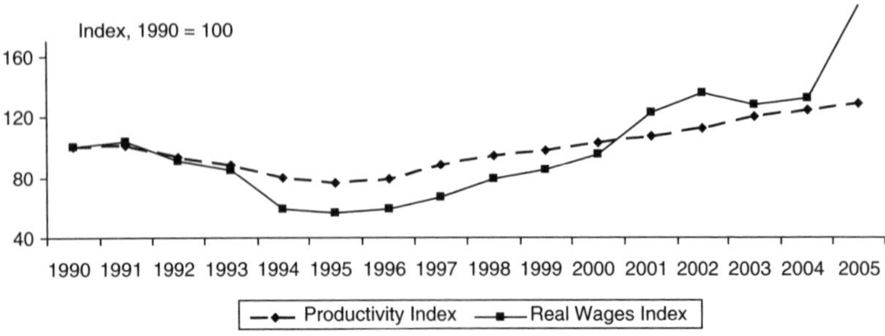


*Figure 7.2*   The dynamics of real wages and productivity in Belarus, 1990–2005

*Source*: Author's calculations on the basis of data taken from the Ministry of Statistics and Analysis.

label for state intervention into the economic process for the purpose of 'buying' social peace. Although the electoral process is considered to be compromised by organisations like the OSCE, the government still needs to secure some degree of support from the population. The result has been the use of monetary and fiscal awards as instruments to satisfy the aspirations of employers (to maintain  production) and wage earners (to enjoy real wage growth). However, one likely outcome of such an accommodation is inflation, which would destroy wage increases, making economic growth a temporary, short-term phenomenon.[45]

Important political events have also put upward pressure on wages. Between 1996 and 2004, all important political campaigns were conducted with promises of paying higher wages, pensions, and transfers. One of the notable increases is related to the 2001 presidential elections, when the average economy-wide wage was increased threefold over a period of 2.5 years, and the year 2004 (the year of the referendum to remove the constitutional restraint on presidential terms for one person), when the minimum wage was increased to reach the subsistence minimum (currently about 65 USD, the highest level among the CIS countries).

The workings of the political business cycle in Belarus have been backed up by a certain psychology of employees. Albert Hirschman[46] claims that there are two channels to express discontent with existing socioeconomic relationships. One is 'exit' (leaving a job, emigration, etc.), and another is 'voice' (bargaining, strike, etc.). In Belarus, the costs of 'exit' are presently higher than the costs of 'voice', which is also strengthened by the virtual absence of public support of the unemployed (the size of the unemployment benefit is less than 20 USD per month, three times lower than the subsistence minimum). Moreover, job creation is almost stagnant. In the first half of 2005, only 6.5 per cent of workers who have moved to a new workplace took newly created jobs. At the same time, only two per cent of all workers lost their jobs because of enterprise closure or scaling down of its economic activity.

Politically motivated wage increases and the protection of jobs do have a reverse side for a small open economy like Belarus. They mean increased pressure on the wage fund, which creates inflationary pressure and thus undermines competitiveness. The conflict between employment and wages could possibly be resolved by either reducing the size of the wage fund or implementing non-accommodating monetary policies that might suffocate growth and decrease employment. Since the latter outcomes are undesirable, the government of Belarus has recently decided to follow a strategy of wage moderation. This also has the consequence of strengthening (at least temporarily) authoritarian tendencies in politics, including new controls on the trade unions. In strictly economic terms, such a strategy is similar to that adopted in post-war Europe. In return for limited wage demands, workers had received benefits via the entitlements of the welfare state, while the employers had been able to reserve more funds for investment, rather than for wage increases. However, in Western Europe this was achieved through negotiation among the government, labour, and employers with the intent of achieving social consensus, not the overarching will of the state as in Belarus.

In Belarus, the consensual elements have been gradually removed from policy-making process. At the end of 2004, the government introduced a new wage-ceiling regulation.[47] This regulation – introduced with no consultation with trade unions – set up the upper limits for the first-grade wage in the wage grid at the level of the budget of the living wage. Although this regulation currently covers only a very small number of enterprises, it foreshadows the elimination of collective bargaining from labour policy. Moreover, it also implies that wage growth could be frozen in the future.

Although Figure 7.1 shows the existence of wage differentiation due to higher wage growth in successfully performing sectors of the Belarusian economy, this also represents a point from which the government has started to reduce wage inequality. Ultimately, this might result in redistribution of incomes from more successful to less successful industries to level wage up to a certain 'economy-wide' target, which is the current stated policy of the government and is written into the National Collective Agreement signed by the Federation of Trade Unions

*Table 7.2* Reduction of wage differentiation in the Belarusian economy, 1994–2004

| | The ratio of maximum wage to minimum wage | The ratio of minimum wage to the average wage | The ratio of maximum wage to the average wage |
|---|---|---|---|
| 1994 | 3.7 | 0.6 | 2.2 |
| 1995 | 3.7 | 0.6 | 2.0 |
| 1996 | 3.8 | 0.5 | 1.8 |
| 1997 | 3.6 | 0.5 | 1.9 |
| 1998 | 3.7 | 0.5 | 1.9 |
| 1999 | 4.0 | 0.5 | 2.0 |
| 2000 | 3.3 | 0.6 | 1.9 |
| 2001 | 3.1 | 0.6 | 1.8 |
| 2002 | 3.6 | 0.5 | 1.8 |
| 2003 | 3.8 | 0.6 | 1.8 |
| 2004 | 3.0 | 0.6 | 1.7 |

*Source*: own calculations on the basis of data taken from the Ministry of Statistics and Analysis.

of Belarus.[48] Thus, it appears that policies of the past few years have been specifically targeted at reducing the wage inequalities produced in the first half of the 1990s (Table 7.2).[49]

## Conclusion

One of the crucial elements of contemporary Belarusian political economy is the growing control of the government over issues of work, pay and collective bargaining. The government seems to be imposing limits on autonomous bargaining to redress wage drift and income inequalities. To this end the government is reworking notions of an 'average wage' as an important element of what can be called Belarusian-style state corporatism. This is not a new organizational form; some of its crucial features emerged in Southern European countries prior to their membership in the EU. This form of corporatism does not only fulfil the political need to minimize dissent from labour, but also serves as a vehicle to resolve economic conflict between employment and the inflation resulting from wage increases in excess of productivity gains. One consequence is that important economic actors, both labour and employers, have turned into consumers of politically driven economic decisions. The result is that the interests of Belarusian political authoritarianism and state management of the economy (including labour market regulation) currently reinforce each other.

# Endnotes


1. T. Beichelt, 'Autokratie und Wahldemokratie in Belarus, Russland und der Ukraine', Forschungsschwerpunkt Konflikt- und Kooperationsstrukturen in Osteuropa an der Universitat Mannheim, *Untersuschungen des FKKS* 26/2001 (July 2001) and European Bank of Reconstruction and Development, *Transition Report 2005, Business in Transition*, London: Oxford University Press, 2005.
2. M. Olson, 'Big Bills Left on the Sidewalk: Why Some Nations are Rich and Others Poor', *Journal of Economic Perspectives*, 10, 2 (Spring 1996), 3–24.
3. D. North, 'Institutions', *Journal of Economic Perspectives*, 5, 1 (Winter 1991), 97–112.
4. A. Naumczuk, E. Mironowicz, P. Kazanecki, P. and G. Gromadzki, 'The Forgotten Neighbour – Belarus in the Context of EU Eastern Enlargement', *On the Future of Europe: Stephan Bathory Foundation Policy Paper*, 4, September 2001, http://www.batory.org.pl/ftp/program/europejski/rap4en.rtf, 12 February 2004.
5. J. K. Laux, 'The Return to Europe: The Future Political Economy of Eastern Europe', in R. Stubbs and G. R. D. Underhill, eds, *Political Economy and the Changing Global Order*, Ontario: Oxford University Press, 2000, 264–73.
6. J. K. Laux, op. cit., p. 270.
7. G. Eyal, I. Szelényi, I. . and E. Townsley, *Making Capitalism without Capitalists: Class Formation and Elite Struggles in Post-Communist Central Europe*, London: Verso, 1998.
8. G. Eyal, I. Szelényi, I. and E. Townsley, op. cit., p. 152.
9. A. Tsygankov, 'Defining State Interests after Empire: National Identity, Domestic Structures, and Foreign Trade Policies of Latvia and Belarus', *Review of International Political Economy*, 7, 1 (Spring 2000), 101–37.
10. A. Tsygankov, op. cit., p. 102.
11. S. Eke and T. Kuzio, 'Sultanism in Eastern Europe: The Socio-Political Roots of Authoritarian Populism in Belarus', *Europe-Asia Studies*, 52, 3, 2000, 523–47.
12. S. Eke and T. Kuzio, op. cit., pp. 524–5.
13. M. Woo-Cumings, 'Introduction: Chalmers Johnson and the Politics of Nationalism and Development', in M. Woo-Cumings, ed., *The Developmental State*, Ithaca, N.Y. and London: Cornell University Press, 1999, 1–31.
14. D. Collier, 'Overview of the Bureaucratic–Authoritarian Model', in D. Collier, ed., *The New Authoritarianism in Latin America*, Princeton, N.J.: Princeton University Press, 1979, 19–32.
15. K. Haiduk, H.-J. Herr, T. Lintovskaya, S. Parchevskaya, J. Priewe and R. Tsikou, *Belarusian Economy at a Crossroads*, Moscow: International Labour Organisation, 2005.
16. G. Rocha, 'Neo-Dependency in Brazil', *New Left Review*, July–August 2002, 5–33.
17. B. Eichengreen and T. Iversen, 'Institutions and Economic Performance: Evidence from the Labour Market', *Oxford Review of Economic Policy*, 15, 4, 1999, 121–38.
18. B. Jessop, *The Future of the Capitalist State*, Cambridge, UK: Polity Press, 2002.
19. O. Holman, *Integrating Southern Europe: EC Expansion and the Transnationalisation of Spain*, London: Routledge, 1996.

20. N. Poulantzas, *The Crisis of Dictatorships: Portugal, Greece, Spain*, London: New Left Books, 1976.
21. O. Holman, op. cit., pp. 35–40.
22. E. Laclau, *Politics and Ideology in Marxist Theory*, London: Verso, 1977, p. 161.
23. P. Hall and D. Soskice, 'An Introduction to Varieties of Capitalism', in P. Hall and D. Soskice, eds, *Varieties of Capitalism. The Institutional Foundations of Comparative Advantage*, Oxford: Oxford University Press, 2001, 1–70.
24. T. Iversen, J. Pontusson and D. Soskice, eds, *Unions, Employers, and Central Banks: Macroeconomic Co-ordination and Institutional Change in Social Market Economies*, Cambridge, MA: Cambridge University Press, 2000.
25. J. Harrod, 'Towards International Political Economy of Labour', in J. Harrod and R. O'Brien, eds, *Global Unions? Theory and Strategies of Organised Labour in the Global Political Economy*, New York: Routledge, 2002, p. 15.
26. A. Lipietz, 'The Post-Fordist World: Labour Relations, International Hierarchy, and Global Ecology', *Review of International Political Economy*, 4, 1 (Spring 1997), 1–41.
27. P. Hall and D. Soskice, op. cit., pp. 5–6.
28. J. Harrod, *Power, Production, and Unprotected Worker*, Princeton, N.J.: Princeton University Press, 1987, p. 20.
29. A. Gramsci, *Selections from the Prison Notebooks*, New York, International Publishers, 1971.
30. P. J. Williamson, *Varieties of Corporatism: A Conceptual Discussion*, Cambridge, UK: Cambridge University Press, 1985.
31. E. Mandel, 'The Laws of Motion of the Soviet Economy', *Review of Radical Political Economics*, 13, 1981, 35–9.
32. H. Ticktin, 'The Political Economy of Class in the Transitional Epoch', *Critique*, 20/21, 1978, 7–25.
33. B. Silverman and M. Yanowitch, 'The Transformation of Work in Post-Socialist and Post-Industrial Societies', in B. Silverman, R. Vogt and M. Yanowitch, eds, *Double Shift: Transforming Work in Post-Socialist and Post-Industrial Societies*, Armonk, N.Y. and London: M. E. Sharpe, 1993, 1–3.
34. M. Burawoy and P. Krotov, 'The Economic Basis of Russia's Political Crisis', *New Left Review*, 198, 1993, 16–38.
35. S. Clarke and S. Ashwin, *Russian Trade Unions and Industrial Relations in Transition*, Basingstoke: Palgrave Macmillan, 2003, p. 23.
36. K. Haiduk, A. Chubrik, S. Parchevskaya and M. Walewski, 'Ryinok Truda Belarusi: Obschii Obzor' [Labour Market in Belarus: An Overview], *Ecowest*, 5, 1, 2006, 44–93, http://research.by/pdf/2006n1r02.pdf, 15 June 2006.
37. A. Hirschman, *Exit, Voice, and Loyalty: Responses to Decline in Firms, Organisations, and States*, Cambridge, MA: Cambridge University Press, 1970.
38. S. Crowley and D. Ost, 'The Surprise of Labour Weakness in Post-communist Society', in S. Crowley and D. Ost, eds, *Labour and Politics in Post-communist Eastern Europe*, Lanhman: Rowman and Littlefield, 2001, 1–12.
39. S. Alasheev and M. Kiblitskaya, 'How to Survive on a Russian Wage', in S. Clarke, ed, *Labour Relations in Transition: Wages, Employment, and Industrial Conflict in Russia*, Cheltenham: Edward Elgar, 1996, 99–118.

40. IMF, Staff Report for the 2001 Article IV Consultations, *IMF Country Report,* 02/223, Washington, D.C.: IMF, 2002, p. 86.
41. Information about them can be found at the web-site 'Trade Union Movement of Belarus', https://www.praca-by.info.
42. K. Haiduk, H.-J. Herr, T. Lintovskaya, S. Parchevskaya, J. Priewe and R. Tsikou, op. cit., Chapter 3.
43. B. Galgóczi, 'Wage Trends in Central and Eastern Europe', *Labour Education: Paying Attention to Wages,* 128, 2002, 39–44.
44. W. Nordhaus, 'The Political Business Cycle', *Review of Economic Studies,* 42, 1975, 169–90.
45. A. Alesina and L. Summers, 'Central Bank Independence and Macroeconomic Performance: Some International Evidence', *Journal of Money, Credit, and Banking,* 25,.2, 1993, 151–62.
46. A. Hirschman, op. cit., 1970.
47. Council of Ministers' Regulation No. 1651, 27 December 2004.
48. For more information, please visit http://www.fpb.by/files/programm.doc.
49. K. Haiduk, A. Chubrik, S. Parchevskaya, and M. Walewski, op. cit., pp. 77–8.

# 8
# Trade Unions and the Labour Market in Four New European Union Member States

*Massimo Congiu*

## Introduction

On 1 May 2004, the EU took the historic step of opening its doors to 10 new countries: eight located in the central and eastern part of the continent, of which no less than six are 'new countries', five founded after the collapse of the Soviet Empire, and, one, Slovenia, during the disintegration of Yugoslavia. In January 2007, these 'new countries' were joined by Bulgaria and Romania. The enlargement of the European Union poses – or imposes – new challenges and several weighty problems for European labour markets and trade unions. The challenge of labour market reform in the pre-2004 EU is now compounded by the challenge of integrating the new states and their reforming and increasingly mobile labour markets. The 2004 accession alone brought into the EU about 30,000,000 workers, many of whom are used to completely different socioeconomic conditions and now must adapt to very different labour cultures and employment futures.

The new EU member states face the combined challenge of post-socialist reform, EU accession and economic globalization with very specific labour market structures and conditions. At the point of accession in 2004, the new member states still had more than 13 per cent of their workers employed in agriculture, compared with four per cent in the EU-15; 32 per cent worked in industry, compared with 28.2 per cent in the EU-15; and 54.5 per cent were employed in the service sector, compared with 67.8 per cent in the EU-15.[1] Female unemployment in the new member states was 15.3 per cent compared with an average 8.6 per cent in the EU-15. Rates of part-time employment are also very different between the new member states (10.3 per cent) and the EU-15 (33.5 per cent), with some countries, such as Slovakia, having part-time employment rates as low as 2.7 per cent.

Labour market transformation has, as a result, been a crucial issue in preparations for EU enlargement and continues to shape policies dealing with economic integration.[2] The regional imbalances are deep and consequences for workers of economic integration are far from clear. This chapter focuses on labour market transformations in Poland, the Czech Republic, Slovakia and Hungary, drawing on interviews with trade union leaders in each country.

## Labour market structure and trade unions

While each accession country differs in the structure of its labour market, they all also share some common characteristics. Average unemployment rates in the new EU members are almost 5–10 per cent, compared with 7.9 per cent in the EU-15. Of these, Poland has the highest unemployment rate (17.6 per cent), Hungary (7.5 per cent) has the lowest (although rates have increased since 2004), and Slovakia (11.4 per cent) and the Czech Republic (7.9 per cent) have unemployment rates between the two. In many accession countries average unemployment rates mask intensely uneven patterns of unemployment, particularly among minority populations such as the Roma population. Thus, for example, in Hungary, the Roma comprise 5–10 per cent of the population and have unemployment rates of between 50 and 60 per cent.

Post-socialist new member states continue their adjustments to the economic reforms adopted since the beginning of the 1990s. These have had important consequences for labour markets, workers, and trade unions. For example, in Poland there are currently about 20 trade unions, the most important being OPZZ (Ogólnopolskie Porozumienie Związków Zawodowych – All-Poland Alliance of Trade Unions), Solidarność and Forum, which has about 300,000 members (Table 8.1).

These are the three trade unions taking part in the so-called tripartite commission that oversees labour politics. With the passing of time and due to political changes, the situation of these organizations has

*Table 8.1*  Trade union membership in Poland, 1993–2003[3]

| Country | Trade Union | 1993 | 1998 | 2003 | Change 1993–2003 |
|---|---|---|---|---|---|
| Poland | OPZZ | 4,500,000 | 2,000,000 | 800,000 | −82.2% |
| | NSZZ Solidarność | 2,000,000 | 1,200,000 | 780,000 | −61.0% |
| | FZZ | – | – | 320,000 | – |
| | Total | 6,500,000 | 3,200,000 | 1,900,000 | −70.8% |

*Table 8.2*   Trade union membership: Solidarność and OPZZ [4]

|  | **Solidarność** | **OPZZ**<br>**(All-Poland Alliance of Trade Unions)** |
| --- | --- | --- |
| 1990 | na | 5,200,000 |
| 1992 | 1,650,000 | na |
| 1998 | 1,300,000 | 3,000,000 |
| 2002 | 904,000 | 1,033,000 |
| 2005 | 801,000 | 1,011,000 |
| 2006 | 722,000 | na |

*Note*: na  not available

completely changed. Solidarność has been in steady decline for more than a decade. As a result, it is less relevant than OPZZ has a little more than 1,000,000 members, but even this union suffered a decline in membership in the 1980s and in the middle of the 1990s (Tables 8.2 and 8.3).

According to Wieslawa Taranowska, vice-president of OPZZ, the diminished status of the unions is due not only to the general public's perception of unions as paper tigers in the present climate of high unemployment, but also to the detrimental effects of government policies in the 1990s, when Solidarność was a leading participant in government. In short, the labour problems of Poland are associated with the political activities of Solidarność, manoeuvring at the highest levels of government, and betraying the nation's social hopes. For OPZZ, the post-communist government's policies are of benefit only to business. Furthermore, the previous social-democratic government modified the labour code three times, complicating the situation for workers and their representatives. As a result, businesses have been given remarkable power by laws such as one forbidding the formation of trade unions in firms with fewer than 10 employees. Ewa Tomaszewska (Solidarność) has suggested that, as a result, people working in trade or in small firms have no real protection or support from government agencies. Of course, individual employees may still join a trade union, but this is difficult in the context of high unemployment and lack of legal protections. Solidarność has gone so far as to argue that the policies of the government are openly against trade unions, and are supported by the media close to those in power.

According to Ewa Tomaszewska, small Polish entrepreneurs believe that their new-found freedoms mean that anything is possible and/or permissible, and, as a result, it is very difficult to convince them that social dialogue is important. Tomaszewska has also suggested that

Eastern Europe entrepreneurs also imagine that Poland offers an environment that lacks clearly defined labour laws and social rules, and where – as a result – business relationships with unions can be problematic. Unemployed workers often have little or no alternative but to accept any conditions of employment, even where the employer does not respect the labour code. The employer has an *embarras du choix* with those who apply for the work offered and can choose freely if some are not willing to accept the conditions, although, with high levels of labour migration to Western Europe, employers are now beginning to feel pressure to maintain workers in regions where surpluses of skilled, semi-skilled, and unskilled workers have dried up. As a result, employers are now putting pressure on the Polish government to reduce the barriers to labour recruitment from Ukraine.

There are, of course, important regional differences in unemployment and in the ways in which the legacies of and practices around state Labour Codes have changed.[5] The unemployment rate in the Czech Republic is 9.3 per cent, but the situation is more critical in Northern Moravia. In the Most region, unemployment remains extremely high (23.6 per cent), in Karviná it is 19.7 percent, in Teplice 17.1 per cent, in Ostrava 17 per cent, and in Chomutov 16.7 per cent. According to the trade unions, the unemployment rate in the smallest towns in these regions can reach almost 50 per cent. ČMKOS (Českomoravská konfederace odborových svazů – Czech–Moravian Confederation of Trade Unions), the main trade union, claims that at present 30 per cent of Czech workers are members of a trade union, a figure that exceeds those of the three other countries. However, this membership rate is decreasing because of the reorganization of industry and the closure of several factories and state firms. The ČMKOS programme calls for full employment from 2002 to 2006 with a series of state subsidies to stimulate vocational education.

## Worker training, skills, and workforce capacities

In recent years, training and skills have emerged as an increasing problem across the region. The number of young people electing to continue their studies instead of looking for a job is increasing. The Czech Republic has one of the highest percentages of young people with certificates of Secondary Education, but only 6.4 per cent of working people attend vocational education classes, compared with the European average of 8.4 per cent and 19.6 per cent in the three best performing European countries: the United Kingdom, Finland and Denmark.

Throughout Central–Eastern Europe the level of investment in vocational training is low. The EU encourages its members to organize permanent systems of vocational education, but for these to be successful the cooperation of private enterprise is essential. However, while some companies in the region do participate in these initiatives, not all do. Indeed, Eurostat has recently reported that 43 per cent of local enterprises have organized vocational classes, compared with 70 per cent of companies in western European countries.

Trade unions are seeking government support for this issue and for the creation of concrete programmes to create new jobs in the public sector while protecting, as far as possible, the most vulnerable members of the labour market, such as women, the handicapped and young adults. The problem of the relative paucity of vocational training has become more marked in recent years. In their 2004 report on vocational training, the German Chamber of Commerce and Industry, in association with Kienbaum Executive Consultants Kft, found that Hungarian firms were becoming increasingly concerned about the lack of skilled workers and the risk this posed for the potential loss of investment capital, especially from German firms and joint ventures. According to Péter Pataky, president of MSZOSZ (Magyar Szakszervezetek Országos Szövetsége – National Confederation of Hungarian Trade Unions), the main Hungarian trade union, this situation has not changed. In some countries, the problem is getting worse.

Zlatka Gospodinova has recently pointed to these problems of worker training in Bulgaria, where increasing demand for skilled workers such as turners, millers, welders and builders, as well as managerial-level employees, has emerged as the economy has grown in recent years.[6] According to Gospodinova, employer organizations have been particularly outspoken about the need for the government to ensure that vocational education responds more effectively to the demands of economic growth and the widespread introduction of new technologies. In turn, the Ministry of Labour and Social Policy and the trade unions have pointed to the failure of employers to invest in training their own workforce. Poaching of qualified workers whose training has been financed by another employer is relatively common and the result is a gamble over the relative merits of such poaching against the expenses and risks of making such investments in the hope of retaining workers.

In Slovakia, Central Office of Labour, the Family and Social Security statistics indicate that the rate of registered unemployment (in March 2006) was 11.4 per cent (1.29% less than the same time last year) with 329,269 persons actively seeking a job. But, as in the Czech Republic,

*Table 8.3*   Regional unemployment rates
in Slovakia[7]

| | |
| --- | --- |
| • Bratislava | 2.7% |
| • Trnava | 7.3% |
| • Trenčin | 6.7% |
| • Nitra | 11.6% |
| • Žilina | 9.4% |
| • Banská Bystrica | 18.4% |
| • Prešov | 15.9% |
| • Košice | 18% |

unemployment rates vary regionally with much higher rates in the eastern regions, where the level of the investment is also much lower (Table 8.3).

Salary levels in the country as a whole are relatively low, but these are also much lower in the eastern parts of Slovakia where, trade unions suggest, the percentage of employees earning a salary lower than the national average might be as high as 60–66 per cent.[8] In these regions infrastructure and services are limited and social problems accumulate. Conditions are particularly desperate among the Roma population, the majority of whom live in the east and among whom rates of unemployment are almost 90 per cent. These problems are also emphasized by KOZ SR (Konfederácja Odborových Zväzov Slovenskej Republiky – Confederation of Trade Unions of The Slovak Republic), the main trade union in the country. This is an independent organization that became a member of the European trade union in 2005. Its ideal partners are the Slovakia social-democratic parties and its programme is based upon solidarity, social justice and democracy. The trade union is well represented in the region and its membership consists of 35 per cent (or 1,500,000) of all employees protected by trade unions. In recent years Slovakia has had the highest GDP growth in the PECO region, which includes Poland, the Czech Republic and Slovenia,[9] but KOZ SR stresses that this growth is misleading:

Nowadays the media broadcast something every day about the 2002 Slovak 'economic miracle'. The government very proudly points out its achievement from 1998 to 2004, and argues that this is a new model for the further development of the economy. But, in comparison to other EU member states which tend to measure and place more stress on their achievements in social policy, the government of Slovakia largely ignores such indicators in its public pronouncements, stressing instead only those aspects of social development that have obviously resulted from improvements in the state of economy.[10]

Trade unions have organized strikes and demonstrations, but participation has been low and hostility from businesses towards their activities has generally increased. In Slovakia, according to Ivan Saktor, president of KOZ SR, trade unions have faced particular difficulties in the private sector, especially among small businesses. Trade union staff members at KOZ SR regularly experience hostility as they try to organize, or conduct inspections and monitoring of the labour code. Problems have been particularly common in construction, agriculture and mining. Businesses are required by law to give trade unions all the papers and information they need, but Slovak trade unionists say that this has been difficult in practice, particularly in dealing with small or Asian businesses.[11]

Victory in the 2006 general election by Smer-Sociálna demokracia (Smer-SD) (centre-left) has already begun to change this situation. Smer was the only political party to strike an agreement prior to the election on post-election cooperation with KOZ SR, and trade unionists have since worked closely with the new government to forge its commitment to becoming more of a social state and focusing more on issues of social justice, including adjustments to the tax system, pensions and health-care schemes, and reform of the Labour Code in order to redress the current disadvantages faced by employees in dealing with employers, and putting each on a more equal legal footing.[12]

In August 2006, the parliament approved the government's new programme with these changes in the social sphere. The *Programme for Government* included the following main chapters:

- Principles and values of the Programme for Government
- Macroeconomic framework, public finance and economic policy
- Social policy
- Healthcare
- Knowledge-based society
- Culture
- Democracy and rule of law
- State defence
- Foreign policy

It stresses the government's commitment to building a welfare state by combining economic growth and performance with employment growth, social cohesion and an improved quality of life for all. The programme also stresses the need for a national employment strategy while also creating a stable business environment and providing support for those who are self-employed and small and medium-sized enterprises. The new employment strategy emphasizes increasing employment and reducing unemployment, fostering investment, increasing job attractiveness, productivity and quality of work, involvement in the knowledge-based economy, and reducing the proportion of low wage earners. The social policy chapter of the government programme also includes some of the important elements the trade unions were seeking prior to the election:

- Labour relations and social dialogue
- Social security
- Family support
- Support of gender equality
- Efficiency of institutions

The Labour Code will be amended to ensure greater protection for certain categories of employees, particularly as flexibilization of work contracts increases. These will include protections for part-time and temporary agency workers who experience discrimination and those who are unfairly dismissed. The amendments will also set the maximum weekly working time, including overtime, establish a scale for steady increases in the minimum wage, and create policies aimed at equalizing labour costs among regions and sectors. To achieve better compliance with legislation and to better protect employee rights, the government further aims to strengthen the labour inspectorates and broaden their rights, as well as develop improved occupational health and safety standards. Finally, the new programme will try to ensure greater levels of efficiency and service in the public sector while deepening the role of social dialogue as a tool for employees and employers to contribute to drafting social and economic policy. To this end, the government supports the trade unions in regaining their position as an effective defender of employee interest, and as an equal party in the social dialogue.[13]

In Hungary unemployment is currently lantly 7.5 percent. As in Slovakia, the Roma are particularly marginalized in Hungary, which has the fourth highest Roma population in Europe after Romania, Bulgaria and Spain. According to the census of 2001, 190,046 people declared themselves as Roma, but Hungarian statistics estimate the number at 570,000–600,000 with some estimates as high as 800,000–1,000,000.[14]

Between 2004 and 2005, unemployment rates increased particularly among young adults. The number of unemployed young adults is steadily increasing and in the last two years it has even doubled, despite the commitment to more flexible labour contracts announced by the government, in the so-called 'hundred steps' programme, which contained several measures, such as fiscal reductions for the first employment for young people and new regulations for occasional jobs and for vocational training. Moreover, before the centre-left victory in the April 2006 general elections, the Prime Minister promised to create 400,000 new jobs. In one year, however, the number of unemployed youth has increased by 10,000 and the unemployment rate for the 15–24 age group has increased from 16.6 per cent to 20.4 per cent, while the average in the new EU members is actually 18.4 per cent.[15] According to the Hungarian Ministry of Labour, young graduates may have to wait at least one year to get a job, even though in the past 10 years the number of university registrations has doubled. At present the labour market is saturated with graduates in Economics or Communication Sciences, while there is a lack of specialists in the fields of logistics and high technology.

The largest Hungarian trade union, MSZOSZ, now has only about 350,000 members, including pensioners, and is experiencing the effects of economic recession throughout the 1990s, when almost 1,500,000 jobs were cut and trade unions lost their place in many workplaces. As a result, over the past decade the importance of trade unions has also decreased. MSZOSZ policies emphasize employment protection, the right to hold a job, and struggles for better working conditions and salaries. Union policies also stress the need for government intervention to stimulate higher employment rates. Employment rates through the CEE are relatively low, but especially so in Hungary. More efficient policies are necessary to reach the level of the European Union, with its rate of 63 per cent employment. Péter Pataki, vice-president of MSZOSZ, argues that despite pre-election claims by politicians that employment has risen or dropped, depending on whether they are in government or in opposition, the actual level has remained the same for the last 10–12 years. Moreover, there has been little improvement regarding salaries, which remain at about 40–45 per cent of the EU average. Moreover, productivity levels remain low at 60.9 per cent of the EU average. Tamás Wittich, former president of MSZOSZ, suggests that in Hungary, collective agreements account for only 40–45 per cent of all labour contracts, and adds that it is not easy to maintain respect for regulations such as working hours, which often exceed the fixed 40 hours, and which do not take into account that many workers must work more than one job in order to have a decent income. This disregard of the rules is compounded by the absence of an efficient system of monitoring and control: at present there are more than 900,000 firms in Hungary and only 200 inspectors. Wittich has estimated that the process of reaching EU standards will take about 30 years. Statistics on the number of accidents at work has not increased, but, as MSZOSZ reports, many businesses no longer report accidents. As in Slovakia, businesses have remarkable power while trade union organizations are weak and, as a result, workers choose not to demand their rights for fear of losing their job.

## Conclusion

Before 1989, 80–90 per cent of workers in the region were members of a trade union. Membership is now only 10–15 per cent. Working people do not really trust trade unions, partly because of their previous roles as transmission belts of the state and partly because they are now seen as weak or lacking influence. The trade union activists come from an experience of socialism, during which time their role was only representative as an expression of the socialist system was largely one of the transmission belts for the wishes of the party of the system. After 1989, trade unions had to learn to act in a completely new way and this has proved to be remarkably difficult. As often occurs in periods of great change, there is a degree of social discontent, which provides good reason for protest, yet, if people are not accustomed to having a voice and fear losing their jobs, they think twice before seeking redress for their grievances. GDP in all reform countries is now increasing and integration into the European Union opens new opportunities and institutional tools for labour organizations. On the other hand, this is itself a contested process and it may be several years before we find out what kind of EU will prevail, a social one or one based on the market model.

## Endnotes

1. Laborstat 2003–2004; UNECE 2003–2004.
2. It was the main subject of the European Conference on Enlargement and Industrial Connections at the University of Modena (Italy) in October 2003.
3. Source:EIRO.http://www.eiro.eurofound.eu.int/2004/03/update/tn0403105u.html
4. Sources: Solidarność International Department and OPZZ Press Office.
5. See J. Pickles and A. Smith, 'Clothing Workers After Worker States: The Consequences for Work and Labour of Outsourcing, Nearshoring and Delocalization', in S. McGrath-Champ, A. Herod and A. Rainnie, eds, *Handbook*

   *of Work and Society: Working Space*, London: Sage Publishers, 2007, pp. [forth-coming].

 6. Z. Gospodinova, 'Low qualification levels an obstacle to economic competi-tiveness', Balkan Institute for Labour and Social Policy (BILSP), 12 December 2006, http://www.eiro.eurofound.eu.int/2006/10/articles/bg0610049i.html.
 7. Source: Slovakian Statistical Office, figures elaborated by ICE Bratislava (Istituto per il Commercio Estero, Institute for Foreign Trade).
 8. Eurostat and OECD.
 9. Source: ICE Bratislava.
10. KOZ SR, 'The truth about the "economic miracle" in Slovakia'.
11. Source: L'ubomír Čierny, KOZ SR press office.
12. Source: TASR, Tlačová Agentúra Slovenskej Republiky – News Agency of the Slovak Republic, 19 June 2006.
13. L. Cziria, 'New government programme includes union demands', Bratislava: Institute for Labour and Family Research, 13 November 2006, *European indus-trial relations observatory online.* http://www.eiro.eurofound.eu.int/2006/09/articles/sk0609019i.html
14. Source: 'Kisebbségek Magyarországon 2004–2005', c. kormánybeszámoló 98–99. oldal; Kiadja a Nemzeti és Etnikai Kisebbségi Hivatal; Felelős kiadó: Heizer Antal (Minorities in Hungary, government figures published by The National and Ethnic Minorities Commission).
15. KSH (The Central Office of Statistics).

# 9

# You '*Can*' Take It with You: Cultural Capital, State Regulation and Tourism in Post-socialist Bulgaria

*Kristen Ghodsee*

## Introduction

The collapse of communism in Bulgaria ushered in an era of dramatic social, political and economic changes. After 1989, Bulgaria slowly abandoned its centrally planned economy for a free market model that encouraged privatization of previously state-owned assets and introduced both domestic and international competition to once monopolistic enterprises. These changes had drastic impacts on Bulgarian employees as they struggled to navigate the new rules in a labour market where the state no longer guaranteed full employment to all citizens and the profit motive began to overshadow the interests and well-being of workers. This chapter examines the impact of these economic changes on ordinary Bulgarians' lives by focusing on women employed in the tourism industry, one of the most important sectors in Bulgaria's post-communist economy and the country's largest generator of hard currency.

In the early 1990s, many Western scholars predicted that women in the former socialist countries would be the hardest hit by the economic transformation.[1] In my own research in Bulgaria, however, I found that there was a large group of women who had actually benefited from the advent of free markets. Many of these were women employed in tourism. This chapter will explore the two main reasons why women in the Bulgarian tourism sector were not negatively affected by the transition away from communism. First, women had acquired before 1989 the kind of education, skills, and experience that would become necessary to succeed in the post-1989 era. And second, state regulations on the management of hotels and restaurants inadvertently favoured women by requiring certain minimum levels of education to work in professional positions in the sector.

The accumulation of cultural capital was uniquely gendered under the communist system. Cultural capital refers to the formal education, work experience, informal training and cultivation of tastes and behaviours associated with the more privileged classes that are embodied in individual men and women.[2] Before 1989, the type of cultural capital one obtained through formal schooling varied by sex, and it was women who earned the appropriate type of education that became valuable after 1989. The Bulgarian communists had concentrated men into technical colleges and professional institutes in order to prepare them for prestigious and better paid jobs in Bulgaria's industrial sector while at the same time funnelling women into universities. The more general education women received at these universities channelled female labour into less prestigious service sectors of the command economy such as law, medicine, academia, banking, and tourism, where wages under communism were lower.

Cultural capital and its value in the economy vary widely across different types of economic systems. In a capitalist economy, cultural capital is an investment that is made in developing the skills and knowledge required for success in the labour market. Under command economic systems, where employment was largely guaranteed by the state, cultural capital had a very different value. The accumulation of cultural capital in individuals was less driven by market imperatives and more related to lofty communist goals of liberating the masses from ignorance. In fact, there was little direct correlation between education and class privilege, which is why women could be more educated than men but receive lower wages. Privilege was more closely associated with political capital, such as being a member of the Communist Party.[3]

The value of different types of cultural and political capital drastically changed with the collapse of communism. After the onset of marketization and privatization in the 1990s, Bulgaria's industrial sector slowly imploded as it lost its traditional export markets in the East and faced new competition from the West. At the same time, professions that had been officially devalued under the command economy became some of the most dynamic and important professions under the new market system – and they required the type of education and training which Bulgarian women had received. Finally, being a member of the Communist Party (*i.e.* having political capital) was no longer enough to secure oneself or one's relatives a job as the state retreated from its guarantee of full employment for all citizens and labour markets were created. Thus, due to a revaluing of their cultural capital[4] brought on by the sudden insertion of Bulgaria into the global capitalist economy, some Bulgarian women were uniquely prepared to succeed in the post-socialist labour market. The case study of Bulgarian women also has broader implications for other post-socialist countries where women exiting communism had accumulated cultural capital that allowed them to succeed in newly created labour markets. It is important to recognize that not all women were the inevitable 'losers' of the transition process and necessary to understand why some groups of women fared better than others.

This chapter is based on 18 months of fieldwork in Bulgaria in 1999 and 2000, during which I conducted over 100 formal interviews with government officials, foreign experts, former Balkantourist managers, tourism entrepreneurs, and ordinary men and women employed in the tourism sector. My research concentrated on the two winter resorts of Borovetz and Pamporovo and the two seaside resorts of Albena and Golden Sands. Finally, I conducted special interviews with professors and students in university-level tourism degree programmes including those at Sofia University, the New Bulgarian University, The University of World and National Economy, and the Dutch–Bulgarian Tourism College in Albena.

## Veneta

Veneta is a hotel manager in the winter ski resort of Pamporovo nestled within the green pine forests of the Rhodopi Mountains in the south of Bulgaria. Her straight brown hair is pulled away from her face in a tight ponytail fastened high on the back of her head. She wears dark sunglasses and a wide headband to keep her ears protected from the cold wind. After watching her lithe, athletic figure swoosh down to the bottom of the slopes in a snug-fitting black and yellow ski uniform, it is easy to forget that she is 41 and not 21-years old. 'This is my dream job,' she tells me over a hot glass of Bulgarian brandy in a nearby café. 'I love to be in the mountains. I love to ski. I love to meet new people. I love to speak English.'

Veneta was born in 1960 in the nearby town of Smolyan, the only child of a Bulgarian father and an East German mother. She was raised during the heyday of Bulgarian communism, when the standard of living of most Bulgarians far exceeded that of their socialist brother countries, before the economic stagnation of the 1980s began to slowly chip away at the nation's confidence in communism. Because she was raised bilingual, she always had an affinity for languages and eventually went to university in Plovdiv where she graduated with a degree in English philology. Her parents had both been important members in the Communist Party in Smolyan, and they had used their political capital to help Veneta get a job as a receptionist in the Sokoletz Hotel in Pamporovo right after her graduation. Because she was fluent in both English and German, Veneta was a valuable asset to the hotel. Throughout the 1980s, she had worked her way up to being a front office manager in charge of all of the other receptionists in the hotel.

Veneta is typical of women employed in the Bulgarian tourism sector–highly educated with many years of experience and fluent in multiple foreign languages. For a variety of reasons having to do with Bulgarian travel prohibitions before 1989 and the access to hard currency and westerners that work in tourism allowed, jobs in Bulgaria's tourism sector have always been considered quite prestigious despite the fact that official wages in tourism under communism were low compared with other sectors of the economy. Women like Veneta were privileged to have employment in tourism. Furthermore, women like Veneta who were employed in seasonal resorts like Pamporovo under communism were often given opportunities to go for additional education and training in the off-season. Veneta used the summer and autumn months to take computer classes and continue her study of English. In November 1989, when Bulgaria's communist leader unexpectedly resigned, Veneta had been preparing for the beginning of the winter season after having spent the autumn taking a course in advanced English literature. 'When the Changes[5] occurred I did not think anything bad was going to happen. I thought our lives would get better. I had no idea what would happen in Bulgaria,' she says.

Under communism, Bulgaria had been the European communist country that was most dependent on the Soviet Union and the COMECON trading bloc for its foreign trade.[6] The 'velvet revolutions' sweeping through Eastern Europe and the final disbandment of the COMECON[7] in 1991 crushed the Bulgarian economy.[8] Between 1989 and 1998, the Bulgarian Gross Domestic Product (GDP) lost more than a third of its value.[9] In the period immediately following the transition, GDP per capita fell from $2,513 in 1989 to $946 in 1991, a massive decline in just two years.[10] The establishment of free markets in Bulgaria also overlapped with banking collapses, hyperinflation, food rationing, and high unemployment.[11] In 1996, when the Bulgarian economy finally imploded, the average annual per capita income was $560, meaning that most Bulgarians had to live on about $1.50 a day.[12] By 2003, per capita GDP had still not recovered to 1989 levels and income polarization had increased.[13]

The economic chaos that followed 'the Changes' put both of Veneta's parents out of work and devastated the local economy in the Rhodopi Mountains. The resort of Pamporovo remained one of the only viable enterprises in the area, and Veneta was able to support herself and her two parents on her salary as a front desk manager. In fact, she earned more in three months at the resort than both of her parents' pensions added up to in a year. But the Changes brought about widespread restructuring in every sector, including tourism. In the early 1990s, the state-owned tourism monopoly, Balkantourist, was broken up, which meant dramatic changes for the Pamporovo resort, and growing uncertainty and instability for people like Veneta, who had never had to worry about their jobs under communism: 'Because I was taking care of my parents, I was very afraid to lose my work. We had heard the stories about Balkantourist, and I remember that I was nervous.'

The success of tourism under communism had been highly dependent on the centralized authority of the state tourism institution, Balkantourist. Centralized tourism managed to survive the first two years of transition almost unscathed, but the 1991 election of a non-socialist government began the erosion of Balkantourist's monopoly. The new 'democratic' government worked with the World Bank and the International Monetary Fund to restructure the Bulgarian economy by drastically reducing the national budget, liberalizing markets, rolling back social programs and rewriting labour legislation to make workers more flexible.[14] It was during this time that tourism promotion was also cut out of the national budget. The fiscal tightening also required the closure of many of Balkantourist's overseas representative offices. Between 1990 and 1992, Balkantourist closed 17 out of its 27 offices abroad,[15] and many Balkantourist employees such as Veneta feared that these cuts would lead to a decrease in tourists: 'We thought the resorts would have to close just like all the factories [had].'

The tourists continued to visit Bulgaria, however, and, as other parts of the Bulgarian economy were driven into insolvency, tourism grew in its importance, particularly because it generated much needed hard currency in order to service Bulgaria's sizable foreign debts. Despite continued success after 1989, Balkantourist was one of the first large state enterprises to be broken up and privatized, leading to a total restructuring of the tourism sector. Ultimately, the state broke Balkantourist up into

89 regionally based, state-owned tourist companies, which accounted for almost all of the state's tourism assets.

The break-up and privatization of Pamporovo worked to Veneta's advantage. Although she had only ever worked at the reception desk, the new hotel managers soon gave Veneta new opportunities: first to work in reservations, then in marketing, and ultimately to become the general manager of the hotel. This was despite the fact that there was high male unemployment in the region, and the new owners would have preferred to hire some of their male 'business associates' into key managerial positions in the hotel: 'Because there was only work in Pamporovo, everyone wanted to get a job in the resort. Men who never worked in tourism suddenly began to apply for positions in the hotel. But because of the Ordinance, they were not qualified.' The 'Ordinance', a key piece of legislation passed by the Bulgarian government in order to prevent the deprofessionalization of the tourism sector, protected the jobs of women like Veneta and opened up important opportunities for them. But in order to understand how women came across these opportunities through state regulation of the tourism sector, it is first necessary to comprehend the process of privatization in tourism in Bulgaria, and the ways in which it allowed women with high levels of cultural capital to dominate one of the most dynamic sectors of the post-communist economy.

## Bulgarian tourism under communism

The development of tourism in Bulgaria was unlike the development of tourism anywhere else in the world.[16] In contrast to many developing countries where hospitality industries were built from scratch by foreign investors and tourism consultants flown in from abroad, Bulgaria developed the vast majority of its tourism infrastructure under communism. The physical and cultural capital of the tourism sector in Bulgaria was developed under very different conditions and for very different reasons than its competitors in advanced capitalist or developing countries. As is the case in many other countries, tourism labour was gendered, but the implications of this gendered division of labour were somewhat atypical in that it did not produce or reinforce the economic marginalization of women.

At the end of communism, in 1989, the rebuilding of the tourism sector under new market imperatives remained heavily informed by the pre-existing socialist forms of tourism. The continued success of tourism in Bulgaria throughout the 1990s and the success of the women employed therein was a direct consequence of the factors informing the historical development of the sector under communism between 1944 and 1989. The communists had invested heavily in tourism infrastructure and had cultivated a steady flow of tourists from the west. With an emphasis on mass seaside and ski tourism through inexpensive prearranged package tours, Bulgarian tourism had carved out a niche market for itself among middle and working class German, British, Scandinavian and French holiday-makers in addition to maintaining a large inflow of tourists from the socialist bloc. It was these same groups of tourists who would continue to come to Bulgaria after 1989, and the new market-driven form of tourism that emerged after the end of communism would also rely heavily on the package tour. Furthermore, since it was women who made up the vast majority of tourism employees under communism, it would be women who would continue to dominate employment in the sector under capitalism. But while there was much continuity, the chaotic privatization process reshaped ownership and power structures in new ways. This allowed some Bulgarians, particularly Bulgarian women like Veneta, to take advantage of the structural changes in the economy that revalued their cultural capital to their advantage.

Bulgaria has been a tourist destination since the early twentieth century, but tourism infrastructure was minimal when the communists took power.[17] From its inception, the Bulgarian tourism industry revolved around the provision of 'social' holidays for the domestic labour force. In 1948, the state tourist organization Balkantourist was formed on the model of the Soviet Intourist set up in 1929. Balkantourist began to develop tourism facilities in Sofia and in the major cities on the Black Sea Coast.[18] The vast majority of early social tourism infrastructure took the form of *pochivni stantzii* (holiday houses). These holiday houses were most often affiliated with a specific trade union or owned by an industrial enterprise. Holidays in the holiday houses were heavily subsidized for all workers, and packages often included the cost of the accommodation and three meals a day.

As social tourism expanded, so too did the number of state organizations that supported it. In 1966, a national Committee on Tourism was formed. This committee was directly accountable to the Council of Ministers, and Balkantourist became its operational body, overseeing the industry as the largest single owner of Bulgaria's tourism infrastructure. Most Bulgarians had the right to 14 days of paid holidays a year in addition to the numerous state holidays. Before 1989, at least 50 per cent of Bulgaria's hotel capacity was reserved for domestic tourists.[19] The goal of social tourism was not only the rejuvenation of the workforce, but also the fostering of national solidarity among the historically and culturally different regions of the country.

In the 1940s, the Bulgarian communists had no real intention of diversifying the country into an international tourist destination. Most improvements in tourism infrastructure were for the expansion of domestic tourism. It was a legal disagreement with Czechoslovakia that first pushed Bulgaria into the international tourism market.[20] Prior to the Second World War, Czechoslovakia invested in several sugar refineries and electricity production facilities in Bulgaria. When the Bulgarian Communists subsequently nationalized them, Czechoslovakia demanded reparations in hard currency. Unable and unwilling to meet the request, the Bulgarians refused to give reparations. After protracted legal wrangling in Paris, Czechoslovakia agreed to accept a barter-style payment: vacation packages on the Black Sea Coast. The restless Czechoslovak intelligentsia was accustomed to taking its holidays on the coasts of Spain and France, but the country's new communist leaders feared that the intellectuals would flee. The Czechoslovak state refused to grant them exit visas to the west, but it deemed the Bulgarian coast a suitable (and politically safe) vacation alternative.[21] By 1951, tourists began to trickle in from socialist brother countries Poland and Hungary. Shortly thereafter, sun-seeking Soviet citizens began to make the pilgrimage south to Bulgaria's shores. Although Bulgaria was building infrastructure, demand by both domestic and foreign tourists vastly exceeded the meagre supply.

After Stalin's death in 1953, many socialist societies experienced a general relaxation of dogma. This coincided with a gradual increase in living standards, a greater emphasis on the international goals of socialism, and a push towards more intra-bloc tourism.[22] Yugoslavia was a potential competitor for Eastern Bloc tourists, but its defection from the Stalinist fold in 1948 caused its tourist industry to focus on Western European tourists to the exclusion of its eastern 'brothers'. Bulgaria was particularly suited to become the so-called 'Red Riviera' because it had a relatively long summer season and its Black Sea coast was clean and free of dangerous sea animals. Throughout the 1960s and 1970s, the Bulgarian resorts became one of the most desired playgrounds of the Eastern Bloc. By 1989, Bulgaria was dependent on the socialist countries for 70.9 per cent of its incoming tourists.[23]

The turning point for the Bulgarian tourism industry came in 1955 and 1956 when the first West Germans came to the country's resorts.[24] Since the two Germanies had been divided, family members separated by the Iron Curtain had searched for a place where they could reunite for holidays. Bulgaria was an ideal destination because both East and West German citizens could travel there with relative ease. The West Germans began paying the cost of the holidays for both families in hard currency. Throughout the 1960s and 1970s, visitor arrivals to Bulgaria steadily increased from both socialist bloc and Western European countries.[25] In 1973, the Zhivkov government finally began committing serious resources to building tourist infrastructure in order to bring in the hard currency needed to bail Bulgaria out of a severe oil crisis.[26] That same year, the Bulgarian government signed contracts for the construction of four five-star hotels by foreign companies.[27] By 1974–5, one-fifth of Bulgaria's foreign exchange was coming from the tourism sector.[28] The early 1980s saw the development of Bulgaria's mountain tourism with the addition of the two downhill skiing resorts of Borovets and Pamporovo. In 1985, international tourism in Bulgaria was the third largest generator of net hard currency income among all other industries.[29]

The late 1980s were incredibly successful for centralized tourism in Bulgaria. Balkan Holidays London, the foreign tour operator for Balkantourist, was one of the three top tour operators in the United Kingdom at that time. They arranged chartered flights to Bulgaria from over 12 airports in Great Britain. Balkan Airlines, Bulgaria's former flag carrier, had no less than a hundred charter flights a week from the UK, Germany, and Scandinavia.[30] Balkantourist also owned a fleet of long-distance buses that brought tourists from Germany on a weekly basis. According to one estimate, Bulgaria spent the equivalent of 20 million dollars on international promotion in 1989 and 1990.[31]

Administratively, Balkantourist was responsible for the central coordination of all international tourism. The organization owned not only hotels, but also restaurants, bars, buses, sports facilities, ski lifts, etc., and had an extensive network of representative offices across the globe. By the late 1970s, Balkantourist was the 17th largest hotel chain in the world.[32] It was the largest of the Eastern European tourism agencies, and was one of the most powerful state-owned enterprises in Bulgaria.

## Tourism employment

In the infancy of Bulgarian tourism, communist leaders considered tourism a bourgeois and unimportant sector because it fell outside of the core communist goals of rapid industrialization. In the late 1940s and 1950s, many of the first employees in tourism were members of the bourgeoisie or former fascist sympathizers because these two groups were the most likely to speak foreign languages. By the 1960s and 1970s, however, tourism's importance had grown, and the number of western tourists increased; the communist regime and the state security services began to worry about the ideological commitment to communism and political reliability of the employees – most significantly, of Bulgarian women who had come to dominate Balkantourist.

Although the very top positions in the enterprise were given to politically well-connected men, women held the vast majority of the technocratic and middle managerial positions. This was true for a variety of reasons unique to the command economic context and communist gender relations. Among Bulgarians, jobs in tourism had become increasingly desirable. In the 1980s, it is said that Todor Zhivkov actually had to prohibit men from being hired in tourism positions in order to concentrate more male labour into the factories and mines that were still considered the most vital sectors according to communist ideology.[33] This division of labour was based on an underlying assumption that most men were physically stronger than most women and should therefore do the work that required physical strength. Women were concentrated in the professions like law, medicine, finance, and tourism, which required less physical labour and also allowed them to more easily combine their productive and reproductive duties to the state. Tourism, in particular, provided an attractive opportunity for women. With the acceptable 'unemployment' of the low seasons, women could more easily combine paid employment with family responsibilities. Since housewives were stigmatized as bourgeois, and work was considered a social obligation, tourism jobs were among the few available that could ease Bulgarian women's double burden.

Furthermore, jobs in tourism represented access to valuable resources. Because of the significant percentage of visitors from Western Europe, employees in the resorts were among the only ordinary Bulgarians who could speak with westerners on a regular basis. Access to westerners also meant access to hard currency. Receiving tips was perhaps the most important benefit of tourism employment. Most western tourists felt obliged to tip despite low levels of service. In fact, the practice of tipping was accepted, even encouraged, by the state. Those employees in tourism who did not receive tips could easily sell leva (Bulgarian currency) to tourists on the black market. Because of the artificial rate of exchange imposed by the state, the market value of dollars was often several times the official one. And, because Bulgarians were hungry for dollars, those employed in tourism were in an ideal position to capitalize on the situation, buying dollars cheaply from the tourists and selling them dearly to other Bulgarians. Access to foreign monies allowed Bulgarians access to the dollar shops that stocked highly desirable imported goods for tourists and foreigners. After 1989, foreign currency also protected Bulgarians from the ravages of hyperinflation and the dramatic devaluation of the Bulgarian currency that prevented most Bulgarians from travelling abroad even once they were free to do so.

In addition to the possibility of earning hard currency, resorts and tourist facilities that were always well stocked provided access to basic amenities even when there were shortages in the rest of the country. Although the stockpiles were kept under tight control, a certain amount of attrition was inevitable. Many women were able to ensure that their families always had access to basic goods by 'borrowing' supplies from the hotels. There were also gifts from tourists of small items such as toiletries, cosmetics, feminine hygiene products, magazines and cigarettes that were very valuable to the workers who 'inherited' them. Many of these objects acquired cult status, and could be sold to other Bulgarian 'collectors'. One of the waitresses I interviewed in the seaside resort of Albena still kept an impressive collection of western women's magazines that she had been given by tourists over the years. During communism, these magazines were very valuable and could be traded for various goods and services.

Besides access to resources, another reason tourism jobs were so desirable was that they were located either on the seaside or in the mountains– beautiful geographic settings far preferable to the insides of factories and offices. No matter how much communism attempted to glorify the miners and steel workers, working outdoors in the sunshine still appealed to the traditionally agricultural society. And work in tourism was seasonal, which meant that women like Veneta could benefit from advanced professional training courses and longer holidays in the off-season. Learning new skills or studying new languages was considered part of the responsibility of a tourism worker. As a result, the tourism labour force in Bulgaria was far more 'qualified' than both the labour force in other sectors and the tourism labour force of other countries.

Bulgarians working in tourism under communism also had more opportunities to travel abroad than Bulgarians employed elsewhere, so they could learn and practise foreign languages with native speakers. Although foreign travel was unlikely for all but the highest-level managers, the mere possibility of foreign travel was enough to raise the social status and respectability of those employed in tourism. Most importantly, jobs in tourism gave Bulgarians like Veneta access to westerners, which meant access to information about the non-socialist world. Veneta could hear western music, smoke western cigarettes, observe western fashions and mannerisms, perhaps even read western books and magazines. She could witness the realities of capitalist culture first-hand. Because the socialist state severely restricted access to foreigners from capitalist countries, a familiarity with western tourists became an important form of cultural capital for Bulgarians employed in the sector.

Contact with westerners and travel experience outside of the socialist bloc could create valuable international networks for the Bulgarians who were able to maintain them. After the 'Changes', these networks provided possible business partners, contacts with western universities and colleges, or, most importantly, foreigners willing to write the letters of invitation needed for most Bulgarians to obtain visas to visit western countries or to pursue educational opportunities abroad. Extended contacts with citizens from other socialist countries could also be valuable to Bulgarians for similar reasons. Thus, not only was communist tourism successful, but the lucky Bulgarian employees, mostly women, benefited from privileges unavailable to other socialist citizens. But in 1989, when privatization began and Balkantourist was targeted for demonopolization, many of these circumstances changed.

## Privatization

The communist state prohibited the private ownership of the means of production in order to prevent individual capitalists from exploiting their workers and extracting surplus value while at the same time reinforcing the Communist Party's monopoly on political power. Bureaucracy, stagnation, and inefficiency in the economy were justified in terms of the hegemonic communist ideals of equality and a 'classless' society. These beliefs structured everyday life in Bulgaria for over 45 years; two generations of Bulgarians knew no alternative. Bulgarians like Veneta's parents who had been members of the Communist Party and had spent their entire lives under the old system very reluctantly adjusted to the new system, and even Veneta herself admits that there were many things about communism that she misses. The sudden and unexpected collapse of communism could not erase entire lifetimes of belief. The idea of taking the 'worker's property', entrusted by the proletariat to the Bulgarian state, and placing it in the hands of private 'entrepreneurs' flew in the face of all established Marxist doctrine. Thus, privatization required not only the physical transfer of assets from the state to the market, but also the accompanying psychological processes that would make these transfers successful. In some ways, women like Veneta had to reinvent themselves in order to get by in the new system – open their minds to different ways of valuing time, labour, money, and even human relationships.

Economic reform and political change were always slow to happen in Bulgaria. Throughout the 1980s, as *Perestroika* and *Glasnost* spilled over into the Eastern Bloc, Bulgaria stubbornly remained an orthodox, Soviet-model, communist country.[34] It made very few market-oriented economic changes: in 1989, 95 per cent of the Bulgarian economy was still controlled by the state.[35] Although Bulgarians and foreigners alike perceived 10 November 1989 as a huge milestone, in reality the Bulgarian Communist Party (BCP) remained functionally in power albeit under a new name: the Bulgarian Socialist Party (BSP).[36] Both Veneta and her parents were among those who voted for the Socialists, hoping to maintain some continuity with the past. The first real economic reforms were not implemented until February 1991, over a year after Todor Zhivkov's resignation.

Before 1989, the 4.9 per cent of the Bulgarian GDP contributed by the private sector mainly came from small tourist businesses, especially handicraft production.[37] At the time, private businesses were restricted to one-person 'enterprises' and/or artisan cooperatives. Decree 56, the law that set the stage for the liberalization of the Bulgarian economy, was retroactively applied from the beginning of 1989 to allow firms that were created illegally under the old law to become legal. It allowed private firms to be registered in any sector. These new firms were allowed up to 10 full-time employees and an unlimited number of seasonal employees.[38] Additionally, Decree 56 required that state-owned enterprises be broken up into either joint-stock companies or limited liability companies.[39] Thus, the legal owners of these new entities had to be other enterprises or public institutions. This allowed enterprise directors to subdivide their enterprises and to appoint themselves, their friends, or their relatives as directors of the newly created 'entities'. Between these two new possibilities for the formation of 'private' enterprises, 342 corporations, 1,643 partnerships and 9,231 one-person firms were registered in 1989 alone.[40] It is difficult to know exactly how many of these were legitimate businesses, because many were probably just shells set up by state bureaucrats, enterprise directors and the nascent Mafia to illegally convert public property into private assets. It was this rampant corruption that made the quick privatization of enterprises like Balkantourist a necessity for the post-communist Bulgarian state. On the one hand, tourism managers and employees feared that the government would break up Balkantourist and sell it off to the highest bidder without regard for the workers' interests. On the other hand, the government worried that managers and employees would sabotage tourism enterprises from within in order to concentrate as many of the assets in the tourism sector into their own hands. In Pamporovo, Veneta told me that during the mid-1990s some hotel workers tried to coordinate efforts to be intentionally rude to tourists in order to drive them away. The hope was that hotels with fewer guests would not be attractive to foreign investors, and that the hotel would instead be sold directly to the workers through a management–employee buyout.

The break-up of Balkantourist separated out functionally independent units that had previously been subsumed under one economic structure. Hotels and restaurants became individual companies, as did auxiliary services such as tourism transport, tour operators and travel agencies, suppliers and retail services, and construction and engineering departments.[41] These tourism companies were later transformed into subsidiaries under the sole proprietorship of the state prior to their privatization. The government took Balkan Holidays, the international branch of Balkantourist, split it off from its mother company and privatized it separately as an independent tour operator. Although a few of the resorts were privatized as a whole, most of the resorts were broken up into smaller pieces consisting of individual hotels or groups of hotels that were sold off to different foreign investors or, more often, local 'entrepreneurs', creating the plethora of new jobs from which Veneta personally benefited. These 'entrepreneurs' were most often members of the newly established Bulgarian Mafia, an odd conglomeration of former Olympic wrestlers, petty thugs, ex-secret police officers, and opportunistic nomenklatura.[42] The different groups came together to drain state-owned enterprises of assets before the privatization process could begin and to illegally run guns, ammunition, and fuel into Serbia during the Bosnian War. Many hotels were initially privatized by members of the Mafia as money-laundering operations. As more Bulgarians were drawn into organized crime, the number of domestic 'investors' increased. This coincided with the marketization of Balkantourist in the mid-1990s. As Balkantourist was broken up into smaller and smaller pieces and sold off to many different owners, employment at the higher-level positions in the hotels expanded exponentially, and Veneta was able to move up the employment hierarchy relatively quickly.

The fragmented and decentralized nature of the privatization process was a key factor in revaluing women's cultural capital in tourism to their benefit. During the communist period, the managerial structure of Balkantourist looked like a pyramid with a handful of politically appointed men at the very top and masses of educated technocrats beneath them doing the actual work of running the tourism sector. Women filled the majority of these technocratic positions in tourism– the middle managerial core. After the restructuring of Balkantourist, many of these women became directors and high-level managers of the new tourist enterprises. Veneta explained: 'It took me almost eight years to become front office manager. It would have taken me much longer to become a hotel manager, but with so many new positions [in tourism] after the Changes, I earned my position [as hotel manager] quickly.'

This is true for a variety of reasons. Firstly, privatization brought with it further duplication of managerial jobs at the high level. The centralized offices for reservations, marketing, accounting and supplies were all closed down. They were replaced with new offices in each of the privatized hotels. In a resort with 30 hotels, one central reservation office could be replaced with 30 reservation offices in each of the individually privatized hotels. This process created a bounty of new positions throughout the tourism industry. In most cases, it was only natural that women take up these positions, since many of them had already been responsible for coordinating these areas before the reorganization. For newly created positions such as the suddenly ubiquitous 'marketing' jobs that appeared after the changes, it was quite common to promote receptionists, who tended to be women. Also, hotels recruited many young Bulgarians from tourism degree programs at the universities. Because of the gendering of the tourism sector under communism and the advantages associated with jobs in tourism, the graduates of these programs were again primarily women.

Graduates with Master's and Doctoral degrees in tourism economics or geography and former Balkantourist employees were also able to take advantage of new positions created in the many private travel agencies and tour operators sprouting throughout the country. But these opportunities were available only to the more educated women in the managerial and higher-level operational positions (Table 9.1). At the lower levels, many maids, laundry workers and especially groundskeepers were put out of work by the hotels' new owners' desire to 'rationalize staffing patterns' – to shed the excess labour employed by most hotels in the communist period. Women in these lower-level positions were considered expendable. While some managed to relocate to other jobs

*Table 9.1*   Job distribution in Bulgarian tourism (1999–2000)

| Job Category | % of Total | % Male | % Female |
| --- | --- | --- | --- |
| Managerial | 12.6 | 8.4 | 15.1 |
| Higher-level operational * | 20.0 | 8.7 | 26.8 |
| Restaurant | 21.5 | 24.9 | 19.4 |
| Bar | 10.2 | 14.2 | 7.8 |
| Kitchen | 8.7 | 10.7 | 7.4 |
| Lower-level operational ** | 19.0 | 24.3 | 15.9 |
| Miscellaneous *** | 8.0 | 8.7 | 7.6 |

*Source*:  K. Ghodsee, *The Red Riviera: Gender, Tourism and Postsocialism on the Black Sea*, Durham: Duke University Press, 2005.
   * Receptionists, tour guides, cashiers, translators, etc.
  ** Maids, bellboys, security, maintenance, shopkeepers, etc.
*** Nurses, beauticians, musicians, artists, craftspeople, entertainers, etc.

within the sector, some (especially the older ones) were forced into an early 'retirement'. In this sense, there was in fact a population of women who were initially pushed out of the sector by 'downsizing'. Overall, however, many new 'professional' jobs were created in tourism after the changes. This allowed educated women to make use of their newly revalued cultural capital. All of my interviews with tourism employees made clear to me that, with few exceptions, education was the key divide between the workers who survived and those who did not.

## State regulation

But simply having the appropriate education and training might not have been enough without careful state regulations put in place to prevent the deprofessionalization of Bulgarian tourism. Although women had an impressive package of cultural capital obtained before 1989, it might have amounted to nothing if capitalist tourism in Bulgaria had followed the path of tourism industries in many capitalist countries where employees in tourism are low-skilled and transient. Furthermore, because members of Bulgaria's domestic Mafia were so heavily involved in the privatization of tourism, it is certainly possible that these new owners might have wanted to replace older, experienced women employees with younger, untrained but better-looking women. It was only through government legislation that privileged cultural capital for professional jobs in tourism that educated women's dominance was maintained.

With the onset of privatization, the state relinquished its power over formerly state-owned enterprises. It was then faced with the challenge of creating a legislative infrastructure that would regulate different industries and tax corporate profits in order to support the state budget. The key challenge in creating post-socialist taxation and regulation was to balance the need to generate state revenues and protect workers' rights with the necessity of ensuring the economic viability and competitiveness of the now private enterprises.

New laws and ordinances on tourism were drafted to help facilitate growth in the sector, not only for privatized state enterprises but also for the rapidly expanding small and medium-sized enterprises in tourism. The Law on Tourism went into effect in June 1998, and two ordinances on the licensing of tourist activities and the classification of tourist objects followed two months later. This legislative framework was an ambitious attempt to codify new standards for the tourism sector. Under this law, more than 2,500 licences were issued by the end of 1999, including those to owners of 243 hotels and 109 family hotels.[43]

These laws formed an essential impetus for the entrance of private businesses into the tourism sector. In an economy often crippled by its constantly shifting legislative framework for business and investment,[44] the Law on Tourism was resilient in its ability to regulate economic activity in the sector. Many small hotels sprang up around the country, catering to a much wider variety of tastes and accommodation needs. Issues of continuing corruption aside, the laws provided a set of guidelines for standardizing the quality of hotels and restaurants throughout the country as well as setting specific standards for the educational experience of the managers. Although sometimes overly bureaucratic, the clearly set-out regulations made tourism one of the easier sectors in which to do business in Bulgaria for both locals and foreigners.

In cases where the government privatized hotels to companies and individuals without experience in tourism, especially the Mafia, these new laws indirectly protected women in managerial positions. Early in the privatization process, many Mafia investors were primarily concerned with money-laundering and left most of the hotel staff in place. They had little interest in actually running profitable enterprises. As privatization proceeded, however, many more Mafiosi and tourism non-professionals bought up tourism assets. The ordinance of the categorization of tourist objects placed restrictions on who could be the manager of a hotel in order to stop the new owners from placing their new hotels in the hands of inexperienced friends, family members or 'business associates', thus jeopardizing tourism's economic viability. The 1998 ordinance required that the manager of any hotel wishing to get or maintain a four or five-star rating have a university degree in tourism, geography or economics and speak two or more foreign languages. Managers of three-star hotels had to have a university or technical college degree in tourism and speak at least one foreign language. Similar educational requirements were explicitly laid out for all key positions in tourism from the receptionists to the maids. These requirements were also kept in the new law on tourism adopted in October 2002. This law regarding the mandatory education of employees effectively legislated that only those with the proper cultural capital could work in tourism.

The debates surrounding the Ordinances were heated, between owners who wanted to remove the restrictions, and employees and tourism programmes at the major universities who wanted to keep the restrictions in place. Maria Vodenska, a professor in the tourism programme at Sofia University, was one of many academics who actively lobbied the government together with Donka Sokolova, the leader of the Bulgarian Association of Travel Agents (BATA), in order to secure the passage of this legislation.[45] There was a great fear among those employed in the tourism industry that the quality of service in the hotels would suffer greatly if the language and university education requirements for high level operational personnel were removed. Certainly, the universities were interested in trying to secure employment for their graduates, but their concerns about quality were also real, especially given that so many hotels were being bought by members of the Mafia with little or no experience in the hospitality sector.

These laws on categorization essentially forced many of the new owners to keep the existing managers and employees in place even after privatization. Newly built hotels wishing to receive a four or five-star rating had to hire university graduates from tourism programmes, again mostly women. Furthermore, most privatization contracts stipulated that the employees of the privatized enterprise should continue to be employed for a minimum period of time following the transaction– usually around three years. In response to the institutional changes taking place throughout the economy, the government legislated measures not only to protect workers, but also to ensure the continued viability of successful sectors of the economy. Although it was not the government's intent to preserve women's employment in the tourism sector, these laws and contract stipulations essentially guaranteed that women would continue to dominate the sector, since few men had the experience or educational qualifications to fill the positions.

## Conclusion

As the vast majority of Bulgarians faced greater insecurity and unemployment in the wake of the end of communism, women in tourism, it seems, have been somewhat unwittingly protected. The education and jobs that were considered less important under communism are now being revalued as the very support structures required for success in a free market economy. Despite forecasts that women in all sectors would be the biggest losers in the transition away from the state-controlled economy, women in tourism are reaping the rewards of being in an industry whose importance has steadily grown over time and across political systems – an industry whose economic vitality the struggling Bulgarian economy cannot afford to lose. By extension, this means that Bulgaria's government was correct in passing laws that protected women's employment in tourism since they have had the greatest role in historically sustaining the now crucial industry.

Women like Veneta, who may not have known what the 'Changes' would bring, are finding that the cultural capital they acquired under the old system, which prepared them for the 'soft labour' of communism, is now providing relative security in the hard times of transition. While there is very little that Bulgarian men and women living under communism for over 40 years have been able to retrieve and 'take' with them into their radically different post-1989 realities, the education and experiences women gained under the old regime constitute one aspect of life that has not only survived, but become a major survival tool for women in a Bulgaria contending with the challenges of global capitalism.

Similar findings to the Bulgarian case can also be seen in other post-socialist countries where women accumulated extensive work experience and education under the communist period. For example, in Hungary, Poland, and Slovakia, Eva Fodor found that women who had worked in the quasi-private sector during communism had more advantages and were more flexible in the new market economy than men who were wholly employed in the public sector before 1989.[46] Julia Szalai found similar patterns in Hungary, where men have made up the majority of the registered unemployed since 1989.[47] Further studies of other post-socialist countries are needed to examine the ways in which certain groups of women have succeeded in the new capitalist labour market. This is important because too often Eastern European women as a whole are portrayed as the economic losers of the transition without serious examination of the differences between women, particularly in terms of the skills they brought with them from the communist period.

In this respect, it may be that class privilege as it is expressed through cultural capital is a more important determination of success in the new market economies of Eastern Europe than merely gender on its own.

## Endnotes

1. For example see: N. Alsanbeigui, S. Pressman and G. Summerfield, *Women in the Age of Economic Transformation: Gender Impacts of Reforms in Postsocialist and Developing Countries*, New York: Routledge, 1994; M. Buckley, *Post-Soviet Women: From the Baltic to Central Asia*, Cambridge; New York: Cambridge University Press, 1997; B. Einhorn, *Cinderella Goes to Market: Citizenship, Gender, and Women's Movements in East Central Europe*, London; New York: Verso, 1993; V. Moghadam, ed., *Democratic Reform and the Position of Women in Transitional Economies*, Oxford: Clarendon Press, 1993; N. Funk and M. Mueller, eds, *Gender Politics and Post-Communism: Reflections from Eastern Europe and the Former Soviet Union*, New York and London: Routledge, 1993; C. Corrin, *Superwoman and the Double Burden: Women's Experience of Change in Central and Eastern Europe and the Former Soviet Union*, Toronto: Second Story Press, 1992; M. Rueschemeyer, *Women and the Politics of Postcommunist Eastern Europe*, Armonk, N.Y: M. E. Sharpe, 1994; and K. Ghodsee, 'Mobsters and Mail-Order Brides: Women and Economic Transition in Post-Socialist Bulgaria', in Berkeley Center for Slavic and Eastern European Studies Newsletter (available on-line at: http://ist-socrates.berkeley.edu/~csees/publications.html, Fall 2000).
2. See P. Bourdieu, *Distinction: a Social Critique of the Judgment of Taste*, trans. Richard Nice, Cambridge, Mass.: Harvard University Press, 1984.
3. P. Bourdieu, *Practical Reason: On the Theory of Action*, Stanford: Stanford University Press, 1998.
4. G. Eyal, I. Szelenyi and E. Townsley, *Making Capitalism Without Capitalists: The New Ruling Elites in Eastern Europe*, London and New York: Verso, 1998.
5. The 'Changes' is how most Bulgarians refer to the collapse of communism and the onset of free markets and liberal democracy beginning in 1989 and continuing into the early years of the 1990s.
6. Vienna Institute for Comparative Economics (VICES), *COMECON Data 1989*, Westport, CT: Greenwood Press, 1990; VICES, *COMECON Data 1990*, Westport, CT: Greenwood Press, 1991.
7. The COMECON or CMEA (Council for Mutual Economic Assistance) was a Soviet-led trading block that promoted socialist economic integration with the other communist Eastern European nations and eventually Mongolia, Vietnam and Cuba.
8. Vienna Institute for Comparative Economics, *COMECON Data 1989*.
9. World Bank, *World Development Report 1998/1999: Knowledge for Development*, New York: Oxford University Press, 1998.
10. World Bank, *World Development Report 1991*, Washington, DC: The World Bank, 1992.
11. For more details, see: K. Ghodsee, *The Red Riviera: Gender, Tourism and Postsocialism on the Black Sea*, Durham: Duke University Press, 2005.
12. National Statistical Institute (NSI), *Statisticheski Godishnik 1998*, Sofia: NSI, 1999, 92.

13. World Bank, *World Development Report 2002: Building Institutions for Markets*, New York: Oxford University Press, 2003.

14. K. Stanchev, 'Bulgaria', *Journal of Southeastern Europe and Black Sea Studies*, January 2001, 140–58.

15. Author's interview with Ms Nedlyaka Sandalska, Chief Executive and Chairperson of the Board of Directors of Balkantourist (Multigroup) in Sofia on 18 August 2000.

16. There are only a handful of scholars who have studied tourism in the socialist context. The two best are D. Hall, *Tourism and Economic Development in Eastern Europe and the Soviet Union*, London: Belhaven Press, 1991; and the special issue of *Annals of Tourism Research*, 17(1), 1990. Most of the literature that does exist was written before the collapse of the Eastern Bloc in 1989.

17. Tourism in Bulgaria dates back to the late nineteenth century when the Bulgarian Hikers' Society was founded in 1895. Most of these early tourists were wealthy Bulgarians inspired by Swiss Alpine hiking. Small rest huts were built to accommodate day hikers. In the beginning of the twentieth century, Bulgaria began to develop its considerable balneological resources (over 600 hot springs), and spa tourism attracted many Bulgarians to springs known for their curative properties. The inter-war period saw the minor developments on the Black Sea coastline, mostly around the towns of Varna and Nessebur. It was during this time that the first tourists from Poland and Czechoslovakia discovered Bulgaria. See: F. W. Carter, 'Bulgaria', in *Tourism and Economic Development in Eastern Europe and the Soviet Union*, D. Hall, ed., London: Bellhaven Press, 1991.

18. P. Doitchev, *Zhivot: Otdaden na Turizma (Life: Devoted to Tourism)*, Sofia, Bulgaria: Literaturen Forum, 1999.

19. M. Pearlman, 'Conflicts and Constraints in Bulgaria's Tourism Sector', *Annals of Tourism Research*, 17, 1990, 103–22.

20. Interview with Mr Peter Doitchev, 'proto-Balkantourist' employee and author, in Sofia, Bulgaria on 19 July 2000.

21. Doitchev, op. cit.

22. Hall, op. cit.

23. World Tourism Organization (WTO), *Yearbook of Tourism Statistics*, Madrid, Spain: WTO, 1990.

24. Interview with Mr Krassen Roussev, Director of the Dutch–Bulgarian International School of Tourism, in Albena, Bulgaria on 23 May 2000.

25. Central Statistical Institute, *Tourism*, Sofia, Bulgaria: Central Statistical Institute, 1990, and NSI, Statistical Yearbook, Sofia, Bulgaria: NSI, 2000.

26. J. Lampe, *The Bulgarian Economy in the Twentieth Century*, London and Sydney: Croom Helm, 1986.

27. These are: The Grand Hotel Varna, The New Otani, and two Novotel Hotels in Sofia and Plovdiv.

28. Carter, 'Bulgaria', 1991.

29. M. Vodenska, 'International Tourism in Bulgaria: Problems and Perspectives', *Journal of Economic and Social Geography*, 83(5), 1992, pp. 17–32.

30. Interview with Mr Velitchko Velitchkov, former Deputy Minister of Transportation and former head of Balkan Airlines, in Sofia, Bulgaria on 25 January 2000.

31. Interview with Mr Krassimir Kanev, Director of Alder Tours, in Sofia, Bulgaria on 20 January 2000.
32. Interview with Ms Mariana Assenova, Deputy Minister of Tourism, in Sofia, Bulgaria on 5 December 1999.
33. Interview with Mr Peter Doitchev in Sofia, Bulgaria on 4 August 2000.
34. E. Kalinova and I. Baeva, *Balgarskite Prehodi 1939–2002 (The Bulgarian Transitions 1939–2002)*, Sofia, Bulgaria: Paradigma, 2002.
35. Z. Mladenova and J. Angresano, 'Privatization in Bulgaria', *East European Quarterly*, 30(4), Winter 1996, 495–516.
36. For more background see: P. Kabakchieva, 'The New Political Actors and Their Strategies', in J. Coenen-Huther, ed., *Bulgaria at the Crossroads*, New York: Nova Science Publishers, Inc., 1996; and P. Kabakchieva, *The Civil Society Against the State: the Bulgarian Case*, Sofia, Bulgaria: Lik, 2001.
37. Mladenova and Angresano, op. cit.
38. M. Jackson, 'A Crucial Phase in Bulgarian Economic Reforms', Paper no. 72, Cologne, Germany: Berichte des Bundesinstituts fur ostwissenschaftliche und internationale Studien, 1989.
39. A joint-stock company consists of shares that are bought and sold by individual shareholders. These shareholders have no liability beyond the value of their shares for the failures of the company. A limited liability company is a partnership where individual partners own the company together; they have more liability than shareholders in a joint-stock company but less liability than a traditional partnership. In both cases in Bulgaria, the state was the only shareholder and the only partner in the early phases of privatization.
40. M. Jackson, 'The Rise and Decay of the Socialist Economy in Bulgaria', *Journal of Economic Perspectives*, 5(4), Autumn 1991, 203–9.
41. Deni Consult, 'A Survey of the Tourist Industry in Bulgaria', Sofia: Deni Consult Ltd, 1997.
42. J. Nikolov, 'Crime and Corruption after Communism: Organized Crime in Bulgaria', *Eastern European Constitutional Review*, 6(4), Autumn 1997. Available online at: www.law.nyu.edu/eecr/vol6num4/feature/organizedcrime.html.
43. Bulgarian Foreign Investment Agency, *Bulgaria Business Guide 2000 – Legal, Tax and Accounting Aspects*, Sofia: BFIA, 2000.
44. For an interesting discussion of the problems with Bulgaria's legislative framework, see T. O'Brien and C. Filipov, 'Current Regulatory Framework Governing Business in Bulgaria', *World Bank Technical Papers*, Washington, DC: World Bank, July 2001.
45. Author's interview with Maria Vodenska in Sofia, Bulgaria on 2 December 1999.
46. E. Fodor, 'Gender in Transition: Unemployment in Hungary, Poland and Slovakia', *East European Politics and Societies*, 11(3), 1997, 470–500.
47. J. Szalai, 'From Informal Labor to Paid Occupations: Marketization from Below in Hungarian Women's Work', in S. Gal and G. Kligman, eds, *Reproducing Gender: Politics, Publics, and Everyday Life after Socialism*, Princeton, N.J.: Princeton University Press, 2000, 200–24.

# 10

# State Policies, Uneven Economic Development and Environmental Regulation in Urban and Rural Lithuania

*Jurgita Maciulyte*

## Introduction

With independence in 1990 Lithuania rejected its previous Soviet model with the aim to liberalize its economy and government, and join the European Union (EU). Convergence with the European model required that the new country devise an environmental policy that was compatible with EU objectives and commitments to economic and environmental sustainability. The implementation of this new model has been shaped by legacies of the Soviet era and by the challenges of restructuring economic and political regimes, while preparing simultaneously for integration into international markets and accession into the European Union. Rapid political, economic and social change has led to the emergence of new stakeholders whose scope for action varies between urban and rural areas, and this has sharpened an important geographical divide between town and country and shaped the conditions of life in each in important ways.[1]

This chapter focuses on these changes in state economic and environmental policy and their consequences for conditions in urban and rural areas. It presents an analysis of the impact of the Soviet legacy on the environment, of the new socioeconomic context that followed the collapse of the USSR, and the economic and social challenges facing Lithuanian environmental policies following accession to the European Union. The chapter focuses specifically on the new mechanisms and forms of action that underpin new environmental policies and how they are connected spatially. First, the chapter identifies the legacies of the Soviet era that has shaped the current state of the environment. The environmental problems of towns and countryside are examined in turn. The chapter then turns to the institutional changes that have occurred since 1990 and the socioeconomic issues with which they are connected. Finally, the chapter assesses the impact of Lithuania's accession to the EU on the environment in urban and rural areas.

## Soviet legacies

### The environment in urban areas

The Soviet occupation of Lithuania imposed industrialization on a country that was still basically agricultural. In the early 1950s, this was accompanied by the immigration of ethnic Russians intended to compensate for the inadequate number of local specialists and accelerate the Russification of the country. Factories were built without concern for the environment. This political and economic choice created pockets of pollution around important historic cities and in the new towns built for major industrial concerns, such as Naujoji Akmene, Elektrenai and Visaginas.

The industrial fabric left behind by this regime remains the main cause of point source air pollution, with a small number of large plants producing nearly half of this pollution: for example the Mazeikiai oil refinery and the town's power station together account for one-quarter of stationary source emissions; the Elektrenai power station for 10 per cent; the Naujoji Akmene cement works for roughly three per cent; and the Achema nitrate fertilizer factory at Jonava and the Lifosa phosphate fertilizer factory at Kedainiai for roughly five per cent together.[2] Atmospheric pollution has declined in the past 10 years as production has fallen, but pollution remains significant in these older industrial centres and in cities such as Vilnius, Kaunas, Klaipeda, and Siauliai (Figure 10.1). Transport produces roughly 70 per cent of all air pollution in the country. Despite measures taken to improve fuel quality, the age of vehicles (only two per cent are less than five years old) and the gradual increase in their number (in 1991, there were 128 cars per thousand population; by 2000, the figure was 297) are responsible for atmospheric pollution in towns. Obsolete energy-intensive technologies and aging equipment also contribute to air pollution. According to the International Energy Agency, Lithuanian $CO_2$ emissions per unit of

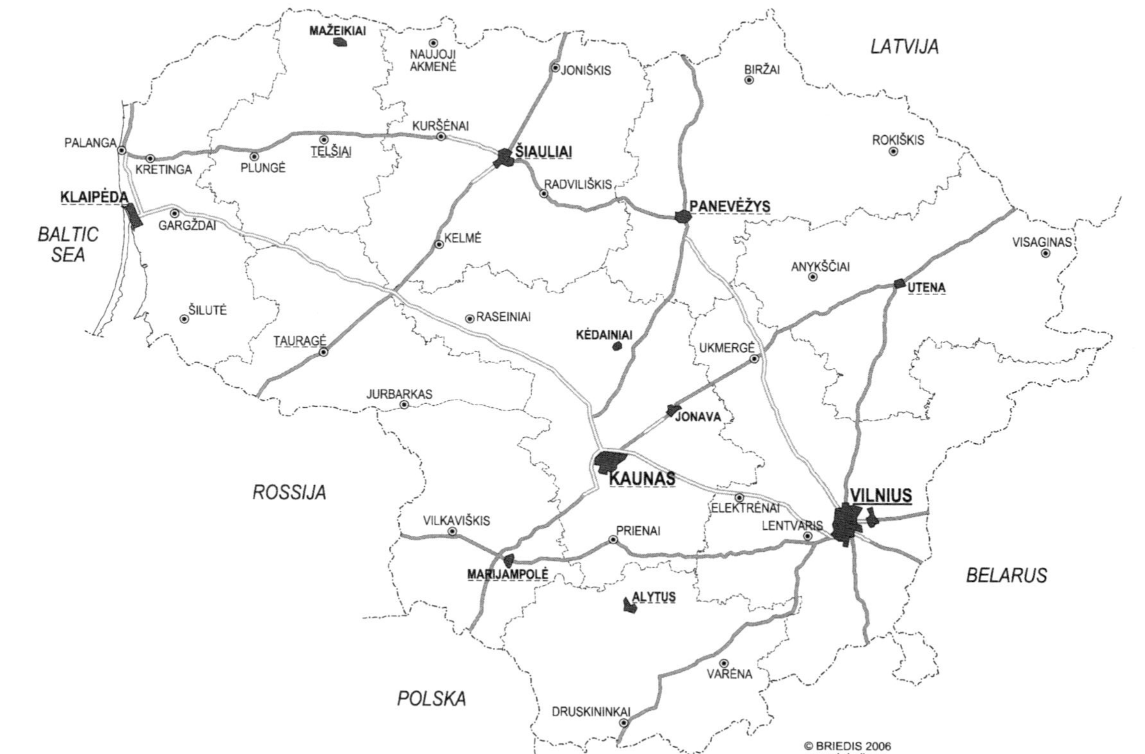


*Map 10.1*  Map of Lithuania

GDP were greater than the European Union average by a factor of between 1.5 and 2.[3] With the privatization of the property sector, centralized heating systems designed to operate in collectively owned properties are now presenting their own problems of pollution management and maintenance.

On gaining independence, Lithuania also inherited an obsolete water use and management system. In 1990, only 22 per cent of waste water released into the environment had been properly treated and 27 per cent had not been treated at all. Despite efforts to improve water treatment, the situation remains a source of concern: only 10 per cent of Lithuanian rivers are considered to be clean, compared with 44 per cent in France.[4] There has been no significant improvement in the water quality of the country's main river, the Neman, which transports a large quantity of pollutants into the Curonian lagoon and the Baltic Sea. Most of Lithuania's beaches have had to be periodically closed because of bacterial contamination, posing a health threat to the local population and a broader ecological threat for the Baltic ecosystem.

Until 1998, waste management was largely unregulated and lacked adequate investment, and as a result waste recycling remains a major problem. Historically, urban residents have not mobilized around water issues and prolonged periods of poor or no infrastructural development have delayed the introduction of household waste sorting, although this is now beginning in the larger towns. Furthermore, Lithuania inherited a radioactive waste dump built in 1963 and used until 1989. Recent analyses have shown that this nuclear dump was not completely sealed and continues to present security problems.[5]

## Under-development in the post-socialist countryside

Soviet occupation and the subsequent collectivization of agriculture introduced a new socioeconomic system in rural areas. The *kolkhoz* and *sovkhoz* structured for economic activity and the social life of farmers. For the Soviet authorities, developing agriculture and intensifying farming meant applying the methods of mechanization, specialization, and centralized production.[6] The shift to specialization, and centralized production began in the 1970s and continued until independence. While specialization was intended to reduce variety, centralized production was to increase the area sown to specific crops and reduce the number of livestock farms to maximize economies of scale. Experience with collective farms showed that the larger the units, the better their production figures were and the lower the investment required to modernize and industrialize agriculture. These production models tended to ignore negative environmental effects. Therefore, preventing pollution and degradation were not priorities for the authorities. Beginning in 1975, factory farms for pigs and poultry developed near towns, and these too soon became major sources of groundwater and air pollution.[7]

The collectivization of farms required wide-reaching restructuring of rural areas. Farm services improvement programmes undertook large-scale projects of drainage, plot consolidation, elimination of isolated farms, creation of irrigated pastureland and meadows, and stone clearing. This work resulted in new land use patterns, including larger land parcels and the concentration of housing close to farm perimeters and village centers. This form of land use created environmental problems as well, the most important of which were soil erosion, loss of wetlands in drained rivers and former marshlands, and radical modification of the farming landscape.

Beginning in the 1960s, even more than in the other regions of the USSR, the rural population in Lithuania was migrating into towns on a massive scale. To stem rural depopulation, Soviet farm policy was redirected towards improving living conditions in rural areas so that they more closely resembled those in the towns. Specific measures were taken to keep young people in the countryside and to improve working and living conditions for farmers. Farm workers received the same

*Table 10.1*  Comparison of housing conditions in urban and rural areas in 1983 (%)

| Communal facilities | Urban | Rural |
| --- | --- | --- |
| Piped water | 87 | 12 |
| Sewers | 86 | 10 |
| Central heating | 75 | 14 |
| Gas | 85 | 36 |
| Hot water | 67 | 8 |

*Source*: Department of Statistics, Vilnius, 1983.

welfare advantages as workers in towns (including holidays, weekly rest day, and retirement at sixty), social and cultural facilities were established (crèches, canteens, arts centres) and detached houses for young couples were built next to the housing blocks.

While these efforts improved the conditions of life of those in rural areas, a gap with urban quality of life remained. The countryside remained a place of arduous labour, poorly functioning supply systems, and low standards of services, public infrastructure and social facilities (Table 10.1).[8] Even the new housing blocks lacked adequate water supply, drainage or waste treatment systems, and few rural areas had proper landfills.

## New environmental policy

### Institutional and legal environmental change

Growing awareness of Lithuania's environmental problems was inseparable from the fight for independence and, correspondingly, the change of political and economic system opened the way for de-collectivization and reform in the social and spatial organization of rural areas. Lithuanian citizen protest against the damage done to their environment by the Soviet regime turned out to be the first expression of the anti-Soviet resistance.[9] In the summer of 1988, a demonstration of thousands of people held by the Greens in Kaunas gathered to oppose the deterioration of environmental conditions, and they also began to give voice to broader aspirations for national independence. The Lithuanian Green movement led to the Lithuanian People's Union and subsequently, on 22 October 1988, to the creation of the popular independence movement, Sajudis.[10]

After the proclamation of national independence, Lithuania set up its own environmental institutions, beginning in 1994. Lithuania signed various international conventions and adopted the National Law in 1992, marking the birth of post-Socialist legislation and sustainable development in Lithuania. In 1996, the Lithuanian Seimas approved an 'Environment Protection Strategy', based on the principles of the Rio de Janeiro declaration, which remains the guiding document for environmental policy.[11] By 2003, the European Commission's (EC) 'Comprehensive Monitoring Report on the State of Preparedness for EU Membership' indicated that in most environmental management sectors: 'Legislation is in place and is in line with the *acquis* [...but that] Lithuania needs to finalize the legal alignment as regards the following areas:...waste management, water quality, nature protection, industrial pollution and risk management, chemicals and noise'.[12]


## Two-speed environmental protection: the urban-rural divide

Although Lithuania has constructed a legal and institutional framework that is in line with European standards, the implementation of environmental protection on the ground remains uneven. Since 1990, progress in environmental regulation and reconstruction has been more effective in towns than in the countryside. Some towns (Vilnius, Kaunas, Siauliai, Birzai, Varena, and Jurbarkas) have constructed or modernized water treatment plants, and the proportion of totally treated water has increased from 22 per cent in 1990 to 60 per cent in 1999. Some towns have improved their household waste collection infrastructure and modernized municipal landfills (Kaunas, Mazeikiai, Visaginas, and Plunge). The economic development of the major towns has also made more strict compliance possible in the modernization and construction of factories. In 2002 alone there were over 150 Lithuanian companies taking part in environmental projects.[13]

Large Soviet-era factories have either been modernized or been under pressure to do so from both European bodies and national authorities. For example, the closure of the dangerous Ignalina nuclear plant raised major political, economic, and employment issues during negotiations with the EU. Since Lithuania has few energy sources and 90 per cent of its energy supply is imported from Russia; closing the plant would have increased the country's economic dependence on Russia and its oil and gas companies, as well as increased energy dependence on fossil-fired stations in Elektrenai, Vilnius and Kaunas.[14] It would also have raised the price of electricity, with direct negative consequences for the economic conditions of the poorest sectors of the population. Technical and financial planning for the closing of the plant is now complete, but the welfare support programme and the creation of a new administrative programs for Ignalina have not been finalized.

Municipal councils in the larger towns have been particularly proactive in enacting environmental projects. They have greater financial resources and a larger number of highly skilled municipal employees than localities in the rest of the country, and they have also received more support from various EU pre-accession structural funds.[15] Many larger projects have been financed by the Instrument for Structural Policies for Pre-Accession (ISPA) fund, a programme that is intended to provide financial help for candidate countries to prepare for EU accession and facilitate the adoption of the *acquis* in the areas of the environment and transport. From 2000 to 2003, 17 major projects were approved in larger towns for wastewater treatment plants, landfills and water supply systems, with awards of some €26 million each year.

Although the main towns are actively attempting to deal with their environmental problems, some of the new policies create new problems. For example, free-market-based policies have led to densification in town centres with negative consequences for available urban green space. In Vilnius, green space in the old city is being replaced by new buildings despite resistance from residents and the legal constraints laid down for town planning. The building of a new high-rise business – and shopping centre near the capital city's historic core has also generated conflict over issues of architectural heritage and harmony, as well as contributing to the dispersal of businesses like small shops and some offices that have had to move out of the city centre to premises where property prices are lower and car access is better.

## Continuing backwardness in the Lithuanian countryside

In the Soviet era, rural areas lagged behind urban areas, but during the years of decollectivization the gap has widened. Exit from the collectivist model has meant the disappearance on a massive scale of the farm associations formed under the *kolkhoz* and *sovkhoz*. Consequently, the family farm system that developed between the two World Wars, has returned, mainly consisting of smallholdings. According to the 2003 agricultural census, Lithuania has 604,031 family farms. 331,980 are smaller than one hectare in size and 272,051 are one hectare or larger, of which 83% are less than 10 hectares in size. Most of the new farms engage in semi-subsistence farming, they market little if any of their produce and they have incomes too low to modernize the farm or improve living standards.[16] Liquidation of collective farms has, thus, also led to unemployment and poverty, 27.4 per cent of the rural population lived below the poverty threshold in 2003, compared with 10.3 per cent in urban areas.[17] The income of farming families is only 55 per cent that of urban families, and although the official unemployment rate was only 9.7 per cent in 2004, the actual rate is likely much higher because semi-subsistence farming 'conceals' or 'disguises' unemployment.[18] Declines in employment and income levels have been further compounded by deterioration in public facilities and sociocultural infrastructure in the rural areas. In 1990, most of the facilities managed by the collective farms (canteens, crèches, arts centres, etc.) were transferred to municipalities or private operators. This change of ownership and municipalities' lack of financial resources led to a significant deterioration in living conditions in the countryside. According to an estimate by the Ministry of Agriculture, rural residents now only receive half the services they had during the Soviet era.[19]

The facilities designed to protect the environment in rural areas were also affected unevenly by the disappearance of the old collective structures. Most of the environmental facilities and treatment plants have no managers and have deteriorated over the last 15 years. Only one-third of large villages have wastewater collection networks and most of these date from the Soviet era. In 2001, only 54 per cent of rural households had mains drainage and 41 per cent piped drinking water, compared with 95 per cent and 91 per cent respectively in towns.[20] Very few villages have water treatment works. Most of the time, wastewater is discharged untreated into streams, drainage channels and lakes, and consequently approximately 80 per cent of country-dwellers use water drawn from wells that does not meet health standards. Poor storage of pesticides has aggravated these soil and water conditions, and fires at pesticide dumps have caused serious contamination for people living nearby and in neighbouring villages.[21] The drainage system continues to degrade because of the rapid pace of transformation, low farm profits, and reduced state investment.

In recent years, the modernization and expansion of meat processing plants has encouraged the creation of large indoor factory farms belonging to industrial groups, some attracted by low environmental protection standards and cheap labour. These are concentrated in the north and centre of the country, which has a large free labour force because of the collapse of collective farms.

During the Soviet era, rural areas also had a military function. Soviet military bases occupied 1.04 per cent of the territory, mainly located around Klaipeda and along the Baltic coast, in the valley of the Neman, and near Vilnius, Kaunas and Siauliai.[22] The main ecological problem they pose is groundwater pollution by petroleum products. Because of high property prices in towns, town councils have managed to clean and rehabilitate their old military areas more quickly, but rehabilitation and reuse of this land is not occurring in the same way or at the same rate in rural areas.[23]

Overall, rural stakeholders have little information or awareness of the environment and quality of life, especially in rural areas. Prior to EU accession, public policy in the countryside was solely 'agricultural'. For 15 years, successive Lithuanian governments focused on the economic problems caused by the collapse of farm production and incomes. Since independence, the government has become more interventionist, providing guaranteed purchase prices, quotas, subsidies for storing or exporting surpluses and measures to protect farmers' access to the domestic market. However, this farm policy is expensive for a young state with few resources, and it has made little contribution to completing the restructuring and modernization of the new farm structures. Nor have any standards for rural development and protection of the environment been established. No projects devoted to modernizing wastewater and drinking water facilities, improving landfill management, or rehabilitating the abandoned buildings and dumps of the former *kolkhoz* and *sovkhoz* have been completed.


## EU Accession and environmental protection

In post-communist society the implementation of new environmental objectives involves complex economic and social issues, and requires more attention. The delay in completing institutional and territorial reform, the lack of financial resources, the new trends in the free market economy, and the absence of a tradition of environmental management have not encouraged sustainable development. However, following Lithuania's accession to the European Union, the country is now obliged to implement European programmes for the environment. As a result, EU recommendations and funding are now playing a significant role in reshaping the environmental regime. As mentioned, the ISPA programme has helped Lithuania align its legislation in this area. European funding has also made it possible to build or modernize wastewater treatment plants, landfills, and a drinking water supply system in major towns. Management of wastewater and household waste is now organized by county, and cooperation between town and county administrations has strengthened the decentralization process.[24]

The country's accession to the EU has also contributed to a change in public policy in the countryside. Convergence with the European model has involved devising a new policy compatible with the principles of European rural development policy. This rural development policy (*Rural Development Plan for 2004–2006*) introduces a comprehensive, coherent rural development policy and pays more attention to the protection of the environment. Now the countryside must take on not only the economic function of agricultural production but also environmental, social and territorial functions (such as water protection, diversification of non-agricultural activities, and green tourism development). Unlike the many other projects previously drafted by the Ministry of Agriculture but never carried out, this Rural Development Plan is due to be supported financially by the EAGGF (European Agricultural Guidance and Guarantee Fund).

The European Commission's rural development programmes (see Table 10.2) have had an indirect impact on the environment because any investment made must meet European environmental protection standards. Support from the Guarantee Section includes agro-environmental programs to encourage farming methods that respect the environment and biodiversity, and consists of grants for organic farming, territorial farming contracts to protect open water bodies, natural meadows and marshland, grants for the afforestation of farmland and support for liquid manure treatment facilities. Farmers in less favoured areas and areas subject to environmental constraints are also eligible for compensation payments. In addition, a special measure of the Cohesion Fund provides for the improvement of drinking water and wastewater management infrastructure in localities with fewer than 500 inhabitants.

Although these European projects offer the rural population new instruments for improving their quality of life and promote sustainable development, it remains to be seen how well rural development and environmental protection projects designed and tested to meet Western European needs and conditions will apply in the Lithuanian context.

Lithuania's experience with pre-accession programmes designed to help countries learn about the new European mechanisms before enlargement shows the difficulties that can arise in implementing

*Table 10.2*  Rural development programme financed by structural funds

| Measures | Agro-environmental measures |
| --- | --- |
| **EAGGF Guidance section** | |
| 1. Investment in agricultural holdings | – Investment must meet European environmental protection standards |
| 2. Aid for the setting up of young farmers | – Holdings must comply with environmental protection standards |
| 3. Aid for processing and marketing of agricultural products | – Investment must meet European environmental protection standards |
| 4. Development of countryside<br>– Management of drainage and irrigation system<br>– Reparcelling<br>– Consultancy for farmers<br>– Diversification of non-farm activities in rural areas<br>– Development of rural tourism and craft activities | – Investment must meet European environmental protection standards |
| 5. Support for forestry | – Forest plantation on non-farm land (disused quarries, landfills, etc.) |
| 6. LEADER+ | – Improvement of quality of life in rural areas |
| 7. Education of rural residents | – Training in good farming practice |
| **EAGGF Guarantee section** | |
| 8. Protection of the environment in rural areas | – Support for organic farming<br>– Territorial farming contracts designed to protect open water bodies, natural meadows and marshland |
| 9. Reforestation of farmland | |
| 10. Support for farmers in less favoured areas and areas subject to environmental constraints | – Protection of the environment in the northern region affected by karstification and the Neman delta region |
| 11. Early retirement for farmers | |
| 12. Aid for semi-subsistence farms | |
| 13. Modernization of livestock farming | – Promotion of extensive livestock farming<br>– Control of liquid manure treatment |
| **Cohesion fund** | |
| Water management in small villages | – Upgrade of drinking water and wastewater treatment infrastructure |

European rural development projects. During the pre-accession period, the Lithuanian countryside made little progress in implementing the new environmental management programs. For example, the agro-environmental measures provided for in the Sapard programme had only marginal effects.[25] Moreover, projects for the reforestation of farmland and the use of new environmental methods in regions with 'fragile' natural conditions (specifically in the northern karst region and Neman delta region) were not carried out.

The record of the first year since the country joined the EU also reveals other difficulties of implementing the European project. Only a part of the funding planned in 2004 for agro-environmental measures was used – in some cases as low as 30% (farmland restoration). Only the demand for farm supports in less favoured areas and areas subject to environmental constraints was bigger than the amount allocated (122.8 per cent).

Constraining factors for the European rural development model in Lithuania are many. First, there are poor administrative capacities at both national and local levels. Second, there is a low civil society participation rate in environmental projects. Third, the construction of facilities to protect the environment on farms (such as the nitrate directive) or the reforestation of farmland require major investments that are only partia lly refunded by the structural funds, or only refunded when all the work has been do ne. The financial impoverishment of many of the new farmers is an obstacle to meeting these environmental standards. Moreover, environmental protection practices are often not the top priority in rural communities hard hit by poverty and serious social problems.

The promotion of the European rural model is also limited by the slow pace of administrative decentralization and territorial reform. European rural development grants are based on a principle of subsidiarity and require decentralization, with regional and local consultation and partnership. However, the institutional and territorial reform of 1994 failed to recognize the autonomy of local authorities and instead privileged one level of territorial authority based on the former Soviet districts. Utilizing these larger regional administrative units[26] has resulted in reduced levels of citizen participation in the management of local affairs, particularly in rural areas. The absence of a local institutional framework in the EU agenda hampers the action and initiative of local authorities, and impairs their ability to implement their own projects. As a result, the disappearance of the collective farms, has provoked a grassroots movement for the renewal of 'rural communities' (*kaimo bendruomenes*). Most of these were founded by women (teachers, arts centre employees, farmers, and members of the Catholic charity Caritas) concerned by social problems and the deterioration of country life since 1990. With support from the Chamber of Agriculture, this movement has expanded rapidly. Between 2000 and 2004, the number of such communities has increased from 159 to 525. With pressure from these new civil society stakeholders, non-profit organizations are playing a more important role in local development in rural areas, although they often lack resources, experience and skills to participate more fully in the EU-funded programmes and projects.

## Conclusion

Ultimately, Lithuania's adoption of various international conventions and its accession to the European Union are likely to improve the protection of the environment. However, the uneven development of town and country will continue to pose challenges. The legacies of Soviet development continue to be important, and they have different consequences in town and country. Most air and water pollution is urban in nature, deriving from large-scale industry with archaic water treatment facilities inherited from the Soviet period and, in some cases, a total absence of wastewater networks. In the countryside, the overall level of pollution is lower but the sources of pollution, particularly of water and factory farms, are more varied and dispersed over wide areas. The countryside also suffers from the underdevelopment of its infrastructure and the degradation of the land caused by Soviet mechanization.

Furthermore, after 1990, the socioeconomic transition has also had differential impacts in urban and rural areas. The ecological situation generally improved in the towns, while the problems in the countryside continued to pile up. The towns, especially the larger ones, have enjoyed a greater level of economic development and this has meant that municipal councils have had more resources to invest in environmental projects. Towns, the symbols of successful transition, have been the focus of the government's reforms and have therefore also been more generously subsidized by the state and EU structural funds. By contrast, the environmental problems of rural areas inherited from the Soviet era have been aggravated by the transition process and have suffered from neglect by the authorities. Since 1990, government action in rural areas (and one-third of the country's population) has focused on the economic and social consequences of de-collectivization, while investments in programmes to deal with environmental problems and the deterioration in living conditions.

The urban municipalities with human and financial resources have been able to initiative and implement a number of projects for local development.[27] On the other hand, the centres of the autonomous municipalities – the main towns of the former Soviet districts – are far removed from the problems of the smaller towns and villages within their jurisdiction. Consequently attention is focused on the problems of larger urban areas, where municipal councillors and mayors live and work. Low population density, distance from urban centres and poor access also hamper the development of the countryside. At the same time, the inertia of the institutions in charge of rural development, their bureaucratic approach and the mentality and behaviour of the political authorities, stamped by the habits of Soviet bureaucracy, are likely to raise other challenges. In either case, the attempts to effect a politics of environmental reconstruction – be it democratic or managerial – may fail to result in more sustainable livelihoods.

## Endnotes

1. Population density varies from 1380 inhabitants per sq. km in the city of Vilnius to only 30 per sq. km in the Trakai district, just 25 km from Vilnius.
2. *Subalansuotos pletros igyvendinimo nacionaline ataskaita. Nuo Rio de Zaneiro link Johanesburgo. Nuo pereinamojo laikotarpio link subalansuotos pletros* [National report on development stability. From Rio de Janeiro to Johannesburg. From periods of transition to development stability], Vilnius: Lutute, 2002.
3. Subalansuotos pletros, op. cit.
4. Subalansuotos pletros, op.cit.
5. Subalansuotos pletros, op.cit.
6. Much of the research of the scientific institutes in charge of development was devoted to finding the so-called optimal size for a plot of land, a block of crops, a work brigade, a village or a depreciation fund, with the aim of minimizing investment and expenditure, and raising incomes and profits as much as possible.
7. Pig factory farms contained from 12,000 to 54,000 animals and accounted for some seven per cent of pork production.

8. Despite the attempts of the Soviet authorities to mechanize farm work, much labour remained manual and required considerable physical effort. Most factory farms had no washrooms or toilets for their employees.
9. This was also true in all the USSR's federated republics.
10. Its leader, Vytautas Landsbergis, defeated the Communist Party at the first multi-party elections held within the USSR in March 1990. He became the first speaker of the Seimas in post-Communist Lithuania.
11. *Lietuvos aplinkos apsaugos strategija: veiksmu programa* [Environment protection strategy: program of action], Vilnius: Lietuvos Respublikos aplinkos apsaugos ministerija, 1996.
12. European Commission, *Comprehensive monitoring report on the state of preparedness for EU membership*, Brussels: European Commission, 2003.
13. Subalansuotos pletros, op.cit.
14. The first reactor in the nuclear plant was closed down on 31 December 2004, and the second reactor is due to be taken out of service in 2009. Once the plant is closed, Lithuania will lose 80 per cent of its energy production. Meanwhile a local development programme will need to be set up to create new jobs for 30,000 largely Russian-speaking residents in Visaginas, whose living depended entirely on the plant.
15. *Structural Funds for agro-environmental projects can be used for (1) the protection of the environment in rural areas; (2) reforestation of farmland; (3) support for farmers in less favoured areas and areas subject to environmental constraints (such as wetlands); and (4) promotion of extensive livestock farming and the treatment of liquid manure.*
16. According to the 2003 agricultural census data, only 13 per cent of Lithuanian family farms produce for the market.
17. *Lietuvos zemes ukis 2003* [Lithuanian agriculture 2003], Vilnius: Lietuvos Agrarines Ekonomikos Institutas, 2004, p. 160.
18. *Lietuvos zemes ukis 2004* [Lithuanian agriculture 2003], Vilnius: Lietuvos Agrarines Ekonomikos Institutas, 2005, p. 160.
19. P. Aleknavicius, *Agrarines reformos ivertinimas* [Agrarian reform estimation], Vilnius: Josara, 1996, p. 80.
20. *Lietuvos zemes ukis 2002* [Lithuanian agriculture 2002], Vilnius: Lietuvos Agrarines Ekonomikos Institutas, 2003, p. 155.
21. *Aplinkos bukle* 2003 [State of the environment], Vilnius: Aplinkos ministerija, 2004.
22. R. Baubinas and J. Taminskas, *Karine gamtonauda Lietuvoje sovietmeciu: ekologines pasekmes* [The use of natural resources by military forces during soviet period: environmental consequences], Vilnius: Geografijos institutas, 1997.
23. For example, in the old Northtown military complex in Vilnius, a new residential area, shopping centres and leisure facilities have been built. Meanwhile, the countryside continues to suffer the pollution from the former bases.
24. By 2009, modern landfills are due to be created in the country's 10 counties (*apskritis*) to replace the 737 public landfills existing in 2003.
25. On 26 November 2001, the European Commission transferred to the Lithuanian authorities the management of Sapard (Special Accession

Programme for Agriculture and Rural Development) aid, involving €30.6 million a year. The programme is planned to help eight major projects defined by the Lithuanian authorities under farm and rural development plan and approved by the European Commission.
26. The administrative divisions enjoying autonomous management range in size from 441 to 2,218 sq. km.
27. Seven major towns and one coastal resort enjoy the status of autonomous administrative division.

# 11

# Building a Social Cause in Post-Communist Countries: Ecological Politics in the Czech Republic

*Sandrine Devaux*

## Introduction

The construction of environmental issues as a 'cause' for mobilizing political action in Czech society occurred in several stages, each with its own specific commitments and goals.[1] By focusing on these processes and stages through which ecological protagonists constructed this politics of the environment we are able to focus on the medium- and long-term social processes and dynamics at work, following a well-established tradition in political sociology that investigates the ways in which the social takes shape as a driver of politics. This chapter examines the constitution of the environment 'cause' and, in particular, the combined roles played by changing social actors in the Czech Republic and international actors.

The term 'cause' is understood in its broadest sense as a problem that is identified by one or more categories of actor as being important for the whole of society, and it is the thesis of this chapter that any such effective mobilization is possible only where there exists a functioning 'public space'.[2] The chapter concludes with an analysis of the relationship between the ecological actors who emerged in the 1980s and the underlying logic of the post-socialist transformation.

Post-socialist attitudes to the environment have been shaped, in part, by the manner in which nature was regarded under the state socialist regime. That period was important not only because it marked a bifurcation of environmentalism in Czechoslovakia from what was happening in the West, but also because it shaped the capacities and understandings of social actors working on environmental issues who are still active today. The Czech Republic is particularly instructive in this respect because so many former scientists and members of protest groups have 'recycled' themselves and are now engaged in careers relating to ecological protection.[3] My first theoretical assumption is, thus, that the construction of a social cause is closely bound up with the configuration of a country's social and political forces and with the way in which outside variables and domestic issues combine together. My aim is to show that in the Czech Republic the environment was produced as a social cause by ecology activists who had already been militant before 1989 and scientists whose careers had led them into environmental institutions, such as think tanks, academic organizations, and governmental agencies, and that this institutional legacy has shaped the practices of the environmental movement since 1989.[4]

Attempts to raise environmental concerns to the level of a national cause after 1989 also cannot be explained without taking into account the professional conversions and the institutionalization of environmental issues that became common elements of government reform, especially as a result of the influence of international lending and development agencies. Our second hypothesis is that the change in political regime after 1989 was at once an opportunity and a constraint for the previous social actors, including those who could be called protesters. Their adjustment to the new system was contingent upon the advent of democratic institutions and practices that opened a space for public debate, the renewal of the political establishment and the creation of advisory bodies through which these earlier actors were able to work. Environmental protectionism in the Czech Republic thus had a threefold parentage – scientific careers, membership in official associations and involvement in dissident and protest groups.

At the strictly environmental level, the Czech Republic, like other post-socialist societies, was obliged to cope with the socialist period's legacy of environmental degradation while developing a capitalist-style economy that was also liable to harm the environment. Pollution in the Czech Republic, resulting from Soviet-model industrialization and intensive farming, had devastating consequences for air quality (especially in the cities where it is aggravated by coal-based heating), ground water and vegetation (particularly in the acid rain-affected forests of North Bohemia). One area, the Black Triangle located near the Polish and former East German borders, is particularly blighted. Other land has been spoiled by lignite mining in North Bohemia and Moravia, as well as being hard hit since the early 1990s by the economic declines that have occurred. These environmental problems are compounded by high levels of nuclear-related risk resulting from the continued operation of Soviet-designed atomic power stations and nuclear waste disposal.

In order to explain the mechanisms and factors involved in the construction of the environment as a political 'cause', this chapter proceeds by three stages: first, it outlines the way the Socialist regime handled the natural; second, it describes how occupational and militant groups seized upon the environment to challenge the 'Soviet-type system' more broadly; and third, it explains how their conversion to the cause gave objective status to ecology in the Czech Republic.

## The Socialist regime and the conservation of the natural patrimony

The 'Soviet-type system' was never monolithic, but was adjusted to local circumstances as it was imported by each country in central Europe. It was through these marginal adjustments that the State socialism was able to establish its own legitimacy by tailoring practice to fit national circumstances. The field of nature conservation provides a good illustration of this, one which had the added element of being influenced in some important ways by the environmental movement in the West beginning in the 1970s.

### The permeability of socialist society to international influences

Any assessment of the relationship between Socialist aims and the environmental goals of the state must also take into account the influence of social movements and the activities of international agencies. One such early reaction to Western environmental concerns was the creation in January 1970 of a Council for the Environment answering to the government of the Czechoslovak Socialist Republic. Twenty years later, it would form the basis for the Ministry of the Environment. While the Council had little room for developing and implementing major initiatives, it did serve to introduce into public discussion the notion of environmental change, and the effects of the economic system on environmental conditions, in conditions in which hitherto only nature conservation had received any attention. The Council was little more than a discussion group lacking any power to contest official policy, despite the fact that it was a state agency and that the state was the primary cause of environmental damage (e.g., open-cast mining, industrial refuse disposal in water, dam projects, air pollution, and the building of Soviet-model nuclear power plants).

The Czech authorities reacted a second time to these broader international influences after the UN Environment Conference held in Stockholm in 1972 by creating a number of new organizations. In 1974 a youth organization devoted entirely to nature study was set up and in 1979 the Czech Nature Protectors' Union (*Český svaz ochranců přirody, ČSOP*) was created. Such organizations presumed the necessity of environmental protection while the socialist economy continued to extract natural resources without regard to the environmental damage they caused.

The Czech Nature Protectors' Union is a good example of an organization formed under socialism that combined a commitment to natural science research on environmental issues with the influence of international debates, and adjusted both to the Soviet model of environmental management. The creation of the Union is indicative of the ways in which the Communist regime was able to demonstrate its interest in environmental issues while also regaining political control over a certain part of the environmental movement. On 11 September 1979, the Union superseded a Nature Conservation Department founded in 1959 within the Prague National Museum. The learned society had obtained independence in 1969 under the name of TIS (the Czech word for yew-tree). Seen as being too critical during the 1970s, the 'voluntary organisation' was disbanded in April 1979 by the Ministry of the Interior. It ceased its activities on 31 December that year.[5]

Ostensibly a voluntary association for attending to practical nature protection needs, the ČSOP was launched at the behest of the Ministries of Culture, Water and Forest Administration, Education, Construction and Agricultural Techniques by a government decision of 23 August 1978 concerning the 'State conception of development and the protection of nature'. Unlike the other official Socialist organisations, the ČSOP did not in 1979 belong to the National Front, the umbrella structure for all 'Socialist organisations'. Instead, it was, by reason of its position in the Socialist education system, directly answerable to the Czech government and the federal Ministry of Culture.[6] Its second Secretary-General, appointed in 1984, was a member of the Czechoslovakian Communist Party nomenklatura. More broadly, there were scientists, Agriculture Faculty teachers, State Institute for Nature and Patrimony Protection employees, people with a natural science background concerned with nature, as well as ordinary voluntary workers. Hierarchical in structure, the ČSOP had a base composed of an extensive network of rural and urban local associations. In 1989, it had 26,000 members spread across 900 of these associations. It was orientated towards environmental conservation and it acted as part of a broader pro-nature movement. Its importance, in part, was its ability to give a degree of official recognition to environmental concerns.

The transition from TIS to ČSOP in the Czech territories suggests that each Eastern country had its own dynamics, independent of international influence and the sovietism in institutions inherited from earlier times.[7] A national tradition could be exploited since it could be integrated in the soviet-type system while supporting specific national interests. The importance of national context may be seen from the different course taken by events in Slovakia, where a Nature and Landscape Protection Union had been founded in 1969. The differences between the patterns of normalization between Prague and Bratislava were quite marked. Whereas the 1977 Helsinki Agreements on the defence of human rights led in Czechoslovakia to the adoption of Charter 77, whose purpose was to condemn the failure of the regime to observe the treaty it had ratified, the Stockholm Conference provided the Communist authorities with an opportunity to weaken the environmental movement by institutionalizing a narrow version of nature conservation in Slovakian institutions. One consequence was that, until the end of the 1980s, the main role of all the official organizations in Slovakia was limited to providing technical information.

## The Socialist and local translation of international stakes

In the West, many scientists and activists rallied around environmental concerns from the 1960s on. In Czechoslovakia political protest was much more limited, particularly because of the influence of state education policies that were directed explicitly at fostering conservative attitudes to environmental issues. As a result, it was mainly scientists who were the first to criticize the negative environmental effects of socialist development plans and it was largely they who sought to create an 'aesthetic' ecology movement ('the ecology of the landscape', in Czech).[8] This action by scientific and academic circles was possible precisely because of the privileged position accorded the exact sciences and the support given by the state to the expansion of technical institutes. The Academy of Sciences' Institute for Land Ecology, for example, helped to create a branch of the Socialist Youth Union concerned with the practical and research side of nature conservation. The 'Brontosaurus' movement for educating young people also formed in this way, following from a well-publicized nature conservation awareness campaign organized in 1974, *Akce Brontosaurus*, in conjunction with the UN-sponsored Environment Year. Such programmes of research and youth education were the two pillars of official organizations up until the demise of the Soviet-style system.

The main activities of the ČSOP and Brontosaurus may be summed up as the creation of education curricula, waste collection, reforestation and the restoration of historical monuments, including religious ones. While Western Europe was ringing with the slogan 'Think globally, act locally', Czech socialist society was focusing much more on local level conservation issues in an effort to cement the ties between the people and their habitat. This kind of nature protection work seems to have been an attempt by the regime to convert environmental concerns into forms acceptable to the 'nationalized' version of socialist ideology. The absence of a genuinely ecological dimension was counterbalanced by a popularization of nature-worship, with large numbers of people joining the ČSOP to enjoy their programmes of nature discovery. The enjoyment of nature became closely integrated into everyday private life and to an ethos of leisure linked with home economics, either through gardening – commonly practised in people's residences and at the country chalets where Czechs spend much of their weekends – or by the gathering of foods such as mushrooms and apples. Some of these nature pastimes fitted in with existing practices such as the 'Brigades' and 'Z Actions' (the names given by the regime to work on beautifying – *Zkrášlovaní* – urban and natural surroundings). Their aim was to stimulate citizen participation in collective tasks, usually devoted to harvesting and the upkeep of natural habitats. There was nothing spontaneous about these operations, of course, and they were often held in line by the youth organizations or neighbourhood cooperatives. As we shall see later in the chapter, this double relationship continued after 1990 as a decisive factor in shaping contemporary debates about ecology and environmental protection.

In the face of the absence of a coherent environment policy, the regime canvassed citizen participation in these nature programmes, portraying 'care' for nature as a way of furthering 'democracy'. Minutes of the local associations bear this out. A ČSOP branch in Krásná Lípa, for example, reported that 'Our organization is small, but our appetite for work is good.'[9] The regime was clearly trying to channel the interests of scientists and ordinary people into specific forms of nature conservation, but ones that made it less likely, and even dangerous, that participants would militate for stronger environmental policies and practices.

These policies were further entrenched by the award in 1988 of the UN Environment Programme's Global 500 Prize to the ČSOP in recognition of its activities, showing how such international praise confirmed the Socialist association's legitimacy on the home front, especially on the eve of the ČSOP's third congress. This was held on 19 and 20 November 1989 to mark the twentieth anniversary of ČSOP and to draw up a new programme for the period 1990–5.

At the same time, however, another tendency was emerging within official institutions as well as the appearance of independent groups disputing the Socialist political order. These initiatives were aimed at stronger claims on the state to deal with serious environmental problems. These groups had occasionally been visible in the 1960s, but they became much more marked and effective during the final ten years of the regime's existence, when issues relating to the protection of nature acquired new standing. Whereas the steps taken by the official associations had tended to accentuate their Socialist conservatism, new groups were beginning to link the problems of the degradation of nature with the ways in which society itself functioned. They introduced the term 'environment' to set themselves apart from the usual theme of 'nature conservation' and its primary focus on animal and plant species diversity.

## The defence of the environment as a way of contesting socialist rule

We have seen how actions by the Czech authorities helped to force the environmental concerns into a Socialist mould. Yet these measures were not without effect on shaping the environmental movement in the country. A number of official scientific institutes became involved in thinking of the environment in aesthetic terms and began criticising the Socialists' projects. At the same time, more radical views were emerging in the mass organizations themselves, leading to the formation of ecological defence groups. In the late 1980s, parallel to what was happening in other areas (such as struggles for human rights, cultural rights and identity politics, and anti-war and anti-nuclear movements), there was a convergence among different environmental defence protagonists: scientists, Charter 77 ecology branch dissidents and young activists adopting a broader view of environmental issues. These groups increasingly began to act politically and their actions began to take the shape of 'protest movements'. These were not what is more often called 'independent currents' or 'seeds of civil society',[10] since these terms tend to presuppose the existence of social actors living in a kind of underground society or, at least, in a space that escaped the system's rules. On the contrary, these environmental actors were importantly embedded in the dynamics and institutions of their own society.

## Criticism by the scientists

The first attempts to give formal expression to an ecological movement thus emerged from inside the regime through the actions of scientists working within their own institutions, specifically the geographers, biologists and chemists working in different departments of the Academy of Sciences. The Ecology Section, founded by the Academy of Sciences Vice-President in 1982, was particularly important in this regard. Housed in the Heritage Institute, it provided the opportunity for scientists, members of the government Environment Council and dissidents to meet once a month. Josef Vavroušek and Bedřich Moldan were especially active in the Ecology Section of the Biology Society of the Academy before becoming pioneer figures in the institutionalization of ecological politics after 1989.

A second movement – the 'Ecologist Front' – had a similar history and consequences. In the mid-1960s, specialists in the Geographic Institute had initiated a study in Moravia of the impacts on wetlands of a major development project on the Morava River. After the repression of the Prague Spring and with a Czechoslovak–Hungarian dam on the Danube also being planned, they began to circulate their findings and organize discussions about the ways in which they might oppose such development projects. Such mobilization among scientists occurred at a time when popular concern about the conservation of open land and ecosystems was increasing. Cooperation was arranged between the Czech Academy of Sciences Biology Section and the Slovak Academy of Sciences Biology and Landscape Section, which became the Biology and Ecology Section in 1975. Through these venues, scientists were able to express their criticisms relatively freely, protected in large measure by the prestige of their positions in the Academy. It was also important that these individuals and organizations did not contest the philosophy of large-scale public works projects as such, often the hallmark of authoritarian regimes. Instead, they offered specific criticisms of the impact of the new infrastructural projects on the surrounding areas and proposed alternative solutions, attempting in each case to maintain their right to offer criticism as a result of the scientific character of the findings and arguments. This is not to suggest that these scientists were successful in their endeavours. In the case of the Gabčikovo-Nagymaros dam, for example, they failed to prevent the government from building the dam and all they were able to do, with the help of ČSOP voluntary members, was salvage the botanical species that were to be submerged under the dam lake.

## The logic of the ecological protest groups

In the Czech Republic, nature conservation took a radical turn only later, and then by following two different paths. Ecology activists had tried to raise popular awareness about the threats from nuclear, power toxic substances and atmospheric pollution. They were particularly concerned about the kinds of 'invisible pollution' that, in the West, had induced scientists to use their capacity as experts to speak out against state and private development projects. In the Czech Republic, the break with the past owed as much to the influence of international debates as it did to the scientific findings about conditions in the region. A new generation of researchers had been influenced by the new lifestyles and environmental concerns being defined in the West and, as a result, the movements that had emerged in the 1980s began to be much more publicly visible, particularly when they began to join forces with political dissident groups who were themselves becoming more interested in creating broader political alliances. Their denunciation of ecological scandals quickly distinguished them from the conservative positions that had been dominant between 1987 and 1989 and, as a result, they were able to make substantial political gains in the last months of the Socialist regime.

These gains were possible, in part, because of wider events in the Soviet bloc as well as the energies of the new Czech protest movements. The Chernobyl disaster discredited Soviet-model nuclear installations throughout Central and Eastern Europe, and, while drawing attention to the dangers the region's power plants represented for the whole of Europe, they significantly weakened the legitimacy of socialist governments throughout the region. At the same time, *perestroika* in the Soviet Union created a political vacuum in the 'satellite' countries, where independent policies became more of a possibility. Although Czechoslovakia remained one of the last bastions of Socialism until the end of 1989, the easing of political constraints had a real influence on the running of society in general and of the official associations in particular. This was reflected in a wider margin of tolerance within the ČSOP and the appearance of sections with strong commitments to ecological politics and their expression in the papers published and topics covered in the ČSOP's journal, *Our Nature*. The change was even more evident in the ČSOP's local papers: *NIKA*, published in Prague, and *Veronica*, published in Brno. At national level, the official line of these groups remained very pro-regime and faithful to the Soviet model of environment protection, with very little mention of the more or less independent groups that were springing up. The ČSOP's leadership had for many years been seeking affiliation with the National Front, which had always been seen to be a path to increased freedom of action and broader mobilization, and on 27 June 1989 this was finally achieved.

In addition, the coming of age of the more militant post-1968 generation brought the old ecology movement into closer alignment with the Charter 77 dissenters. The latter, who had been chiefly concerned with defence of human rights and political freedoms, became more and more interested in ecology seen as the citizens' right to contribute to public policy dealing with the environment in which they lived. From being small working groups inside Charter 77, the ecologists acquired greater standing and soon began to work vigorously to open up space for debate in ever wider domains of society. One concrete outlet for this work was the publication of the *Ecological Bulletin*[11] and the subsequent establishment of an Ecology Forum.[12] A common feature of these new movements was the role of students. They put their social standing and the permeability of the official youth networks to good use in the public airing of environmental problems.

A different strategy emerged with the Mothers of Prague League. Particularly active during the 1988–9 winter, when the city was shrouded in tenacious smog, this group was primarily concerned with the health of their children in the heavily polluted capital city. They had a strong feminist orientation with ties based on personal relations with other contemporary movements such as the Ecology Society. The women and their children demonstrated in the streets of Prague in August 1989 carrying banners demanding more pedestrian zones and cleaner air. The result was the emergence of other associations like *České Děti* (Children of Bohemia), *Zelený Kruh* (the Green Club), *Ekologická Společnost* (the Ecology Society), and, later, *Děti země* (Children of the Earth) or *Hnutí Duha* (the Rainbow Movement) that opposed official censorship about the dangers of pollution and the state of the environment and argued for more transparency and awareness of the health consequences of environmental pollution.

Attempts to create a 'public space' for the discussion of environmental and health issues originated with these movements. Their aim was two-fold: on the one hand, to open debate about environment issues by taking them out of the hands of the scientists and, on the other, to contest government censorship of environmental information. Pro-dissident journals, like *Ekologický Bulletin*, played an important role in this process by distributing unofficial information which might alert the population, particularly students and people already concerned by the effects of specific cases of pollution in areas such as North Bohemia.[13] Many of these young activists, although engaged in a form of political protest, were of course also products of the Socialist regime. They embraced the cause of ecology while pursuing their studies, especially in such subjects as biology and chemistry, and they were members of officially-sponsored nature conservation associations. Besides their social contacts in these associations, many of them came from severely polluted areas in North Bohemia. One result was the creation of Children of the Earth in September–October 1989, superseding a group originating in the 1970s. Among the founders were Jindřich Pertlík and Miroslav Patrik, who had met at high school in Bilina in North Bohemia, where they had been members of the archaeology and natural science club. Later, when they were university students, they set up a cell, the 'demolition squad', within the Prague 6 ČSOP. On 18 September 1989, sixty people from all over the Czech Republic met together in a Prague 6 cultural centre and, on 27 October, decided to change this ČSOP cell into an independent association called Children of the Earth with members drawn from a student network that had been built around scientific university careers and centres of interest.

The Rainbow Movement, one of the country's main ecological associations at the present time, perhaps surprisingly, did not emerge from concern about environmental damage. It was founded by two friends who had met at Brno high school. The Movement's motives were less about mobilizing for local causes and more to do with recruiting young people who were concerned about planetary futures and committed to introducing a global vision of ecology into the Czech Republic. The title of the Movement's journal, *The Last Generation*, says much about how some of the country's youth envisioned the future in the late 1980s.

These groups, largely concerned with the urban environment and with the impact of new technology, focused on the nuclear issue, a problem posed by the Dukovany atomic power plant, which was designed on the Chernobyl model, and the scheme, begun in 1983, for building the Temelín plant using more recent Soviet technology. Their agenda also included motor vehicle pollution, water and groundwater pollution, and waste management, as well as opposition to the use of Freon which, by then, was known to be a major factor in causing ozone depletion. A particular trademark of this group was their commitment to alternative lifestyles opposed to the type of consumer society imposed by the Socialist regime.

The environmental cause thus, on account of the Socialist regime's institutionalization of the nature conservation field, grew following a process different from that experienced by Western capitalist societies, especially because the development of ecological movements came later. This was why the political ecology movements developed later and in a specific context of opposition to an authoritarian regime, although this did not ensure their being considered as legitimate after 1989. Again, while it is undeniable that the slew of water, air, forest and other conservation laws adopted in the Socialist countries was inversely proportional to the government's interest in the subject, the regime did institute a number of bodies and organizations whose influence on the Czech Republic's present image of environmentalism can scarcely be doubted. A significant example was the popularity of the youth organization, *Brontosaurus*. The ČSOP's survival into the post-Socialist era, its national scale and its naturalist orientation bear witness to the vigour of this current of thought, today expressed in a new magazine, *KRÁSA, Našeho domova*.[14] In the early months of 1990 the old one, we may note, hailed the renaissance of the Boy Scout movement with a three-part survey entitled 'Ecology in the Boy Scout Holiday Camps' to salute the eminent role of this kind of youth organization in developing ecological education.

In summary, if state implication in nature-linked mass organizations had the advantage for the regime of making participation in protest movements more difficult, the manner in which relations with nature had been conceived by both the government and the protest movements had a shaping effect on the lines of tension among the nature conservation actors and the cause's redefinition after 1990.

## The actors' permanence and the cause's redefinition after 1989

The fact of basing our analysis on the environmental cause's construction allows us to apprehend the complexity of the processes at work in every area of society and to have a relational view of several rationales evolving simultaneously. This stands in opposition to an approach centred on the 'structures of political opportunities'.[15] Two perspectives are possible for understanding how the environment makes its presence felt in Czech society. One is the rapid and very visible surge in civic organizations of all sizes (from local associations to national entities) concerned with nature. The other is the multiplication of environmental knowledge-amassing bodies connected with academia, or even with the governing authorities. Fifteen years later, we can observe a clear change in the internal functioning of the associations and their place in the 'public space'.

## The reshaping of ecological actors after 1989

In the new political context, three tendencies seem to be at work where the formulation of the environmental issue is concerned. First, a network of ecology activists, who joined the 1980s movement and continue to work within the associations, persists. Second, there is a naturalist view, supported by the organizations dating from the Socialist period and based on an earlier tradition of protecting local heritage, that had been manipulated by the Socialist regime (like ČSOP, *Brontosaurus*). Third, there is the professional development of a fringe group of scientists, some of whom held political posts after the regime change and founded ecology-related institutions sometimes on close terms with the government. This professionalization, applicable also to the younger generation, is responsible for the creation of new types of association.

The ecology field is fairly representative of the way association life has developed since the early 1990s, and of the related trend towards professionalization. Both have occurred by way of creating salaried positions for certain members and recruiting young staff with university training in voluntary organization management and in special skills (environment or social work).[16] The greatest difference from other fields is the wide diversity in types of organization. Whether new or old, however, all the organizations obey the same trend. Some, like Brontosaurus in Prague, have a combined amateur and professional structure. The amateur wing, in the shape of voluntary associations, runs youth organization work while the professional wing looks after the dissemination of ecological information. Even in the smaller structures, association directors draw salaries. All this contributes to the stability of the 'ecology market'.

Nature conservation society members continue energetically with their work. They defend their choice as a way of distinguishing their action from that of the ecology societies. The proof of the naturalist movement's vitality lies in the ongoing life of the ČSOP, which today claims 10,000 members spread across 408 base organizations. The enduring feature of the environmental groups is their bias towards urban problems – transport, organizing the no-car day, preserving townscapes threatened in their view by *intra muros* shopping malls. The associations derived from the Socialist regime, for their part, continue their work on the countryside and woodlands. The actors find their positions altered by the state of progress of the various cases of interest to them. Not only did the demise of the Soviet-type system fail to put a halt to the environmental damage with which it was associated, but the transition to a market economy brought with it new dis-amenities. As early as 1989, the resumption of the planned start-up of the Temelin nuclear power station not far from the Austrian border stirred ecologists into action at local and national – even international, with the intervention of *Greenpeace*'s Czech branch – levels. Again in 1999, the calling-off of the *Hnutí Duha* campaign against the power station brought about a redeployment of the ecology actors and a decision to fight on by *Nesehnutí* (the independent social and ecological movement), an association formed by the secession of the more radical members.

Permanence is, on the whole, the mark of the protest organizations that arose during the very last months of the Socialist regime's existence, like *Děti Země*, *Hnutí Duha* and *Pražské matky*. The first two of them are still the main nationwide ecology associations in the Czech Republic, along with Greenpeace. As we have seen, the ecology debate during the 1990s was fired principally by members of the old protest movements who were trying to build the cause in the new political context.

The ecology spectrum also includes more localized associations, set up during the 1990s, specializing in certain topics, such as *Jihočeské matky* (the Mothers of South Bohemia), agitating mainly against Temelín; *Přátele přírody* (the Friends of Nature in Ústi nad Labem), whose cause is the conservation of the Labe River Valley; the Old Defenders of the Jizerské Mountains in Liberec, concerned with replacing spruce monoculture in the Mountains by a wider variety of tree species; or the VITA association in Ostrava in North Moravia, one of the country's most devastated regions, whose main activity is organizing ecology education seminars and 'public sector management'. Other organizations – such as the Transportation Centre and Ekowatt, which provide cost estimates for renewable energies – are less preoccupied by a local environment problem than by particular technical fields. They are the creation of young science or law graduates who, while engaged in defending the environment, find employment in ecology organizations that are funded in part by European programmes or by Czech and/or British foundations. One such organization is called the Environment Workshop (Workshop for short); it is a perfect example of these new organizations' hybrid character. They combine the provision of legal advice with market services as regards observance of environmental standards and the right of citizens to have a say in local decisions. This is also the role of the Ecology Law Service in Brno and Prague, set up by young Law graduates. While their main function is advice, they also investigate cases dealing with specific environment problems (e.g. saving the Šumava national park, Environment Information Act, Atom Act), and seek to stimulate popular involvement by promoting citizen participation in decision-making procedures – particularly, as with the Workshop, the contract-awarding procedures for building shopping centres in the main cities. The Workshop, whose members are architects, lawyers, chemists and biologists, holds special interest for us since it embodies the trajectory of ecology groups since the early 1990s and the way in which the former ecology activists have inflected their personal careers since the change of regime.

## The renewal of involvement and the development of occupational careers

This research is in its early stage, and the hypotheses outlined in this paper need further testing. However, preliminary results suggests that the distinguishing marks of Socialist activism are accentuated in the post Socialist context. The revision of their commitment and its shift into a professional career is common to all the ecology activists, just as their relation to their 'source' organization produces a certain number of career stereotypes.

As to the former ecology activists, our hypothesis is that their pre-1989 commitment had a structuring influence on individual militant careers. Whereas in 1989 – in a context of broader social and political possibilities, including the recycling of dissident convictions into politics – careers were potentially reversible, certain activists persevered in what we shall call a 'contra' posture, despite their theses touting themselves as 'apolitical'. Spurning a political label could well be a strategy for avoiding a clash with the authorities and for keeping their movements viable. But the stance of being different with respect to defined policy in a Soviet-type system does not carry the same meaning in a democratic one. Protestation means accepting the rules of the political games (bargaining with political authorities), which several ecological associations were not keen to do at the beginning of the 1990s. Their uninterrupted commitment also shows in the ecology activists' 'alternative' personal image – ranging from clothes without synthetic fibres and use of recycled paper to wearing beards and longish hair.

Other cases can illustrate the point, with subtle differences due to career bifurcations. The Workshop's founder, Petr Kužvart, was not an organization member. He was, however, a friend of scientists and dissenters. He formed part, he says, of the 'grey sphere', from which he published ecological papers as samizdat. After acting as counsellor to Josef Vavroušek, the first Federal Environment Minister, he drew on his strengths as a lawyer to set up an independent association which lobbied local and national authorities in defence of nature, landscape and, especially, urban environment. His influence was far from negligible, since it was he who originated the text of Act No. 123 of 1998 concerning the right to information on the environment. So, although he was a practising lawyer, his public stands made him a representative of radical ecology.

Other personalities are linked with the former Socialist regime's official institutions. Many of the ecology militants still active in associations today were first involved in ČSOP local branches. In the opposite direction, scientists have become converted to ecology activism. One example is a Brno geographer, Jaroslav Ungermann, whose Geographical Institute closed in 1993. He joined the association Veronica, a branch of the ČSOP dealing with ecology education and the provision of expertise. Back in the 1960s, he had been an active member of the 'ecologists' front', where he followed the case of the Morava River development scheme. In that particular connection, his mastery of several foreign languages was of great help in establishing partnerships between Veronica and Austrian, Hungarian, French and Anglo-Saxon scientific colleagues. His case confirms the adjustability of social resources acquired under the Socialist regime.

The third career model which we have identified concerns environmental institution actors themselves. It enables us to understand the connections and networking that exist among some of the institutions in charge of environmental affairs. There is a distinction to be made between 'institutions' and 'organizations' / 'associations', even though they all (whether they be civil or public) have the status of voluntary body, since a function of the former is to produce cognitive standards. It is possible that certain ecology associations do the same but, at this point in our research, we are led to think that the institutions do this in a more striking way. The personalities who worked for the State institutions prior to 1989 seem to possess an academic, social and political capital that has enabled them to redeploy themselves in other organizations close to the new government and to hold high-ranking jobs, while pursuing their commitment.

Let us first consider the case of Josef Vavroušek, a former clerk who, from 1970 to 1990, became head of the Science and Technology Development Advisory Institute and, from 1982, was a member of the Ecology Section of the Czech Academy of Sciences' Biology Society. Despite his official functions, he was regarded as a leading light of Czech ecology and, in the final days of the Socialist regime, he began engaging in activities of a more political nature. In September 1989, he launched the Independent Intelligentsia Circle, whose aim was to restore the values of European culture and encourage dialogue among the different segments of society. On 19 November 1989, he co-founded the Civic Forum, along with other ecologists, such as Ivan Dejmal, the editor of a samizdat and member of the Civic Forum coordinating committee for Prague. In 1992, as Federal Environment Minister, Josef Vavroušek created the Sustainable Development Society, which sought ways of achieving sustainable development. Two former Environment Ministers and a former member of Brontosaurus – who had been a paid employee of the Landscape Ecology Institute and became Deputy Director of the Applied Ecology Institute of the Forestry Faculty of the city of *Kostelec Nad Černymi Lesy* – sat on its Executive Committee.

The Czech Academy of Sciences' Ecology Section was a breeding ground for ecological scholars as distinct from ecologists in the usual sense. This is confirmed by the career of one of the Section's founders, Václav Mezřický, who was at the time a legal expert in the Institute for State and Law. In 1992, after serving as Czech Environment Vice-Minister, he helped, in his capacity as a specialist in environment law, to set up a think tank, the Eco-policy Institute.

The last of the career itineraries we should like to mention is that of Bedřich Moldan, a chemist and former Vice-President of the Ecology Section of the Czech Academy of Sciences' Biology Society. He says that he received the backing of ČSOP members when he was appointed as the first Czech Minister for the Environment, at a time when half the Cabinet was still composed of Communist Party members. Despite his membership in the Civic Forum and his status as MP for the Civic Movement, he was denounced for collaborating with the secret police and resigned from the Ministry in 1991. The rest of his career brought into play two of his strengths: one in the environmental field, the other in the field of international relations. During the 1990s, he consolidated his position as a protector of nature by occupying the Presidency of the ČSOP from 1991 to 1997 and, in 1992, he founded the Centre for Environment Issues at the Charles University in Prague. While he cannot be strictly termed an ecology activist, he is an apostle of sustainable development in the Czech territories. It should be remembered that this concept is used mainly by the more or less governmental institutions and very little by the ecology associations, although they acknowledge it implicitly in their field work. Moldan's role traces back to the time, in 1986, when he was put in charge of the Czech Republic's plan for an Environmental Problem Scientific Committee. In 1992, he sat on its Executive Committee before becoming its Secretary-General in 1998. On a broader plane, he has performed many duties connected with the environment in European and international bodies and chaired the UN

Sustainable Development Commission in 2000–1. Here again, the possession of academic, social and political assets explains the reorientation of a professional career that had been deeply engaged in official institutions before 1989.

The number of the Academy of Sciences' Ecology Section former members currently active in environmental defence institutions leads us to advance two hypotheses. One is that the scientists counted both on the highly specialized expertise they had acquired while working in official organizations and on their list of contacts to redirect their careers in the new political circumstances. The other is that this expertise and participation in international networks confers on building the cause a more institutional, and therefore more 'respectable', character. Certain ecological institutions close to the government employ the language of sustainable development. As this is less used by the associations, it acts as a dividing line between the different actors. Closeness to political power, along with European programme and Anglo-Saxon foundation funding, are a big reason why the environment gets redefined in line with international usage. In 2000, for example, the Ecopolicy Centre was entrusted with bringing public environment policy up to date and implementing Agenda 21 for sustainable development in the town of Kladno, north of Prague. We suggest that the configuration of the cast of actors responsible for nature matters under the Socialist regime in the Czech territories has influenced the definition of the environmental cause since the early 1990s. Indeed, because of their scientific knowledge and notoriety (at national and international level), and their skills to bargain with political authorities, they managed more easily to access the political sphere and to be listened to by governments.

The choice of the Czech example does not imply that this paper disputes the idea of an environmental heritage shared by all the former Soviet bloc countries; it has just located the Czech developments in the specific situation of Socialist era actors, both official and protest. What interests us is the way in which that heritage is incorporated into and assimilated in a particular national situation. The activity of certain foreign or international organizations does, indeed, tend to give the impression that the environmental scene in central Europe is homogeneous. Generally speaking, the Anglo-Saxon foundations which support, or engender, the spread of civic practices – that is, those which have acted as defenders of civil society since 1990 – have tried to justify their intentions by stressing the likenesses among national situations. Yet Socialist societies, despite their adoption of a certain number of political ground rules and institutions drawn from the Soviet model, had their distinctive features, with social currents and power goals peculiar to each national territory. What is important to us is the future development of these configurations. The movement has already seen itself institutionalized with the creation of an Environment Ministry in 1990, with the codification of the environment through the adoption of EU norms occurring shortly thereafter.[17] In our view, the differences among national situations find their explanation in the varying play of internal forces, especially as regards the intermeshing of associations, official agencies and Ministry.

## Conclusion

Ecology presents an undeniably interesting terrain for understanding the process by which certain issues managed to filter into Socialist societies and mould them. Today ecological movements continue to contribute to the reconfiguration of key forms of social action. We have seen that the pre-1989 relationship with nature proceeded from both the imported Soviet model and the revival of a national naturalist heritage. While this collective form of the relationship with nature is in conformity with the country's political history, individual signs of an interest in nature did not disappear. Paradoxically, it was the reshaping of the naturalist cause under international influence which helped to consolidate the issue in its Socialist form. The creation of new organizations led to the constitution of networks of people who shared the same interests and took part in socially and politically recognized collective actions. We agree with the thesis that the Socialist authorities sought to channel naturalist sentiment to prevent it from escalating into ecologist demands. It remains true, however, that these organizations brought into contact and educated several generations of Czechs. The enduring survival of the ČSOP is an indication of the deep-rootedness of these social practices. So is the part played by the membership in the ČSOP of the present Minister, who was President of the ČSOP for a number of years, in investing him with the mantle of environmental specialist.

The originality of these societies also lies in the place attained by the scientists, on account of not only their knowledge and the privileged position they occupied in the Soviet-type system but also their ability to articulate environmental problems. Having acquired specialist skills in their research institutes and drawing benefit from certain international circuits, they managed quite quickly to recover their status and confirm their reputation as experts after the regime change.

This was not quite the case with the members of what we have labelled 'protest groups'. Some activists, the ones most closely associated with dissident circles, embarked on political careers of varying durations; but, for the most part, they remained ecology cause militants and did not abandon their dissenting stance. A majority of them adopt an alternative lifestyle and continue to level criticism at the way society is developing. At the same time, they, like all the Czech association actors, are attracting fresh resources and receiving European and international support. Our thesis therefore is that the protest role assumed by these activists when they were young students in the late 1980s has had a lasting structuring effect on their social career paths. The scientists already had professional careers, whereas the activists drew status and social identity from their 'political' activities.

In the Czech Republic, to conclude, a configuration of the players concerned formed around the twin issues of nature conservation and environmental protection, a configuration that reflects the tension between fidelity to the national (including Soviet) model and assimilation of international standards. The modes of socialization during the Communist period and the present conjugation of activism and professional careers are decisive, in explaining the developmental differences between the Czech and the Western model.

## Endnotes

1. P. Lascoumes, *L'Eco-pouvoir: Environnements et politiques* [Ecological Power: Environments and Policies], Paris: La découverte, 1994, 9–15.
2. J. Habermas, *L'espace public. Archéologie de la publicité comme dimension constitutive de la société bourgeoise* [Public space], Paris: Payot, 1993.
3. We use the term of career in the sense given by Erving Goffman. It means the moral aspect of the career and its impact of the personality and on the representation's system of an individual. See E. Goffman, *Asiles : études sur la condition sociale des malades mentaux et autres recluse* [Asylum], Paris: Editions de Minuit, 1990, 179–80.
4. For a parallel argument, see P. Pavlinek and J. Pickles, *Environmental Transitions: Post-Communist Transformations and Ecological Defense in Central and Eastern Europe*, London: Routledge, 2000.
5. See M. Vaněk, *'Nedalo se tady dýchat. Ekologie v českých zemích v letech 1968 až 1989'* [It was impossible to breathe here: The ecology in the Czech countries from 1968 to 1989], Praha: Ústav pro soudobé dějiny AV ČR, 1996 and D. Zajoncová, *'TIS, Svaz pro ochranu přirody, krajiny a lidi. Dobrovolná ochrana přirody v období totality'*, Oborová prace: faculty of philosophy, Masaryk University in Brno.
6. See M. Damohorský, 'Vývojové tendence Českého svazu ochránců přírody' [The trends of ČSOP], in M. Potůček, M. Purbráqkek and P. Háva, *'Analýza*

*událostí veřejné politiky v České republice'* [The Analysis of public policies in the CR], *Institut sociologických studií*, FSV UK, Prague, 1994, 117–37.

7. It was the same case with the Panrussian Society for the protection of nature (VOOP). It was founded in 1924, but took a soviet form in the 1950s, while it was created on the pattern of the European scholarly societies from the nineteenth century.

8. See H. Librová, *Sociální potřeba a hodnota krajiny* [The social importance and value of the landscape], Brno: Blok, 1987.

9. *Naši přirodou*,1, 1987, 22.

10. L. Sochor, 'Peut-on parler de la "société civile" dans les pays du bloc sovié-tique?' [Can we talk about civil society in countries of the soviet bloc?], *Communisme*, 8, 1985, 79–80; M. Molnar, *La démocratie se lève à l'Est, Société civile et communisme en Europe de l'Est: Pologne et Hongrie* [Democracy wakes up in the East: Civil society and Communism in Eastern Europe; Poland and Hungary], Paris : Presses Universitaires de France, 1990.

11. Ivan Dejmal, ecologist, former dissident, founder of the *Ecological Bulletin*, of the Ecological Society in 1989 and co-founder of the Society for the sustainable development in 1992, the second minister of the Environment, interview, 22 October 2004, Prague.

12. Vaněk, op. cit., p. 258.

13. See P. Pavlinek and J. Pickles, *Environmental Transitions*, 2000, for a detailed treatment of these environmental movements in Northern Bohemia prior to and after 1989.

14. *The beauty of our house*, Review of the ČSOP, founded in 1904 and republished from 2001.

15. See S. Tarrow, *Democracy and Disorder: Protest and Politics in Italy, 1965-1975*, Oxford: Clarendon Press, 1989.

16. We can mention the Department of Ecology and Environment at the Faculty of Agriculture in the Charles University in Prague and the Department of Environmentalism at the Faculty of Social Sciences in the Masaryk University in Brno.

17. Ministries of Environment were created in Poland in 1971 and in Hungary in 1988.

# 12
# Informal Practice, Cultural Capital and Politics in the Czech Republic, Slovenia, Bulgaria and Romania

*Åse B. Grødeland*

## Introduction

A key feature of communism was the organization of society into formal and informal spheres. Formally, communist society was defined by a vast number of laws and rules and regulations, and the economy was regulated by short-term and long-term plans. As laws were frequently idealistic – and consequently also often unrealistic[1] – and plans (carrying the status of law) were often too taut to be implemented, informality became a useful tool to circumvent the former and secure fulfilment of the latter. It was also used by the general public as a strategy for coping with everyday life: having a contact in the right place gave access to consumer goods that were in short supply and otherwise impossible to obtain. Finally, informality was used to gain privileges such as the right to study at a good university or to secure easy military service, a good position or nice housing.[2]

Transition has removed some of the purposes for which informal practices were used during communism, as the planned economy has been replaced by the market and the shortages that were so widespread before 1989 have been replaced by (relative) abundance.[3] Besides, the emphasis on the rule of law has largely sought to enhance formal at the expense of informal society.[4] Consequently, to the extent that informal practice in communist states was a response to specific systemic circumstances and situations rather than a part of the national culture, one would expect it to gradually disappear as a result of transition.

There is, however, also the possibility that transition as such has produced circumstances that either require or encourage informal responses. Politicians and business people in East Central and Southeast Europe have on numerous occasions successfully manipulated – in some cases ignored altogether – laws and regulations to their advantage.[5] Some observers of post-communist states see informality primarily as a result of transition.[6] For example, Ledeneva has argued that 'it is not that the components of the rule of law are absent. Rather, the ability of the rule of law to function coherently has been subverted by a powerful set of practices that has evolved organically in the post-communist milieu.'[7] A Romanian lawyer provides one explanation: 'as a jurist, I have to confess that I feel totally helpless in front of this avalanche of laws, especially when it is about adapting to a completely new system that is foreign to every one of us...' (CoE-2, Ro[8]).

Transition has affected post-communist states in East Central and Southeast Europe differently. First, while all these states have introduced markets and Western-style democracy, the number of transitions they have experienced varies either as a direct result of the collapse of communism or shortly after, and some gained their independence as a result of war. Thus, general economic and political reforms have been accompanied by post-war reconstruction and statebuilding. Finally, several post-communist states in East Central and Southeast Europe applied for EU membership in the late 1990s and immediately after embarked on a lengthy and demanding process of implementing institutional and legal changes as required by the EU. These all have important consequences for the future of informal practices in both politics and the economy.

This chapter focuses on the Czech Republic, Slovenia, Bulgaria and Romania, each of which has introduced a market economy, moved from one-party rule to democratic rule and implemented the *acquis communautaire*. The Czech Republic and Slovenia joined the EU in 2004 and Bulgaria and Romania in early 2007. Unlike Bulgaria and Romania, the Czech Republic and Slovenia did not exist as independent national states prior to the collapse of communism. Slovenia gained independence in 1990, having fought a brief war with Serbia. The Czech Republic became independent in 1992, following the peaceful dissolution of Czechoslovakia.

Second, the timing of transition differs amongst post-communist states. In Slovenia, for instance, economic restructuring dates back to the early 1980s and following Slovenian independence, was continued by the very same people who originally initiated and implemented it. In

Czechoslovakia the communists were not only voted out of office but also prevented from holding any positions of significance as a result of lustration. Although the colour of government alternated in the 1990s, both the conservatives and the social democrats emerged from Obcanske Forum – the very movement that toppled the communist regime – and both were equally committed to reform.

Reform in Bulgaria and Romania, by contrast, was carried out partly by 'rapidly reformed' communists and partly by a politically inexperienced opposition – both of whom lacked the necessary political mandate to implement radical reform. As a consequence, in Bulgaria the state of the economy deteriorated during the 1990s, culminating in an economic crisis in 1996. During this period, Romania was ruled by 'reformed communists' who were – at least initially – not so eager to introduce adequate and efficient reform; consequently reform progressed much more slowly in Romania than elsewhere.

Third, the impact of reform has to some extent been conditioned by the pace and sequences of transition. While Slovenia and the Czech Republic were able to put the most difficult initial stage of transition behind them relatively quickly, Bulgaria and Romania were still recovering from the worst effects of economic reform when the EU accession process started. Moreover, Slovenes and Czechs were much more exposed to the West during communism than Bulgarians and Romanians. Consequently, they were more familiar with the economic and political models they were emulating and therefore also more willing to endure a period of hardship while implementing these models.[9] West European investors were also much more willing to invest in the Czech Republic and Slovenia than in the other two countries.[10]

While the communist experience or transition may explain informal behaviour in post-communist states, it may also be the case that informal practices can be interpreted in terms of more deeply embedded practices associated with 'national culture', shaped by historical events and social norms that are fairly resistant to change.[11] If informal practice is *embedded in a country's historical past* – i.e., is a part of the wider national culture – then it is unlikely to change significantly as one political and economic system is replaced by another one. If this is the case, informal practices during both communism and transition may simply reflect the national culture as applied within different political, economic and social contexts.[12]

If, on the other hand, informal practices are *functional* – i.e., if they have emerged as a response to the institutional and legislative shortcomings of communism or the disruptions caused by transition – then one may expect them to gradually wither away as 'chaos' is replaced by institutional order and clear rules and regulations allowing for the formal solution of problems. In other words, one would expect informality to be less extensive in countries with a (relatively) stable institutional, legal and economic setting than in countries whose institutional and legal setting is less stable and whose economies are weaker. The need for informal coping strategies as a means by which to cope with transition may therefore be more pronounced in Bulgaria and Romania than in Slovenia and the Czech Republic.

Finally, it should be noted that informality is by no means a feature typical only of transitional post-communist societies. There is also considerable evidence of informality in old Western-style democracies. In such democracies informal practices are often encouraged – for instance in businesses to enhance efficiency, although they occasionally also produce negative effects, such as corruption.[13] However, conventional wisdom seems to assume that stable democracies – unlike states in transition – are in a better position to address such negative effects, given that they are characterized by less red tape, more active civil societies, a better informed public and a stronger commitment to the rule of law. Certainly, opportunities for harmful informal behaviour are more limited and sanctions more likely (and potentially more serious) than is currently the case in transitional post-communist states.

This chapter seeks to establish: (a) whether informal practices in post-communist states have evolved in response to transition and the problems they cause, whether they have been carried over from communism or whether they have their roots in pre-transition political culture, and (b) whether informal practices are less widespread in Slovenia and the Czech Republic than in Bulgaria and Romania. It does so by providing examples of how informal practices manifest themselves in politics, i.e., of how efforts are made to influence politicians more generally and decisions made by elected political bodies in particular, presenting partial findings from 80 in-depth interviews with various politicians carried out in Prague, Ljubljana, Sofia and Bucharest during the winter of 2003–4.

The interviews were carried out as part of a three-year project investigating informal relations not only in politics, but also in public procurement and the judiciary in the Czech Republic, Slovenia, Bulgaria and Romania. The project, funded by the Norwegian Council of Research (award no 156856/730), was carried out by the Norwegian Institute for Urban and Regional Research in collaboration with Centre for Social and Economic Strategies at Charles University/GfK-Prague (Czech Republic), Faculty of Police and Security Studies, University of

Maribor/CATI (Slovenia), Vitosha Research (Bulgaria) and Romanian Academic Society/Gallup (Romania).[14]

## Contacts, informal cultures and informal networks

A study conducted by Miller, Grødeland and Koshechkina[15] in the late 1990s suggested that informal practices in local government institutions in post-communist states were widespread. We have no reason to believe that their use is any less common in politics – at both high and low levels.

Informal influence in politics may be exerted in a number of different ways. Informal outcomes may be sought through the lobbying of individual MPs or non-elected party representatives, or through the funding of political parties in return for political influence. Individuals or groups of individuals linked together either formally (in a formal network or an interest group), or informally (for instance in an informal network), who engage in lobbying may simply present a number of arguments in support of their agendas, may offer some incentive in return for specific outcomes, or may try to pressure politicians into complying with their wishes. They may also approach politicians directly themselves or indirectly through a contact. The contact may know the politician(s) personally or may be particularly skilled in the art of lobbying – and thus also in a better position to influence the latter.

We are primarily interested in finding out *how* informal influence is exerted in politics – i.e., in the end result of informal efforts – and in direct as well as indirect influences. We have therefore found it useful to approach the subject by focusing on the use of contacts and informal networks in this sector. There are numerous definitions of both 'contacts' and 'informal networks'. We define a 'contact' as 'a person who is able to and willing to help someone' and an 'informal network' as 'an informal circle of people able to and willing to help each other'. People linked together in an informal network derive some benefit from interacting with other people in the network. Therefore, they have an interest in maintaining the network over time and a sense of obligation towards other people in it.

People who make use of such contacts and networks often do so with a view to deriving some benefit – for instance to solve a problem, to speed up an official procedure or for personal gain. A contact may be approached on an on-off basis to solve a specific problem or promote a certain outcome, or repeatedly and over time. In many such interactions, there is an element of reciprocity involved in the sense that the person who seeks the assistance of a contact normally offers something in return, either immediately or at some point in the future. A failure to offer something in return may result in the loss of the contact and one therefore has a sense of obligation towards him/her to return the favour rendered.

The two terms – as defined above – are not mutually exclusive: a contact may of course also be part of one or more informal networks. Similarly, people linked together in informal networks may resort to 'contacts' outside their networks. A contact may convey a request on behalf of one individual or a group of individuals. An informal network may convey a request on behalf of, or through, several people linked together in the network or on behalf of one single individual. Our definitions of contacts and informal networks therefore do not allow us to distinguish between the individual and the collective. They do, however, allow us to distinguish between requests made directly by an individual or a group of indivduals linked together either formally or informally, on the one hand, and requests conveyed indirectly through a contact on behalf of an individual or a group of individuals linked together either formally or informally, on the other. The distinction is also useful in that contacts are often sought on an on-off basis for solving one particular problem or issue, whereas informal networks are linked together by people whose shared interests are usually more long-term.

It also makes sense to distinguish between individual contacts and informal networks in terms of social capital: although a contact may be a very powerful individual with access to considerable financial and/or other resources, and for this reason may be highly influential, the informal network is able to draw on the collective resources of all the people it links together. This, in turn, gives informal networks an advantage in terms of influence. The distinction between contacts and informal networks thus allows us not only to study informal practices as such; it also allows us to study different aspects of the manner in which informality manifests itself in key areas of society.

Contacts and informal networks are in themselves neither positive nor negative. Both can be used for legitimate or illegitimate purposes. To the extent they are used for legitimate purposes, they may help people gain something to which they are entitled by law – for instance publicly available information, assistance from public offices and the like. Informal networks may also facilitate trust and professionalism in society, as people linked together in the network often work within one singular branch (for instance business or politics), are usually well qualified and know they can rely on each other. However, informal networks may also be used for more clandestine purposes, such as giving people access to something to which they are not entitled, undermining fair competition and professionalism in society and promoting illegitimate interests, thus facilitating corruption.

## Methodology

Informal networks are usually investigated through case studies of concrete institutions and the link between people working in these institutions. The bulk of these studies focus on information flows in business companies with the aim of improving efficiency, though studies have also been undertaken on how businesses enhance their profitability through informal networks.[16] Network theory has also been applied to investigate informal links at the political level.[17] The latter usually requires access to detailed information such as media footage, telephone or meeting logs, which are difficult to obtain, or they call for direct observation – even participation – over time. An added drawback with the case study approach is that, although it may generate very detailed and accurate information about one network, it fails to put the activities of this network in a broader context.

In this chapter, I am primarily interested in the ways in which contacts and informal networks manifest themselves in society more generally, and in politics in particular. Second, I deal with common informal as opposed to formal practices in these sectors. And third, I focus on the negative aspects of informal practices and specifically on corruption. Detailed case studies on these issues are not feasible and so, for my present purposes, I deal with qualitative data analysed by a combination of qualitative and quantitative methods. This has the added advantage of allowing me to deal more systematically and in a more representative manner with the qualitative part of the study.[18]

Work on the project commenced in March 2003 and was completed in March 2006. Data for the project was collected in three stages: 1) in-depth interviews; 2) roundtable discussions and 3) national quota-based surveys (N=600 × 4). The in-depth interviews and roundtable discussions were completed in late 2003, early 2004 and the summer of 2004, and the national surveys were carried out in 2005. We conducted a total of 360 structured, open-ended in-depth interviews – 90 interviews per country with nine categories of respondents. Half of these interviews were carried out with respondents operating at the national level, whereas the other half were carried out at the regional (capital) level to allow for comparison of informal practice at different administrative levels.

More specifically the following categories of respondents were interviewed: 1) elected representatives; 2) public procurement officials; 3) prosecutors and judges; 4) national business representatives; 5) international business representatives; 6) political party representatives in charge of party finances; 7) media representatives; 8) national and international NGOs; and 9) EU and Council of Europe representatives and national government officials working in the field of anti-corruption. Each interview lasted for approximately one hour and was conducted in the local language by professional interviewers. All interviews were carried out according to a pre-prepared interview guide, consisting of five main sections: 1) general views on the rule of law; 2) general views on the use of contacts; 3) general views on informal networks; 4) personal exposure to and use of contacts and informal networks; and 5) general views on how to strengthen the positive aspects of networks while limiting their negative aspects.

English language transcripts of the interviews were coded in QSR NUD*IST (version 4) – a software for qualitative data analysis – according to a detailed coding scheme consisting of more than 60 nodes (or coding categories) and sub-nodes. The text unit – the basic unit to be coded – was defined as a respondent's answer to a question, starting when the respondent started to speak and finishing when the respondent either stopped talking or was interrupted by the interviewer. Some double-coding did occur in cases where the respondent's answer to a question addressed issues covered by more than one node. In some cases, respondents provided answers to one question when answering others. In such cases, more than one answer from one and the same respondent was coded at the same node. Some respondents failed to answer all the questions. The total number of text units (N) in the tables below therefore does not always correspond to the total number of respondents interviewed. Once the data set had been coded, the total number of text units coded at each node was recorded and percentages were calculated. This allowed for the creation of tables based on the numerical findings from the four national data sets qualitative (N=90 per country).

We also wanted to establish (a) whether there were any major differences between the nine categories of respondents interviewed, within each country; and (b) whether there were any major differences between these categories across countries. For this purpose we created nine independent variables – one for each category of respondents included in the project.

All statements made by all respondents belonging to the public procurement category were coded at a 'public procurement node', all statements made by all respondents from the national business category were coded at a 'national business node', and so on. Each independent variable was cross-tabulated against all the dependent variables (nodes and sub-nodes)[19] and the total number of text units retrieved from each cross-tabulation put into tables.

Analysing qualitative data statistically is in itself not sufficient, however. To give an example, several respondents may hold the view that informal networks are more common now than they were before 1989. But they may have different opinions as to in what way informal networks are more common now and why this is the case. It is, therefore, necessary to combine the statistical findings with a content analysis of what the respondents actually said. Findings below were generated from this combined analysis: numerical findings are presented in table form[20] and 'illustrated' with verbatims from the in-depth interviews.

## Politics and requests for assistance

Analysis shows that contacts and informal networks are frequently used in politics in both East Central and Southeast Europe.[21] To find out how they are used, we asked the politicians several questions about their personal experiences. One of these was what types of requests they had received from people. By phrasing the question in such a way it appeared less intrusive to the respondent, but it also allowed us to investigate how common were requests for favours compared with more legitimate types of requests, such as access to publicly available information or help to get something to which one is entitled by law.

Czech respondents reported that they primarily received requests for something legal or for favours, Slovenian and Bulgarian respondents were mostly approached for favours, and Romanian respondents received requests for information, something legal or favours in roughly the same measure (with requests for information being slightly more common than requests for favours) (Table 12.1).

In *Slovenia* and *Romania* requests for information were often made by people who either did not know how to obtain, or were unable to obtain, the information they needed from elsewhere. Such requests appear to be a left-over from communism: 'many times the problem is that they are not informed about what they are entitled to...a certain class of people are still so uninformed that they do not know their way around,

*Table 12.1*   Type of requests received by the respondent (in per cent)

|  | Czech Republic | Slovenia | Bulgaria | Romania |
|---|---|---|---|---|
| Requests for information | 9 | 36 | 8 | 35 |
| Requests for something legal | 36 | 23 | 28 | 31 |
| Requests for favours | 36 | 40 | 57 | 27 |
| Other /Don't know | 18 | 2 | 8 | 8 |
| N= | (11) | (53) | (53) | (26) |

*Note*: N=the total number of text units. Each text unit represents an answer to a question given by one respondent. As decimals are rounded up or down to the nearest whole number, numbers do not always add up to 100.

they do not know how to get information, how to use the internet, how to communicate with officials, etc.' (El-r-3, Sl).

In all countries people requesting something legal generally sought assistance to obtain something to which they were entitled by law. *Bulgarians* and *Romanians* frequently turned to politicians because they were unable to obtain their legal rights by following normal, regular procedures – mostly due to the slowness of public administration. Such requests therefore appear to be a response primarily to transition: 'some simply can't get what they're entitled to the regular way' (PP-4, Bu); 'usually I am approached by people that did not get the answers they were entitled to obtain, or that did not receive any answer. In these cases I go and ask what is happening with the different issues' (El-r-2, Ro); and 'often people want my help to break the bureaucratic barriers' (El-r-10, Ro).

Some of the *Bulgarian* respondents found it difficult to draw a line between legitimate and illegitimate requests for information. In *Bulgaria*, *Romania* and the *Czech Republic* requests for which the requester felt that he or she was legally entitled were also sometimes masked requests for favours: '...the greater part of the requests is of that nature...' (PP-1, Bu); 'they are asking for some advantages. Sometimes it is really hard to tell what is an advantage and what they are entitled to by law' (PP-6, CzR).

Requests to speed up official procedures were common in all countries, though somewhat more so in *Bulgaria* and *Romania*: 'people have often turned to me with a request for something they are entitled to by law and yet they did so because they wanted to save both time and money' (PP-7, Bu); 'and there were the requests when people were asking for something they were entitled to by law but wanted to get faster' (El-r-4, Ro).

*Table 12.2*  Whether respondent has received requests for favours (in per cent)

|  | Czech Republic | Slovenia | Bulgaria | Romania |
|---|---|---|---|---|
| Has received requests for favours | 95 | 84 | 96 | 87 |
| Has not received requests for favours | 5 | 13 | – | 9 |
| Other/Don't know | – | 3 | 4 | 4 |
| N= | (19) | (31) | (24) | (23) |

*Note*: N=the total number of text units. Each text unit represents an answer to a question given by one respondent. As decimals are rounded up or down to the nearest whole number, numbers do not always add up to 100.

## Requests for favours

As shown above, elected representatives and political party representatives in all countries were frequently approached for favours. When specifically asked whether they had received requests for favours a large majority of the respondents in all countries included in our project answered that they had (Table 12.2).

Some respondents in the *Czech Republic* said that they were not often approached with requests. Those that were, however, pointed out that requests were often similar to those they received during communism. To some extent this was also the case in *Slovenia* and *Bulgaria*: 'I meet people who believe the function of the MP is something like that of the regional party secretary years ago under communism. They are convinced that this person (the MP) is omnipotent and can fix everything...' (El-r-4, CzR); 'people turn to you because they think that you can influence the judiciary, police and administrative bodies, to change some laws or (secure a) different interpretation of them, anything...' (El-r-2, Sl); 'sometimes...people come to slander their superior, they...want to get rid of him...' (El-r-3, Bu).

The most frequent type of request in *Slovenia* and *Bulgaria* was requests for assistance to obtain jobs. Such requests were usually made by ordinary people: 'requests mainly and most often relate to employment...' (PP-1, Sl); 'they relate to employment, because it is difficult to get – especially employment in Ljubljana, at the coast and maybe in Maribor and Celje'(PP-2, Sl); 'sometimes they think that because you are a person with a high-ranking position you can for example call a company and ask them to employ someone – such things' (El-r-2, Sl); 'in view of the high unemployment rate, most of the requests I have received are connected with finding a job for someone' (PP-2, Bu).

Requests to help speed up official procedures and to facilitate contact with other people were also fairly common in these two countries: 'requests refer to certain procedures that they wish to speed up, also to gain certain rights, for example scholarships...' (PP-7, Sl); 'most often they would like to speed up a procedure that would happen anyway if they would wait for a while' (El-r-8, Sl); 'of course there are also a lot of requests for contacts with people who hold important positions' (PP-7, Sl); 'the majority are those who want you to introduce them to somebody else...only one phone call of mine can open the doors for them – and after that it is up to them' (PP-1, Bu).

Other requests were less innocent, such as intervening in lawsuits, securing particular outcomes from state bodies or facilitating changes in, or favourable interpretations of, legislation and formal rules. Such requests were fairly common in *Bulgaria* and *Romania*: 'many people do not realise that they are asking (about) illegal things. They think it is their right to accomplish certain outcomes' (PP-10, Ro); 'people are usually (more) interested in solving their problems and less in what the law forecasts' (El-r-5, Ro); 'others have other types of requests – if it is possible to "bend" the law or find the right legal loophole to resolve their problem, because there's always some legal way of doing it' (PP-4, Bu); 'there are requests that are not granted, for instance, for money or for achieving a certain position...people mostly ask me to interfere in lawsuits...' (El-r-3, Bu).

Other respondents, especially those in *Bulgaria* and *Romania*, were approached for advantages of some sort: 'there are cases when they request something which they can only receive through the protection of a politician' (PP-5, Bu); 'personal profit – these are probably the most frequent requests...' (El-r-5, Bu); 'the interventions appear in case of a competition: someone wants my help because he considers himself better than his competitors' (El-r-10, Ro). However, not all elected representatives were considered equally useful to approach by the general public and, even if they were, many requests simply did not reach the representative in question: 'in order to reach me, one has to come through one or several links. And I guess I get to hear only about a few such requests...usually such kinds of requests are stopped on the way' (El-r-6, Ro).

That many people face serious hardship also means that there was some understanding between our respondents and those making the requests: 'having in mind how hard people's lives have become, we cannot judge them (i.e., people) for the fact that they try to solve their problems through contacts more and more often. They turn to me with their various requests. Generally they deal with finding a job or arranging a meeting with other politicians on whom the settlement of a major issue depends – property issues, business problems' (PP-1, Bu).

### Requests made by informal networks

When asked about general requests, the respondents spoke about direct, individual requests. However, we also asked them what kind of requests they received from informal networks. Some of the *Czech* politicians thought such requests were non-existent or rare and those who had not received any did not consider themselves important enough. Other respondents claimed that such networks were often trying to get favourable business deals for themselves, although they frequently tried to cover their requests up as something beneficial to the community: 'in 80 to 90 per cent (of the cases) it is always about personal interest...' (El-r-3, CzR); 'somebody comes with sort of a generally beneficial plan to build something, for example a playground, and then you find out that he is linked to other people, who for all kinds of reasons, have an interest in the construction. It is difficult to see through it...' (El-r-10, CzR).

Most of the *Slovenian* respondents said they had been approached by informal networks, but they did not go into the details. Those who did provide specific information referred mainly to economic networks, but also to business networks that were looking for favourable business deals. Some politicians were more frequently approached than others: 'for example construction lobbies' (El-r-7, Sl); 'this relates more to my position as mayor than to my position as a member of parliament, because as mayor you make the budget and you also have a say in public procurement... the mayor is under more pressure... In the case of... parliament it is more (about) legislation, while here it is business... there are a lot of companies that operate in this region and of course they want business and of course they try to influence you in one way or another, so they are using their contacts, their network...' (El-r-1, Sl).

The *Bulgarian* respondents who said that they had been approached by informal networks claimed that these were primarily financial networks, networks of friends, or old-style communist networks: 'it happens mostly when you talk with representatives of the business sector... you know that he has "higher" protection. Then you have no choice but to be useful for him and solve the case as soon as possible' (El-r-6, Bu); 'such a person emphasizes that he knows so-and-so...' (El-r-4, Bu); 'representatives of the gas distribution companies have approached me. They wanted to get certain budget preferences and to retain their old positions...' (El-r-2, Bu).

In *Romania* formal networks, such as trade unions, sometimes use informal means to try to influence politicians. Informal networks do not always clearly state what they want to achieve or their stated motives differ from their real motives. Occasionally they make life difficult, even for MPs: 'it is possible that some persons who ask for something are in fact informers. I think that this institution of informers remains in the blood of the Romanians' (PP-3, Ro); 'at one moment I was responsible for offering solutions for the land restitution requests based on law no. 10. I had solved some requests favourably, but some person who wished to block these restitutions appealed to another connection and managed to stop the process. So the people who were to receive the land had to go to court to solve their requests' (El-r-4, Ro).

### Attempts at influencing the politicians

As can be seen from Table 12.3, a majority of the statements made by the respondents in all countries suggested that people requesting something from them usually tried to exert influence one way or the other.

In the *Czech Republic* and *Slovenia* attempts at influencing the respondents tended to be rather 'innocent', in the form of persuasion or friendly behaviour: 'of course they try to influence me. They try to explain... how very important it is... I cannot say that when I helped somebody I was not invited to some of their actions, where they gave me some refreshment. That happened a few times... friendly behaviour...' (PP-6, CzR); 'they try to influence mainly through persuasion. I only experience this' (PP-5, Sl). In some cases, however, those seeking assistance from

*Table 12.3*   Attempts at influencing the respondent when making requests (in per cent)

|  | Czech Republic | Slovenia | Bulgaria | Romania |
|---|---|---|---|---|
| Attempts to influence the respondent | 78 | 77 | 70 | 82 |
| No attempts to influence the respondent | 11 | 18 | 27 | 12 |
| Other/Don't know | 11 | 5 | 3 | 6 |
| N= | (9) | (22) | (30) | (17) |

*Note*: N=the total number of text units. Each text unit represents an answer to a question given by one respondent. As decimals are rounded up or down to the nearest whole number, numbers do not always add up to 100.

*Slovenian* politicians appealed to people known to, or close to, them and occasionally there were threats. As a rule, however, requesters were respectful of MPs and attempts to influence them with bribes were rare: 'they try to get the (desired) solution also through other people...' (El-r-1, Sl); 'friendship...promises of privileges and non-material...contra-favours, etc.' (El-r-8, Sl); 'they said that I will benefit financially if I help them' (El-r-7, Sl); 'they actually threatened (me) and demanded that I pose a question in parliament to the minister...' (El-r-5, Sl).

Efforts to influence respondents in *Bulgaria* frequently appeared to be motivated by desperation. There were displays of emotion, appeals to family members of the politicians and flattery. More worryingly, however, illegitimate means such as bribes or threats were equally common and were often successful: 'well, some people weep...many perform dramatic scenes, they sob, cry...become hysterical and bring children or sick people with them. Other people who know members of my family go to them and try to influence me through them' (PP-3, Bu); 'they have...offered me favours: "if you do this, I will do that"...' (El-r-7, Bu); 'people threatened me, saying that if I failed to agree with their political proposals, "you will see what will happen to you...you won't see your family (again)..." I refused to comply' (El-r-2, Bu).

In *Romania*, stories of attempts at influencing the respondents in legitimate ways were few and far between. Most respondents referred to cases of friendly behaviour, attempted bribery, threats or even black-mail: 'in some cases different persons tried to persuade me (to solve the same problem)' (El-r-4, Ro); 'they pledge for themselves, use persuasion, behave friendly, try to offer me favours' (El-r-1, Ro); 'they...promise political support...' (PP-1, Ro); 'I was for example threatened. Starting with SMS, letters and oral threats. Even a fellow MP has threatened me with actions of the criminal world...' (PP-3, Ro).

## Politicians and their responses to requests for assistance

Informal networks and powerful and influential people[22] are active in politics in Central East and Southeast Europe, mostly seeking to obtain illegitimate favours of some sort, especially in Bulgaria and Romania. What is more, requests are often accompanied by pressure. When talking about how requests they had received were accompanied by offers of payment or threats, several respondents added that they had of course not accepted the payment offered or given in to the threats made. When specifically asked what requests they would turn down, a majority of the respondents in all countries said they would not accept requests

*Table 12.4*   Respondent's response to requests made by powerful and influential people (in per cent)

| | | | | |
|---|---|---|---|---|
| More difficult to say no to powerful and influential people | 33 | 33 | 44 | 30 |
| Equally difficult to say no | 58 | 29 | 22 | 50 |
| Less difficult to say no to powerful and influential people | 8 | 24 | 6 | – |
| Other/Don't know | – | 14 | 28 | 20 |
| N= | (12) | (21) | (18) | (10) |

*Note*: N = the total number of text units. Each text unit represents an answer to a question given by one respondent. As decimals are rounded up or down to the nearest whole number, numbers do not always add up to 100.

that were in any way illegal. Yet almost one-third or more of the statements made by respondents in all countries indicated that it would be more difficult to turn down requests made by powerful and influential people than requests made by others (Table 12.4). More than two-thirds of the statements made by the respondents in all countries indicated that they found it difficult to say no such people. Some of the *Czech* and *Slovene* respondents thought it was more difficult to turn down these requests because people tended to respect authority and power for fear of repercussions: 'I would say yes, because each person would automatically think that the next time this person might obstruct you from something...' (PP-8, Sl).

*Czech* and *Bulgarian* respondents indicated that they might need the assistance of those making the requests at some point in the future, implying that it would be difficult to get this assistance if they ignored their requests: 'unfortunately it is true (that it is more difficult to turn down such requests), because you may need some help from the influential person in the future...' (PP-7, CzR); 'if it concerns highly placed persons, sometimes you have no choice. You have to help. It is a mutual process. Doing a favour means establishing a contact with a person who might be useful to you at a later stage. In our circles we help each other, it is a normal thing' (El-r-6, Bu).

According to quite a few of the *Czech* and *Bulgarian* respondents it was more difficult to turn down requests made by powerful and influential people as they were better informed and also more persistent than others. *Czech* and *Romanian* respondents also suggested that the consequences of turning down such requests might be rather unpleasant, although one of the Czechs thought it was possible to turn down such requests: '...the influential person can be unpleasant – pushing you in a much more unpleasant manner than the ordinary person' (El-r-8, CzR); 'an empowered person usually knows about the possibilities and when you must refuse, you have to explain in a very well argued way why you cannot do something. He didn't come to you by chance' (El-r-4, Bu); 'it is probably more difficult as these people often have influence over other people you need (in order) to perform your political activity...' (El-r-10, CzR); 'if I am approached by an influential person and I have to refuse him, of course then I think about all the possible consequences...if a certain action may cause me harm then I do not intervene' (El-r-7, Ro).

## The influence of informal networks in politics

As noted above, informal networks carry considerable clout (Table 12.5). Of course, this does not mean that politicians automatically comply with their wishes, although if politicians perceive informal networks as being influential their requests may be more successful.

*Czech, Bulgarian* and *Romanian* politicians thought informal networks actually did achieve a great deal although Romanian networks, in particular, were not necessarily perceived as being stable: 'I think that in the sphere of politics, informal networks are becoming increasingly active. Perhaps they underlie the process of disintegration of the political parties since theses and opinions carry increasingly less weight while the strength of informal contacts is acquiring much greater significance' (PP-2, Bu); 'they work extremely well...the interest circles are very tight and the high places are practically closed since no one from the outside may get in' (PP-8, Ro); 'yes, they are (influential). It is just that they do not last...' (PP-1, Ro).

*Table 12.5*   The influence of informal networks in the respondent's own sector (in per cent)

| | Czech Republic | Slovenia | Bulgaria | Romania |
|---|---|---|---|---|
| Informal networks are influential | 89 | 100 | 90 | 59 |
| Informal networks are not influential | – | – | 10 | 24 |
| Other | – | – | – | 12 |
| Don't know | 11 | – | – | 6 |
| N= | (9) | (20) | (20) | (17) |

*Note*: N=the total number of text units. Each text unit represents an answer to a question given by one respondent. As decimals are rounded up or down to the nearest whole number, numbers do not always add up to 100.

Some of the politicians we interviewed spoke about the influence of particular types of networks. Communist networks were thought to exert some influence in the *Czech Republic, Bulgaria* and *Romania*. In *Slovenia*, however, the influence of such networks has declined substantially: 'under communism there (were) nomenklatura networks…today, they are in hiding, but I am sorry to say they still have a very strong influence…' (El-r-2, CzR); 'there are at least two very visible such networks (in Romania): that of the former Securitate officers, and that of former Communists. Unfortunately for the others, they have been successful…for the last 14 years. And Iliescu[23] is the best proof of that: he has managed to occupy high positions for all this time…' (El-r-6, Ro); 'the former party networks have influence in the regional parliaments, mayors' offices, in the media, local business…' (Leg-9, Bu); 'I certainly believe that an informal network exists among political workers from the previous system. However, I think that this network includes only a small circle of people' (El-r8, Sl).

*Czech* respondents spoke about a network that had formed around former president Vaclav Havel and also about a cross-cutting network of MPs sitting on the same parliamentary committees. In most cases, however, they were hard to identify. *Slovenian* respondents spoke about networks of acquaintances and people who had studied together: 'The Prague Castle…(is) an example. Under Havel there used to be a network of friends that was influential and these people helped each other' (PP-2); 'due to their informal character it is hard to identify them. What connects them is common interest, not ideology' (PP-7, CzR); 'yes, different networks (are active in politics). Networks of acquaintances you have, whether through the political party, sports, interest activities, people that studied together (with you)…' (El-r-2, Sl); 'it is generally a mix of politics and business' (El-r-9, Sl).

Politicians in the *Czech Republic, Bulgaria* and *Romania* conceded that informal networks influenced the composition of party lists during elections. In *Bulgaria* and *Romania* networks also facilitated (political) employment, resulting in obligations that might later produce benefits: 'inside the party of which I am a member, in 90 per cent of the instances it is not the quality, skills and results that decide the positions on the list of candidates, but the network…' (El-r-3, CzR); 'old families do have serious influence (in our party) – they have their own elections, their own favourite candidates…the Jewish lobby has a serious influence in all political parties. The former special services also exert serious influence…' (El-r-3, Bu); 'some business structures and informal structures are moving up and seek to insert their people in local governments and thus in the future to try to define the activities of these local structures' (El-r-8, Bu).

The majority of statements made by respondents in the *Czech Republic* and *Slovenia* focused on the influence exerted by informal networks in terms of lobbying. Network influence in this area was considered to be particularly important, although *Bulgarians* made fewer references to lobbying: 'mainly (for) lobbying people. They mainly go to the parliament but also to our office, and it is generally known who has good contacts with whom, with which politician, and can influence him' (PP-2, CzR); 'you can see (it) from different activities that occur when laws are prepared and adopted... (for instance) the law on gambling: there they achieved a tax exemption of approximately 1 billion tolars a year... this does not happen in other sectors' (El-r-10, Sl); 'we help our supporters. We strive to help them when they need something, whether to make contact with someone or to implement some project of theirs' (PP-4, Bu).

Some *Bulgarian* respondents reported that in their country informal networks were also used for directly criminal purposes. One even went so far as to suggest that the networks operating in the political sphere are so powerful that they have captured the state: 'the political life in our country is practically governed and directed by various informal networks... it is not a secret that a great part of the politicians come to power with the votes and support of the local business. Those are bought seats, which you have to deserve later. So when they get to power then the real work begins. If you follow carefully what actions for example a municipal councillor has taken it will not be difficult to understand who he or she is working for. Those are well-known things and the worst is that nobody is even trying to cover them up' (PP-1, Bu).

Finally, as seen in Table 12.6, a majority of the statements made by our respondents suggested that informal networks facilitate corruption.[24]

*Table 12.6* Whether informal networks facilitate corruption (in per cent)

|  | Czech Republic | Slovenia | Bulgaria | Romania |
| --- | --- | --- | --- | --- |
| Facilitate corruption | 67 | 73 | 82 | 83 |
| Do not facilitate corruption | 11 | 14 | 9 | – |
| Other/Don't know | 22 | 14 | 9 | 17 |
| N= | (18) | (22) | (22) | (24) |

*Note*: N=the total number of text units. Each text unit represents an answer to a question given by one respondent. As decimals are rounded up or down to the nearest whole number, numbers do not always add up to 100.

## Conclusions

Politicians in East Central and Southeast Europe are frequently approached for favours, and not only by ordinary people (directly, as well as indirectly, through contacts), but also by informal networks. Ordinary people usually seek the assistance of politicians to solve their everyday problems. They request assistance to find a job or help to get rid of an annoying boss. Requests for favours, such as speeding up an official procedure or intervening in a lawsuit, are also fairly common. Elites and informal networks primarily seek business preferences and/or political influence.

There is also a difference in the manner in which the two convey their requests. Those representing informal networks are usually confident and direct. They make it clear to politicians whom they represent, frequently offer a counter-favour or payment in return for favourable outcomes, and if necessary they also use coercion. Not surprisingly, respondents found it easier to turn down requests made by ordinary people. However, politicians were not exclusively victims. They were able to exert considerable pressure on business for their own personal gain. More than two-thirds of the statements made by politicians as well as by other categories of respondents suggest that informal networks facilitate corruption, even in politics.

Our data suggest that ordinary people use informality as a coping strategy for dealing with excessive bureaucracy and complex rules and regulations brought about by transition. Contrary to what we expected, however, this approach appears to be widespread not only in Bulgaria and Romania but also in the Czech Republic and Slovenia. As such, the Czech Republic's and Slovenia's earlier adjustment to EU membership may not have made it easier for ordinary people to deal with official institutions, at least not in the short run. On the other hand, manifestations of informal practices in Bulgaria and Romania were more extensive and harmful than in the Czech Republic and Slovenia, suggesting that institutions, rules and regulations at the national level function better in the latter two countries where there is less scope for informal outcomes.

However, inefficient public administrations appear to be only part of the story. Politicians in all countries suggested that ordinary people frequently turn to their elected representatives and expect them to solve any odd problem they may have, often out of habit. During communism, party secretaries and elected representatives had the power to solve a wide range of issues. While the tasks of elected representatives have since changed, not everybody is aware of this. Less educated people, in particular, used to turn to party officials and elected representatives whenever they had a problem to solve and did not know exactly whom to turn to. For many of the same reasons, they now turn to elected representatives expecting them to help. In this context, at least, informal practices during the transition appear to be rooted in pre-transition political culture.

We did not come across any examples of informal practices that could be linked to the broader national culture of the countries included in our project. It could perhaps be argued that elites and informal networks seeking personal gain in politics are no different from elites and networks elsewhere, whether post-communist or not. In this sense, they may exhibit more general human values. While this may no doubt be the case, such behaviour may have different motivations in post-communist and Western societies. Quite a few judges and prosecutors interviewed as part of our project, particularly those in Bulgaria and Romania, argued that attitudes toward the law are shaped by both communist and pre-communist values; stealing from the state and circumventing laws, for example, are both deemed acceptable, particularly as laws are often interpreted as reflecting the interests of particular groups rather than the common good. Stealing from or in any other way harming other people, however, is widely condemned. Moreover, transition has provided people with more opportunities to break or circumvent laws. In this sense promoting personal interests informally may be easier to justify morally in post-communist states than in old democracies, particularly if the traditional roles played by informal networks – such as *bliski* networks in Bulgaria – no longer operate within codes and institutions that regulate individual and group norms and behaviour to the same extent as in the past.[25] Whether or not these processes and practices of informality will continue may well rest on the extent to which the processes of European Union harmonization and institutionalization begin to stand in for at least some of these group norms.[26]


## Endnotes

1. M. Goldman, *The Spoils of Progress: Environmental Pollution in the Soviet Union*, Cambridge: Massachusetts Institute of Technology, 1972.
2. Å. B. Grødeland, T. Y. Koshechkina and W. L. Miller, ' "Foolish to give and yet more foolish not to take", in-depth interviews with post-communist citizens on their everyday use of bribes and contacts', *Europe-Asia Studies* 50(4), June 1998, 649–75.
3. Though the average person's purchasing powers are still low.

4.  For an account of perceptions of the rule of law in East Central and Southeast Europe, see Å. B. Grødeland, 'Informal Networks and Corruption in the Judiciary: Elite Interview Findings from the Czech Republic, Slovenia, Bulgaria and Romania', Paper presented at World Bank conference on 'New Frontiers of Social Policy', Arusha, Tanzania, 12-15 December 2005, available at http://web.worldbank.org/.../0,,contentMDK:20692493~pagePK:2100 58~piPK:210062~theSitePK:244363,00.html

5.  For examples of corrupt politicians in East Central and Southeast Europe, see M. Brusis, I. Kempe and W. van Meurs, 'Central and Eastern Europe and the Baltic States. Political Corruption', in R. Hodess, T. Inowlocki and T. Wolfe (eds), *Transparency International. Global Corruption Report 2003*, London: Profile Books, 2003, pp. 181-82; Open Society Institute, EU Accession Monitoring Program, *Monitoring the EU Accession Process: Corruption and Anti-corruption Policy*, Budapest: Open Society Institute, 2002, pp. 106–8 and pp. 451–516.

6.  W. L. Miller, Å. B. Grødeland and T. Y. Koshechkina, *A Culture of Corruption? Coping with Postcommunist Government in Europe*, Budapest: Central European University Press, 2001.

7.  Ledeneva quoted in A. Mungiu-Pippidi, 'Informal Institutions and Societies. Post-Communist Modernization Strategies in East Central Europe', State-of-the-art paper for ECPR Research Group on Informal Institutions in Eastern Europe.

8.  Quotations are marked as follows: El-r (elected representative) and PP (political party representative); N-bus (representative of national – i.e. local company); I-bus (representative of international company); Med (media representative); NGO (NGO representative); Proc (public procurement official); Leg (judge or prosecutor); G-off (government official working in anti-corruption); EU (EU representative); CoE (Council of Europe representative). The number of the respondent is also indicated, as is the country in which the interview took place: CzR refers to interviews conducted in the Czech Republic, Sl refers to Slovenia, Bu refers to Bulgaria and Ro refers to Romania. CoE-2, Ro indicates that the respondent represents the Council of Europe, is respondent number 2 from this organization and based in Romania.

9.  For details, see Å. B. Grødeland and A. Aasland, 'Informality and Informal Practice in East Central and Southeast Europe', Paper prepared for 12 IACC, Guatemala, November 2006. The paper is available at the IACC web site: www.12iacc.org.

10.  Whereas Slovenia had considerable economic interactions with West European countries prior to the collapse of Yugoslavia, Czechoslovakia's economy was primarily geared towards COMECON. However, the country benefited from the '1968-factor', its radical break with communism in 1989 and its location in the middle of Europe, and soon started attracting foreign investments.

11.  What is more, changing such behaviour will require a level of consensus in society, a concerted effort on the part of the authorities, as well as a fairly long-term perspective. For a detailed account of historical and cultural factors that may explain informal relations in post-communist states, see Grødeland and Aasland (12 IACC).

12.  As the communist period lasted for some three generations in all countries included in this project, elements of the national culture may have been

co-opted into the communist culture. In Romania, for instance, Ceausescu frequently referred to 'socialist culture'. It is therefore possible that when people refer to the national culture, they may essentially be speaking about features typical of communism and vice versa. Informality during transition may also be motivated in part by the national culture, in part by the communist experience and in part by circumstances caused by transition.

13. See for instance F. Saliger, 'Korruption und Betrug durch Parteispenden', in *Neue juristische Wochenschrift*, 58(16), 2005, pp.1073–78; H. von Arnim (ed.), *Korruption – Netzwerke in Politik, Aemtern und Wirtschaft*, München: Knaur, 2003.

14. The project also had two international consultants: Dr A. Ledeneva (SSEES, University College London) and Dr H. Pleines (Forschungsstelle Osteuropa, Bremen).

15. Miller, Grødeland and Koshechkina (op. cit.).

16. See for instance M. J. Garmaise and T. J. Moskowitz, 'Informal Financial Networks: Theory and Evidence', in *The Review of Financial Studies*, 16(4), Winter 2003, 1007–40. Garmaise and Moskowitz used a dataset detailing brokerage activity in the US commercial real estate market for their study.

17. For a study mapping connections between former president of Peru, Fujimori, and representatives of the media and business interests in Peru, see L. Moreno Ocampo, 'Corruption and Democracy. The Peruvian Case of Montesinos', Paper presented at the 11th IACC, Seoul, 26 May 2003.

18. Whereas in-depth interviews are frequently used to study informal networks, surveys are less commonly used. While some more recent studies have made use of internet surveys to collect data, it is still a widely held view amongst people studying networks that surveys are better avoided. For an account of the former, see R. Cross, N. Nohria and A. Parker, 'Six Myths about Informal Networks – and how to overcome them', in *MIT Sloan Management Review*, Spring 2002, 67–75. D. J. Watts argues that surveys are not a very reliable way to obtain high-quality data on networks 'not only because people have a hard time remembering who they know without being suitably prodded, but also because two acquaintances may have quite different views of their relationship. So it can be hard to tell what is actually going on. The method also requires a lot of effort on behalf of the subjects and particularly the investigator. A much better approach is to record what it is that people actually do, who they interact with, and how they interact' (D. J. Watts, *Six Degrees: The Science of a Connected Age*, New York/London: W.W. Norton & Company, 2003, p. 26). As we are not interested in how people in networks are linked with each other, but more with their impact in the political sphere, in the judiciary and in public procurement, however, the flaws Watts refers to are not relevant to our study.

19. Each respondent's answer to a particular question was coded at the same node and treated as an independent variable.

20. As can be seen from some of the tables, the number for 'other/don't know' is in some cases quite high. This is not a result of people not having an opinion. Statements that did not fit into the coding scheme were coded as 'other' during initial coding.

21. For a fuller version of this chapter, see Å.B. Grødeland, '"Red Mobs", "Yuppies" and "Lamb Heads": Informal Networks and Politics in the Czech

Republic, Slovenia, Bulgaria and Romania', *Europe Asia Studies* 59(2), March 2007, 217–52.
22. Respondents tend to use the two terms interchangeably. For a detailed discussion, see *Europe–Asia Studies* 59(2), March 2007, 217–52.
23. Iliescu was elected as president for the National Salvation Front Council in December 1989 and was leader of the Provisional Council for National Unity from February to May 1990. In May 1990 he was elected president. He was re-elected in popular elections in October 1992 for a four-year period. From 1996 to 2000 he was Senator for the Social-Democratic Party and from 2000 to 2004 President of Romania. He was replaced as President of Romania in 2004 by the President of Democratic Party, Trajan Basescu.
24. For examples, see Grødeland in *Europe–Asia Studies* 59(2), March 2007, 217–52.
25. B. A. Cellarius, *In the Land of Orpheus: Rural Livelihoods and Nature Conservation in Postsocialist Bulgaria*, Madison: University of Wisconsin Press, 2004.
26. Given the relatively small sample of respondents, we cannot draw very firm conclusions based on findings from our in-depth interviews, although they were designed and organized in such a way that we have no reason to assume that they are not representative. Findings from the large-scale quota-based elite surveys that are currently being analysed should give us a better idea with regard to how representative the findings above are.

# 13
## Conclusion: State, Society and Hybrid Post-Socialist Economies

*John Pickles*

### Introduction

What happens when a world turns, when the very fabric of institutions, practices and the norms that sustains them shifts from one register to another? What are we to make of the tearing of a fabric that once bound lives and regions to a stabilized, hegemonic, economic regime? And precisely how is such a regime deterritorialized and recomposed, giving new meaning or opportunities to some and wreaking havoc on the lives and livelihoods of others? How are post-socialist economic subjects and spaces produced and how are we to understand the processes of recombination that restructure these subjects, spaces and the regional economic systems of which they are a part?

These are among the many challenges that have faced scholars of and policy-makers in post-socialist countries in Central and Eastern Europe since the 1980s. Economic stagnation and the eventual collapse of the bureaucratic centralist model of economic planning have given way to various forms of state withdrawal, privatization and re-composition of social forces. Private property and exchange relations have become more important drivers of economic lives. Economies have been re-institutionalized and re-socialized through the acceptance of coordination mechanisms and regulations resulting from European Union accession, the integration of financial institutions into international markets, and alignment of trade and industrial policies with those of broader European and international norms and requirements. EU accession has shaped the integration of regional production and trading networks, trade facilitation programmes have expanded and upgraded road and rail networks, expanded citizenship rights have invigorated inter-regional labour migration, and standardized property rights and banking systems have encouraged foreign direct and private investments in industry, services and personal property throughout the region. At the same time, local social forces and national (sometimes nationalist) governments have struggled to mediate the effects of these transnational institutions and norms. In some cases, state institutions have provided legislative and political support to local individuals, groups and sectors as they struggle to adjust to rapidly changing economic conditions and requirements. In other cases, whole sectors have been abandoned by the state. In some of these, such as in the Bulgarian tourist industry, workers have found that the very skills that once functioned as limits on occupational mobility in a market economy now provide them with enhanced opportunities. In other cases, struggles over resources have structured new forms of local and national power in less benign and less legal ways. The post-socialist economy has indeed been contested ground.

## Institutions and variation in post-socialist economies

*State and Society in Post-Socialist Economies* focuses primarily on the roles played by specific institutions and social practices in shaping the trajectories of democratization and economic restructuring of Central and Eastern Europe. The individual chapters speak to Max Weber's injunction that to understand 'the spirit of capitalism' we need to build up a picture of economic development from its integral and concrete pieces, rather than from an abstract and general model. Thus, in different ways, each chapter attends to the concrete specificities and economic complexities of post-socialist transformations. In so doing, each focuses on some specific set of instruments, policies, technologies, actors, social formations, and/or emerging regional systems, and each shows how these articulate with continental and global processes of harmonization and integration on the one hand and wrenching change and dislocation on the other. As the authors show so nicely, not all processes of harmonization and integration have the same results; lead industries in high value sectors are able to innovate and their workers are able to exercise newfound positional powers and capacities, while low-value sectors struggle to adapt to increasing global competition and see their unskilled workforce become less competitive in regional as well as international terms; in new joint-stock companies some insider owners struggle to hold on to their control against the broader tendencies of outsider stakeholder consolidation, while other insider owners see their interests aligning more with professional managers against external boards of directors; female workers in the Bulgarian tourist industry are better positioned than the more privileged male workers to mobilize their structural disadvantages under state socialism (confined to accounting and translation positions) into resources of opportunity in the post-socialist economy; and Central and Eastern European environmental activists continue to work in and through the state socialist institutions that provided relatively secure bases from which to act against the party state, now as they turn their attention to the ecological challenges of deregulated economies.

In these and other ways, the authors in this volume have focused on the concrete and often very plain details of institutional practice and social action that are shaping the post-socialist regional economies of Central and Eastern Europe. Each of the authors responds differently to Polanyi's (1944) challenge to move beyond the even then 'old-fashioned' theories of linear transition to capitalism, and instead they seek to map out sectorally, institutionally and geographically diverse trajectories of post-socialist economic development and the varieties of economic regime that have arisen. For some, European Union accession represents one pole of this issue, providing institutional support and pressure for common trajectories of change. But even here, as any observer of the new Member States at the European Parliament and Commission in Brussels will testify, there remains great variation in the ways in which the EU project is accepted and adopted in countries like Poland, Slovakia, or Romania.

## Economic governance, diverse trajectories and regional economies

What are the lessons of *State and Society in Post-Socialist Economies* for how we understand the role of these historical legacies, institutional specificity, and emerging forms and patterns of economic governance in Central and Eastern Europe? As Béla Greskovits suggests, there are 'reasons to doubt that the advanced societies evidently represent the future of less advanced economies either in a west-east context or specifically within the group of East European new EU-members'. Post-socialist economies have to be understood in terms of the industrial legacies of state socialism and the specific patterns of regional investments that were made at this time in heavy and light industries. These patterns were reworked by the market reforms of the 1990s, producing various levels of semi-core and semi-peripheral patterns of economic development organized around various combinations of heavy/light and complex/basic leading industrial sectors. These conditions and subsequent investment decisions by transnational corporations produced regionally distinctive socioeconomic regimes across Eastern Europe. There remain, however, serious constraints on industrial upgrading in the leading sectors of these reforming peripheral economies, where – unlike the historical situation in Western Europe – the state itself is more, not less, likely to become part of the developmental problem rather than its solution. The result, for Greskovits, is that Eastern European capitalism is more rather than less stable over time and may well represent 'a fairly permanent and self-sustaining configuration'.

The emergence of different, distinct and self-sustaining developmental models in Central and Eastern Europe poses real challenges for how we study reform economies. As Arjan Vliegenthart argues, the production of a specific type of Central and Eastern European capitalism can only be understood in the context of the combination of the legacies of the communist period, the process of privatization and the transnationalization of the state. By interrogating these in combination, the differential adoption of either Anglo-Saxon or continental European models of corporate governance does not have to be seen as leading to forms of economic and regional convergence with these models. As the case of the Czech Republic illustrates, the Czech state played a crucial role in securing the conditions for foreign investment and opening the economy. Initial efforts to control this process and generate a form of national capitalism and a specific post-socialist state regime (what Jan Drahokoupil refers to as the Klausian welfare national state (KWNS)) failed to reproduce itself in the late 1990s. The result was further rounds of deregulation and the production of a new state form (which he refers to as the Porterian workfare postnational regime (PWPR)) in which foreign capital came to play a much more central role. One consequence has been that capitalism with Czech characteristics has begun to converge with the other Visegrad-Four countries. But there is no necessity in this convergence. Instead, it has to be seen as a series of contingent attempts to solve specific problems of the post-socialist economy which, in turn, are producing a regionally specific mixture of national and transnational capital and a distinctive post-socialist model of 'embedded neoliberalism'.

Similar contingent struggles have been occurring at the level of the post-socialist enterprise, producing distinctive patterns of national corporate governance and diverse micro-models of corporate control. In Russian companies there is a particularly clear shift emerging from one form of corporate governance based on the initial redistribution of corporate stock and the dispersal of employee property through voucher privatization to one in which corporate ownership is being rapidly concentrated and insider control exercised by dominant owners who manage the company or closely oversee hired professional managers. While these emerging patterns of Russian corporate governance superficially appear to be similar to those in EU-oriented and globally oriented businesses, in practice Russian governance models exhibit quite different features that continue to be influenced in important ways by the interests of specific institutional stakeholders and the specificities of Russian historical and cultural formations. As with the Czech cases earlier, Russian corporate governance has been strongly influenced by the privatization process, by social networks and by government involvement, which in turn have resulted in a model that remains strongly shaped by the interest politics of stakeholders. Business integration and consolidation of ownership by strong external owners or shareholder groups are occurring and these, in turn, seem to be promoting a gradual separation of ownership and operational management. The dominant manager and worker ownership patterns of the early reform years are gradually being supplanted by external shareholders and ownership groups whose interests are increasingly better served by external control and delegated management. As a result, pressure is increasing for the state to create more effective and accessible legal institutions and regulate more transparent business practices.

Increasingly uniform patterns of corporate governance emerged across Central and Eastern Europe, particularly as the *acquis communautaire* were signed in preparation for EU accession. The harmonization of laws and regulations and the integration of economies across the region created a broader European economic space within which transaction costs have been rapidly reduced for all concerned. Nonetheless, as the essays in this volume have shown, the consequences for the political economic regimes across the region have been neither uniform nor expected. Instead, the liberalization and transnationalization of the economy have been shaped by national traditions, socialist institutional legacies and the existing structures of social power in ways that are more than incidental or transitional. Gerald Creed's suggestion that local communities of work and exchange were effective in 'domesticating socialism' to the practices, norms and values of pre-socialist communities may suggest a parallel in contemporary post-socialist Europe.[1] Here reform economies might be understood to be similarly 'domesticating' neoliberalism and transnationalism by the concrete practices of work and exchange. It is to some of these more social practices of reforming economies that I now turn.

## Social mobilization and economic lives

If the state plays an active and contested role in the transformation of reforming economies, who are the actors that rework state legacies, mobilize new state institutions, contest their policies and build the economy? The creation of markets, privatizing of property and the regulation of company practices are all occurring with input, guidance and pressure from transnational institutions, particularly but not only the European Union. In this sense, economic transformation is often interpreted in terms of a general process of convergence around a set of common goals, standard norms and harmonized practices.

The authors in this volume have shown how research on divergent and hybrid forms of capitalism deepens this analysis of convergence and harmonization. This is not, of course, to argue that such processes of convergence and harmonization in a European common space are not occurring; they obviously are, and rapidly. Nor is it to argue that these processes of convergence and harmonization are not also processes of integration into wider spaces of economic life and practice. Economic globalization and the integration of sourcing, production and employment into much wider networks of trade and investment are occurring throughout the region. Instead, the chapters in this volume have focused on the ways in which specific industrial mixes, varieties of capitalism, and economic regimes are already and always regionally differentiated social and economic formations. These may, for example, be of a Keynesian Western European type or a Southern European authoritarian type, with specific characteristics of each. Thus, the liberal market economies of the US and UK and the stronger social-democratic 'social partnership' of coordinated market economies in northern Europe, such as Germany and Sweden, remain quite distinct social formations with specific social forces binding together concrete socioeconomic compromises. The role of the state in each of these settings is also quite distinct. While post-war Keynesianism in Western Europe depended only to a limited degree on government direction of investment in the private sector, in Southern Europe the state did act in significant ways to direct public and private investments. But Southern European states were also characterized by less established mechanisms of social compromise and intense inequality in the distribution of wealth and incomes – an absence of a considerable middle class that prevented alternatives to authoritarian orders from emerging. The result was a more general climate of social unrest and a state that often turned to populist–authoritarian measures. In the social-democratic states of

Western Europe forms of social compromise were more broadly institutionalized and the presence of a considerable middle class enabled alternatives to authoritarianism to emerge.

In the second part of the book, authors have turned their attention more directly to the social forces and processes at work in these processes of economic transformation. By focusing on employment practices, wage-setting procedures, and differential access in decision-making, authors have shown how social actors, and especially different forms of labour, remain crucial in shaping specific forms of economic practice and institution. With changes in lead sectors within the economy and the corresponding transformation (and most recently opening) of labour markets, trade unions are now struggling to redefine their role in post-socialist economies and in ways that maintain some presence in leading industrial sectors, extend their role in rapidly emerging service sectors, and demonstrate a new-found independence from party and state. They are doing this in an EU context in which models of social dialogue and trilateralism (negotiated policies among government, business and labour) are themselves being challenged by more market-based models in conditions of rapidly emerging processes of economic flexibilization and the emergence of precarious labour markets.

Even here, however, the story of economic transformation is far from monolithic. After 1989, the majority of Bulgarians faced similar threats of unemployment, economic insecurity and precarious work contracts. Tourism was one of the most important sectors in Bulgaria's communist economy and the country's largest generator of hard currency, and it was widely thought the downturn in the industry after 1989 would be particularly sharp and fall differentially on female workers in the industry. Against expectations, jobs which had once been considered less important and had been more heavily feminized became important sites of social capital as the industry was restructured. Limited by the kinds of job opportunities they could take before 1989, women had entered the tourist industry in differentially large numbers and in that industry had acquired the kind of education, skills and experience that coincidentally became valuable in the post-1989 era and often at higher levels than male workers. State regulations aimed at professionalizing the management of hotels and restaurants for more demanding Western European consumer markets further inadvertently favoured women by requiring certain minimum levels of education to work in professional positions in the sector.

These social and gender differences also have their parallels in significant regional differences in economic well-being across the region.

Nowhere are these differences sharper than between town and countryside. Long histories of urban primacy and collective resource extraction from rural communities have generated patterns of regional inequality in infrastructure, health and income. At the same time, the relatively recent histories of industrialization and policies of recruitment into urban and industrial economies mean that many urban residents maintain familial links with their rural grandparents and cousins who remain important suppliers of household foodstuffs. The result is patterns of combined and uneven development sustained by macroeconomic policies and the micro-practices of weekly and seasonal commuting between city and countryside. One interesting result of these processes is that these economic practices and their sustaining institutions produced distinct 'natures' and environmental and health conditions in urban and rural areas. European accession policies are worked through this palimpsest of natures and economies with important results. For example, EU rural development grants require co-funding and consultation with stakeholders at the local level. Such policies are standard requirements to ensure a broader pattern of participation in projects and are an attempt to deal with issues of regional unevenness and social cohesion. But the history of regional development and struggles over administrative reforms have been such that the autonomy of rural local authorities has not always been formally recognized while larger regional administrative units have been privileged, as the case of Lithuania shows. With weak and underfunded local authorities, local public involvement necessary for EU financial support is limited and there are few mechanisms enabling the local authorities to raise the co-funding necessary for such projects. Those capacities are lodged at the level of regional authorities, where there is little public involvement. By contrast, urban municipalities have the administrative capacities, financial means and experienced staff to implement EU programming with relative ease.

Post-socialist transformations are, then, complex articulations of dislocations and rupturing breaks that are, in turn, always worked through local and historical resources and institutions. Even anti-state political movements in the 1980s need to be seen in this light, as the case of the Czech ecological movement shows. State policies to reproduce conservative and nationalist ideologies drew on conservation logics and public programmes of nature awareness to frame a distinctive and popular vision of the new socialist citizen. But, in order to sustain such a commitment, the state invested deeply in training and research programmes in academies and universities, which in turn were closely linked to state management institutions. A technical cadre of teachers and researchers committed to environmental health and justice thus emerged in and through the institutions of the state, preparing the ground for what emerged in 1989 as a broadly based and institutionally secure environmental and more broadly political movement. Such movements also emerged in churches and other institutions across Central and Eastern Europe in the 1980s, resulting in the velvet revolutions of the day. These patterns of social change deriving from the very institutions of state socialism are less surprising if we also understand the ways in which the planned economy always presupposed complex forms of informal economic practices operating through overlapping social networks. Emerging in part from pre-socialist legacies of communal exchange and in part in response to overly taut planning requirements, social networks of exchange and informal practices of support became even more important as access to consumer goods and foodstuffs became ever more difficult in the late 1980s and early 1990s. Social networks and informal practices became an important to gain access to goods and privileges otherwise not available. These informal practices and networks have not diminished with transition, but are being adapted to new conditions that have either required or encouraged informal exchange in struggles over basic needs and social surplus. The post-socialist economy is, in this reading, as much about the deepening and extending of informal economics networks, sustaining under market conditions economies of jars and gifting, and enabling formal transactional economies to function in conditions of deep personal local and group influences and obligations.

## Conclusion

As post-socialist economies restructure their institutions, regulations and practices, they are being rapidly integrated into broader European and global production networks and labour markets, and harmonized with EU and WTO regulations. The everyday practices of the economy (banking, insurance, work-time, and struggles over social surplus) are all rapidly converging around clear and distinct general models of economic governance. But these patterns of convergence remain complex and multiple, and they are always mediated through local configurations of historical legacy, institution, region, gender and influence. In these many ways, post-socialist economies are hybrid rather than transitional economies, forging recombinant regimes in which concrete economic practices are shaped by the legacies of past investments, geographies and norms, and in which state and society constantly interact with broader institutional and economic imperatives to shape concrete economies. *State and Society in Post-Socialist Economies* contributes to analyses that keep open, rather than close off, this dialectic of change and the always present mediation of the global and the local.

## Endnote

1.  Gerald Creed, *Domesticating Revolution: From Socialist Reform to Ambivalent Transition in a Bulgarian Village*, University Park: The Pennsylvania State University, 1998.

# Selected References


Adam, J., 'Transformation to a Market Economy in Czechoslovakia', *Europe-Asia Studies*, 45, 4, 1993, pp. 627–45.

Affanasiev, M., *Korporativnoye upravleniye na rossiiskikh predpriyatiyakh* [*Corporate Governance in Russian Enterprises*], Moscow: Interekspert, 2000.

Åslund, A., *Building Capitalism*, Cambridge: Cambridge University Press, 2002.

Avdasheva, S., 'Biznes gruppy kak forma restrukturizatsii predpriyatii: dvizhenie vpered ili shag nazad?' ['Business Groups as a Tool for Enterprise Restructuring: Moving Forward or Backward?'], *Rossiiskii zhurnal menedzhmenta*, 3, 1, 2005, 3–26.

Benneworth, P. and Henry, N., 'Where Is the Value Added in the Cluster Approach? Hermeneutic Theorising, Economic Geography and Clusters as a Multiperspectival Approach', *Urban Studies*, 41, 5/6, 2004, 1011–23.

Berglof, E. and von Thadden, E-L., *The Changing Corporate Governance Paradigm: Implications for Transition and Developing Countries*, Centre for Economic Policy Research Working Paper No. 263, London: CEPR, 1999.

Bieler, A. and Morton, A.D., eds, *Social Forces in the Making of the New Europe. The Restructuring of European Social Relations in the Global Political Economy*, Basingstoke: Palgrave, 2001.

Black, B., Kraakman, R. and Tarassova, A., 'Russian Privatization and Corporate Governance: What Went Wrong?', *Stanford Law Review*, 52, 2000, 1731–808.

Blasi, J., Kroumova, M. and Kruse, D., *Kremlin Capitalism: the Privatization of the Russian Economy*, Ithaca: Cornell University Press, 1997.

Bockman, J. and Eyal, G., 'Eastern Europe as a Laboratory for Economic Knowledge: The Transnational Roots of Neoliberalism', *American Journal of Sociology*, 108, 2, 2002, 310–52.

Bohle, D., 'Internationalization: An Issue Neglected in the Path-Dependency Approach to Post-Communist Transformation', in M. Dobry, ed., *Democratic and Capitalist Transitions in Eastern Europe. Lessons for the Social Sciences*, Kluwer, 2000, 235–62.

Bohle, D. and Greskovits, B., 'Europeanization and the Variety of Competition States in Central-Eastern Europe', unpublished manuscript, 2006.

Bohle, D. and Greskovits, B., 'Capitalism Without Compromise? Strong Business and Weak Labor in Central-Eastern Europe's New Transnational Industries', *Studies in Comparative International Development*, Spring 2006.

Bourdieu, P., *Distinction: a Social Critique of the Judgment of Taste*, trans. Richard Nice, Cambridge, Mass.: Harvard University Press, 1984.

Bourdieu, P., *Practical Reason: On the Theory of Action*, Stanford: Stanford University Press, 1998.

Boyer, R., 'The Political in the Era of Globalization and Finance: Focus on Some *Régulation* School Research', *International Journal of Urban and Regional Research*, 24, 2, 2000, 274–322.

Boyer, R., *The Regulation School: A Critical Introduction*, New York: Columbia University Press, 1990.

Brenner, N., *New State Spaces: Urban Governance and the Rescaling of Statehood*, Oxford and New York: Oxford University Press, 2004.

Bryant, C.G.A. and Mokrzycki, E. 'Introduction. Theorizing the Changes in East-Central Europe', in C.G.A. Bryant and E. Mokrzycki, eds, *The New Great Transformation? Change and Continuity in East-Central Europe*, London: Routledge, 1994.

Bunce, V., *Subversive Institutions: The Design and the Destruction of Socialism and the State*, Cambridge M.A.: Cambridge University Press, 1999.

Burawoy, M., 'The State and Economic Involution: Russia through a China Lens', *World Development*, 24, 6, 1996, 1105–17.

Burawoy, M. and Krotov, P., 'The Economic Basis of Russia's Political Crisis', *New Left Review*, 198, 1993, 16–38.

Cardoso, F.H. and Faletto, E., *Dependency and Development in Latin America*, Berkeley: University of California Press, 1979.

Carothers, T., 'The End of the Transition Paradigm', *Journal of Democracy*, 13:1, 2002, 5–21.

Cellarius, B.A., *In the Land of Orpheus: Rural Livelihoods and Nature Conservation in Postsocialist Bulgaria*, Madison: University of Wisconsin Press, 2004.

Cernat, L., *Europeanization, Varieties of Capitalism and Economic Performance in Central and Eastern Europe*, (London: Palgrave), 2006.

Clarke, S. and Ashwin, S., *Russian Trade Unions and Industrial Relations in Transition*, Basingstoke: Palgrave Macmillan, 2003.

COMTRADE database of the United Nations Statistics Division. Available from <http://intracen.org/tradestat/sitc3–3d>.

Cornelius, P.K. and Kogut, B., eds, *Corporate Governance and Capital Flows in a Global Economy*, Oxford: Oxford University Press, 2003.

Creed, G., *Domesticating Revolution: From Socialist Reform to Ambivalent Transition in a Bulgarian Village*, State College, PA.: The Pennsylvania State University Press, 1998.

Crouch, C. and Streeck, W., eds, *Political Economy of Modern Capitalism: Mapping Convergence and Diversity*, London: Sage, 1997.

Crowley, S. and Ost, D., eds, *Workers After Workers States. Labor and Politics in Postcommunist Eastern Europe*, Lanham, Boulder, New York, Oxford: Rowman & Littlefield, 2001.

Crowley, S. and Ost, D., eds, *Labour and Politics in Post-communist Eastern Europe*, Lanham: Rowman and Littlefield, 2001.

Csaba, L., *Kelet-Európa a világgazdaságban* [*Eastern Europe in the World Economy*], Budapest: K.J.K., 1984.

Cull, R., Matesová, J. and Shirley, M., 'Ownership and the Temptation to Loot: Evidence from Privatized Firms in the Czech Republic', *Journal of Comparative Economics*, 30, 2002, 1–24.

CzechInvest, *Clusters: Programme Approved by Government Resolution No. 414/2004 on 28 April 2004*, Prague: CzechInvest/Ministry of Industry and Trade, 2004.

Dangerfield, M., 'Ideology and the Czech Transformation: Neoliberal Rhetoric or Neoliberal Reality?' *East European Politics and Societies*, 11, 3, 1997, 436–69.

De Melo, M., Denizer, C. and Gelb, A., *From Plan to Market: Patterns of Transition*, Policy Research Working Paper 1564, Washington D.C.: The World Bank, 1996.

De Melo, M., Denizer, C., Gelb, A. and Tenev, S., *Circumstance and Choice: The Role of Initial Conditions and Policies in Transition Economies*, Washington D. C.: The World Bank, IFC, October 1997.

Deryabina, M., 'Restrukturizatsiya rossiiskoi economiki cherez peredel sobstvennosti i kontrolya' ['Restructuring of the Russian Economy Based on Redistribution of Ownership and Control'], *Voprosy Ekonomiki*, 10, 2000, 5–69.

Doitchev, P., *Zhivot: Otdaden na Turizma [Life: Devoted to Tourism]*, Sofia, Bulgaria: Literaturen Forum, 1999.

Dolgopyatova, T., *Rossiiskie predpriyatiya v perekhodnoi ekonomike: ekonomicheskie problemy i povedeni [Russian Enterprises in the Transition Economy: Economic Problems and Behaviour]*, Moscow: DELO, 1995.

Dolgopyatova, T., 'Modeli i mekhanizmy korporativnogo kontrolya v rossiiskoi promyshlennosti' ['Models and Mechanisms of Corporate Control in Russian Industry'], *Voprosy Economiki*, 5, 2001, 46–60.

Dolgopyatova, T., *Corporate Control in Russian Companies: Models and Mechanisms*, Working paper WP1/2002/05, Moscow: SU HSE, 2002 (also available at http://www.hse.ru/science/preprint/default.html#wp1).

Dolgopyatova, T., ed., *Russian Industry: Institutional Development*, Moscow: Publishing House of SU HSE, 2003.

Dolgopyatova, T., 'Sobstvennost' i korporativnyi kontrol' v rossiiskikh kompaniyakh v usloviyakh aktivizatsii integratsionnykh protsessov' ['Corporate Ownership and Control in Russian Companies in the Context of Integration'], *Rossiiskii Zhurnal Menedgmenta*, 2, 2, 2004, 3–26.

Dolgopyatova, T. and Iwasaki, I., *Exploring Russian Corporations: Interim Report on the Japan-Russia Joint Research Project on Corporate Governance and Integration Processes in the Russian Economy.* IER Discussion Paper Series B No. 35, (Tokyo: Hitotsubashi University, Institute of Economic Research., 2006) (also available at http://www.ier.hit-ac.jp/).

Drábek, Z., 'IMF and IBRD Policies in the Former Czechoslovakia', *Journal of Comparative Economics*, 20, 2, 1995, 235–64.

Drahokoupil, J., 'From Collectivization to Globalization: Putting Populism in Its Place', *Slovak Foreign Policy Affairs*, Spring 2005, 65–74.

Drahokoupil, J., 'Post-Fordist Capitalism in the Czech Republic: The Investment of Flextronics in Brno', *Czech Sociological Review*, 40, 3, 2004, 343–62.

Drahokoupil, J., 'State of the Capitalist State in East Central Europe: Towards the Porterian Workfare Postnational Regime?' in B.S. Sergi, W.T. Bagatelas and J. Kubicova, eds, *Industries and Markets in Central and Eastern Europe*, Aldershot, UK: Ashgate, 2006.

Drobyshevskii, S., Radygin, A., Gorshunov, I. and Izryadnova, O., *Investitsionnoe povedenie rossiiskikh predpriyatii' [The Investment Behaviour of Russian Enterprises].* Naychnye trudy IEPP N 65, Moscow: IEPP, 2003 (also available at http://www.iet.ru/publication.php?folder-id=44&category-id=116&publication-id=1174).

Dyson, K., *European States and the EMU*, Oxford, UK: Oxford University Press, 2002, http://brie.berkeley.edu/~briewww/pubs/wp/wp128.htm.

Eichengreen B. and Kohl, R., 'The External Sector, the State and Development in Eastern Europe,' BRIE Working Paper 12, 1998.

Ekiert, G., 'The State after State Socialism: Poland in Comparative Perspective', *IWM Working Paper*, 6/2001, 2001.

Ekiert, G. and Hanson, S.E., eds, *Capitalism and Democracy in Central and Eastern Europe: Assessing the Legacy of Communist Rule*, Cambridge University Press, 2003.

European Bank of Reconstruction and Development, *Transition Report 2005: Business in Transition*, London: Oxford University Press, 2005.

Eyal, G., Szelényi, I. and Townsley, E., *Making Capitalism without Capitalists: Class Formation and Elite Struggles in Post-Communist Central Europe*, London: Verso, 1998.

Eyal, G., 'Anti-Politics and the Spirit of Capitalism: Dissidents, Monetarists, and the Czech Transition to Capitalism', *Theory and Society*, 29, 2000, 49–92.

Eyal, G., *The Origins of Postcommunist Elites: From Prague Spring to the Breakup of Czechoslovakia*, Minneapolis and London: University of Minnesota Press, 2003.

Eyal, G., Szelenyi, I. and Townsley, E., *Making Capitalism Without Capitalists: The New Ruling Elites in Eastern Europe*, London and New York: Verso, 1998.

Fassmann, M. and Černějová, H., *Czech Republic: National Social Dialogue on the Formulation, Implementation and Monitoring of Employment Policies*, Geneva: International Labour Office, 2003.

Federocwicz, M. and Aguilera, R.V., eds, *Corporate Governance in a Changing Economic and Political Environment: Trajectories of Institutional Change*, Basingstoke: Palgrave, 2003.

Ferguson, T., 'From Normalcy to New Deal: Industrial Structure, Party Competition, and American Public Policy in the Great Depression', *International Organization*, 38, 1, Winter 1984, 41–94.

Fish, S., 'The Determinants of Economic Reform in the Post-Communist World', *East European Politics and Societies*, 12, 1, 1998, 31–78.

Fodor, E., 'Gender in Transition: Unemployment in Hungary, Poland and Slovakia', *East European Politics and Societies*, 11, 3, 1997, 470–500.

Frieden, J., 'Invested Interests: the Politics of National Economic Policies in a World of Global Finance', *International Organization*, 45, 4, Autumn 1991, 425–51.

Frieden, J., 'Real Sources of European Currency Policy: Sectoral Interests and European Monetary Integration', *International Organization*, 56, 4, Autumn 2002, 831–60.

Frieden, J., 'Classes, Sectors, and Foreign Debt in Latin America', *Comparative Politics*, October 1988, 1–20.

Genov, N., 'State and Economy in Eastern Europe: Trends in Establishing Social Dialogue', in Z. Mansfeldová, V. Sparschuh and A. Wenninger, eds, *Patterns of Europeanisation in Central and Eastern Europe*, Hamburg: Krämer, 2005.

Gereffi, G., 'Mexico's "Old" and "New" Maquiladora Industries: Contrasting Approaches to North American Integration', G. Otero, ed., *Neoliberalism revisited*, Boulder, CO.: Westview Press, 1996, 85–105.

Gereffi, G., 'Global Production Systems and Third World Development', in B. Stallings, ed., *Global Change, Regional Response*, Cambridge: Cambridge University Press, 1997, 100–42.

Ghodsee, K., *The Red Riviera: Gender, Tourism and Postsocialism on the Black Sea*, Durham: Duke University Press, 2005.

Gibson-Graham, J.K., *The End of Capitalism (as we know it): a feminist critique of political economy*, Oxford and New York: Blackwell, 1996; reprinted by the University of Minnesota Press, Minneapolis, 2006.

Golikova, V., Dolgopyatova, T., Kuznetsov, B. and Simachev, Yu, 'Spros na pravo v oblasti korporativnogo upravleniya: empiricheskie svidetel'stva,' in *Razvitie Sprosa na Pravovoe Regulirovanie Korporativnogo Upravleniya v Chastnom Sektore. Seriya 'Nauchnye doklady: nezavisimyi economicheskii analiz'* ['The Demand for Corporate Law: Empirical Evidence', in *Evolution of Private Sector Demand for Regulation of Corporate Governance. Series 'Academic Reports: Independent Economic Analysis'*], no. 148, Moscow: Moskovskii obshestvennyi nauchnyi fond, Necommercheskaya organizactiya "Proecty dlya budushego", 2003, 229–339 (also available at http://www.mpsf.org/lib.html).

Gould, J., *Beyond Creating Owners: Privatization and Democratization in the Slovak and Czech Republics, 1990–1998*, PhD, Columbia University, 2001.

Gourevitch, P., *Politics in Hard Times*, Ithaca and London: Cornell University Press, 1986.

Grabher, G. and Stark, D., *Restructuring Networks in Post-Socialism: Legacies, Linkages and Localities*, Oxford: Oxford University Press, 2006.

Grahl, J. and Teague, P., 'Is the European Social Model Fragmenting?', *New Political Economy*, 2, 3, 1997, reprinted in C. Pierson and F.G. Castles, *The Welfare State Reader*, Malden, MA: Polity Press, 2000, pp. 207–233.

Graziani, G., 'Globalisation of Production in the Textile and Clothing Industry: The Case of Italian FDI and Outward Processing in Eastern Europe', BRIE. Working Paper 128, 1998, http://brie.berkeley.edu/~briewww/pubs/wp/wp128. htm.

Greskovits, B., 'The First Shall Be the Last? Hungary's Road to the European Monetary Union', forthcoming in K. Dyson, ed., *Enlarging the Euro-Zone: External Empowerment and Domestic Transformation in East Central Europe*, Oxford: Oxford University Press, 2006 forthcoming.

Greskovits, B.,'Beyond Transition: The Variety of Post-Socialist Development,' in R. Dworkin *et al.*, eds, *From Liberal Values to Democratic Transition*, Budapest: Central European University Press, 2003, 201–25.

Greskovits, B., *The Political Economy of Protest and Patience: East European and Latin American Transformations Compared*, Budapest: Central European University Press, 1998.

Åse Berit Grødeland, '"Red Mobs", "Yuppies", "Lamb Heads" and Others: Contacts, Informal Networks and Politics in the Czech Republic, Slovenia, Bulgaria and Romania', *Europe-Asia Studies*, 59, 2, March 2007, 217–52.

Guriev, S. and Rachinsky, A., 'The Role of Oligarchs in Russian Capitalism', *Journal of Economic Perspectives*, 19, 1, 2005, 131–50.

Guriev, S., Lazareva, O., Rachinskii, A. and Tsukhlo, S., *Korporativnoe upravlenie v rossiiskoi promyshlennosti. Seriya 'Nauchnye doklady: nezavisimyi economicheskii analiz'* [*Corporate Governance in Russian Industry. Series 'Academic Reports: Independent Economic Analysis'*], no. 149, Moscow: Moskovskii obshestvennyi nauchnyi fond, CEFIR, 2003 (also available at http://www.mpsf.org/lib. html).

Haiduk, K., Herr, H.-J., Lintovskaya, T., Parchevskaya, S., Priewe, J. and Tsikou, R. *Belarusian Economy at a Crossroads*, Moscow: International Labour Organization, 2005.

Hall, D., *Tourism and Economic Development in Eastern Europe and the Soviet Union*, London: Belhaven Press, 1991.

Hall, P.A. and Soskice, D.W., *Varieties of Capitalism: the Institutional Foundations of Comparative Advantage*, Oxford: Oxford University Press, 2001.

Hellman, J., Jones, G. and Kaufmann, D., 'Seize the State, Seize the Day: State Capture, Corruption, and Influence in Transition Economies', *World Bank Policy Research Working Paper*, 2444, 2000.

Hellman, J., 'Winners Take All. The Politics of Partial Reform in Postcommunist Transitions', *World Politics*, 50, 1998, 203–34.

Hirschman, A., 'A Generalized Linkage Approach to Development, with Special Reference to Staples', in *Economic Development and Cultural Change. 25. Supplement. Essays in Honor of Bert Hoselitz*, Chicago: University of Chicago Press, 1977, 67–98.

Hoen, H.W., ed., *Good Governance in Central and Eastern Europe: the Puzzle of Capitalism by Design*, Cheltenham, UK and Northampton, MA: Edward Elgar, 2001.

Hollingsworth, J., Schmitter, P. and Streeck, W., *Governing Capitalist Economies: Performance and Control of Economic Sectors*, New York, Oxford: Oxford University Press, 1994.

Hollingsworth, J.R. and Lindberg, L.N., 'The Governance of the American Economy: The Role of Markets, Clans, Hierarchies, and Associative Behaviour', in W. Streeck and P.C. Schmitter, eds, *Private Interest Government: Beyond Market and State*, London: Sage, 1985.

Hollingsworth, J.R., Schmitter, P.C. and Streeck, W., 'Capitalism, Sectors, Institutions, and Performance', in J.R. Hollingsworth, P.C. Schmitter and W. Streeck, eds, *Governing Capitalist Economies: Performance and Control of Economic Sectors*, Oxford and New York: Oxford University Press, 1994.

Husák, P., *Budování Kapitalismu V Čechách: Rozhovory S Tomášem Ježkem [Building Capitalism in Bohemia: Interviews with Tomáš Ježek]*, Prague: Volvox Globator, 1997.

Iversen, T., Pontusson, J. and Soskice, D., eds, *Unions, Employers, and Central Banks: Macroeconomic Co-ordination and Institutional Change in Social Market Economies*, Cambridge, MA: Cambridge University Press, 2000.

Jessop, B., *The Capitalist State*, Oxford: Oxford University Press, 1982.

Jessop, B., 'The Crisis of the National Spatio-Temporal Fix and the Tendential Ecological Dominance of Globalizing Capitalism', *International Journal of Urban and Regional Research*, 24, 2, 2000, 323–60.

Jessop, B., *The Future of the Capitalist State*, Cambridge, UK and Malden, MA: Polity Press, 2002.

Jessop, B., 'The State and the Contradictions of the Knowledge-Driven Economy', in J.R. Bryson, P.W. Daniels, N.D. Henry and J. Pollard, eds, *Knowledge, Space, Economy*, London: Routledge, 2000.

Jessop, B., *State Theory: Putting the Capitalist State in Its Place*, University Park, PA: Pennsylvania State University Press, 1990.

Kalinova, E. and Baeva, I., *Balgarskite Prehodi 1939–2002 [The Bulgarian Transitions 1939–2002]*, Sofia, Bulgaria: Paradigma, 2002.

Kapelyushnikov, R. and Dyomina, N., 'Vliyanie kharakteristik sobstvennosti na rezul'taty eckonomicheskoi deyatel'nosti rossiiskikh promyshlennykh pred-priyatii' ['The Effects of Property Features on Economic Performance of Russian Industrial Enterprises'], *Voprosy Ekonomiki*, 2, 2005, 53–68.

Karl, T., *The Paradox of Plenty: Oil Booms and Petro-States*, Berkeley and Los Angeles: University of California Press, 1997.

Kaufmann, D., Kraay, A. and Mastruzzi, M., *Governance Matters: Governance Indicators for 1996–2002*, Washington: World Bank, 2003.

King, L.P., 'Does Neoliberalism Work? Comparing Economic and Sociological Explanations', *American Journal of Sociology* (under review).

King, L.P., 'Does Neoliberalism Work? Comparing Economic and Sociological Explanations', *New Political Economy*, (2006).

Klaus, V., *Rok Málo Či Mnoho V Dějinách Země? [Is a Year a Lot or a Little in the History of a Country?]*, Prague: Repro-Media, 1993.

Kleiner, G., Kachalov, R. and Sushko, E., 'Economic State and institutional environment of Russian industrial enterprises', *Voprosui ekonomiki*, 9 (in Russian), 2005, 77–9.

Kramer, A., 'Nemůžeme Si Dovolit Štědrost K Těm, Kteří Nechtějí Pracovat, Says Zdeněk Škromach', ['We Cannot Afford to Be Generous to Those Who Do Not Work (Interview with Zdeněk Škromach)'], *Právo*, 18 September 2004, 1.

Kudrna, Z., Bauer, M., Cvrček, T., Janoušová, J., Knot, O., Koleček, L., Kreuzbergová, E., Nezdara, O., Schwarz, P., Streblov, P., Střelková, J. and Vychodil, O., *Vzestup a Pád Investiční a Poštovní Banky [The Rise and Fall of Investiční a Poštovní Banka]*, Prague: e-Merit, 2002.

Kurth, J., 'The Political Consequences of the Product Cycle: Industrial History and Political Outcomes', *International Organization*, 33, 1, Winter 1979, 1–34.

Laux, J.K., 'The Return to Europe: The Future Political Economy of Eastern Europe', in R. Stubbs and G.R.D. Underhill, eds, *Political Economy and the Changing Global Order*, Ontario: Oxford University Press, 2000, 264–73.

Lampe, J., *The Bulgarian Economy in the Twentieth Century*, London and Sydney: Croom Helm, 1986.

Lavigne, M., 'Ten Years of Transition: A Review Article', *Communist and Post-Communist Studies*, 33, 2000, 475–83.

Lindberg, L.N., Campbell, J.L. and Hollingsworth, J.R., 'Economic Governance and the Analysis of Structural Change in the American Economy', in J.L. Campbell, J.R. Hollingsworth and L.N. Lindberg, eds, *Governance of the American Economy*, Cambridge: Cambridge University Press, 1991.

Lipietz, A., 'The Post-Fordist World: Labour Relations, International Hierarchy, and Global Ecology', *Review of International Political Economy*, 4, 1, Spring 1997, 1–41.

Lipietz, A., *Mirages and Miracles: The Crises of Global Fordism*, London: Verso, 1987.

Lipton, D. and Sachs, J., 'Creating a Market Economy in Eastern Europe: The Case of Poland', *Brookings Papers on Economic Activity*, 1, 1990, 75–133.

McCarthy, D. J., Puffer, S.M. and Shekshnia, S.V., *Corporate Governance in Russia*, Cheltenham, UK and Northampton, MA: Edward Elgar, 2004.

McDermott, G.A., *Embedded Politics: Industrial Networks and Institutional Change in Postcommunism*, Ann Arbor: The University of Michigan Press, 2002.

Mallya, T.J.S., Kukulka, Z. and Jensen, C., 'Are Incentives a Good Investment for the Host Country? An Empirical Evaluation of the Czech National Incentive Scheme', *Transnational Corporations*, 13, 1, 2004, 109–48.

Martin, A. and Ross, G., *The Brave New World of European Labor: European Trade Unions at the Millennium*, New York, Oxford: Berghahn Books, 1999.

MF, *Informace O Stavu Systémové Implementace Partnerství Veřejného a Soukromého Sektoru [Information on the State of Systemic Implementation of Public-Private*

*Partnerships]*, Ministry of Finance of the Czech Republic, 2004 [cited 23 November 2004]. Available from http://www.mfcr.cz/static/PPP/InfoPPP.htm.

MF, *Rozpočtový Výhled 2003–2006: Koncepce Reformy Veřejných Rozpočtů [Budgetary Prospect 2003–2006: The Concept of Public Budget Reform]*, Prague: Ministry of Finance of the Czech Republic, 2003.

Mladenova, Z. and Angresano, J., 'Privatization in Bulgaria', *East European Quarterly*, 30, 4, Winter 1996.

Michalopoulos, C. and Tarr, G., eds, *Trade in the New Independent States*, The World Bank/UNDP: Washington DC, 1994.

Moran, T., 'Multinational Corporations and Dependency: A Dialogue for Dependentistas', *International Organization*, Winter 1978, 79–100.

Myant, M., 'Czech Capitalism – Towards a European Model?', aper presented at the Managing the Economic Transition, 13th Research Seminar 'What Type of Capitalism in the Post-Communist Economies?', Cambridge: Cambridge University, 2004.

Myant, M., 'Employers' Interest Representation in the Czech Republic', *Journal of Communist Studies and Transition Politics*, 16, 4, 2000, 1–21.

Myant, M., *The Rise and Fall of Czech Capitalism: Economic Development in the Czech Republic since 1989*, Cheltenham, UK and Northampton, MA: Edward Elgar, 2003.

Myant, M., *Transforming Socialist Economies: The Case of Poland and Czechoslovakia*, Aldershot: Edward Elgar, 1993.

Myant M., and Smith, S., 'Czech Trade Unions in Comparative Perspective', *European Journal of Industrial Relations*, 5, 3, 1999, 265–85.

OECD, *White Paper on Corporate Governance in Russia*, 15 March 2002.

Orenstein, M.A., *Out of the Red: Building Capitalism and Democracy in Postcommunist Europe*, Ann Arbor: The University of Michigan Press, 2001.

Ó Riain, S., 'The Flexible Developmental State: Globalization, Information Technology, and the "Celtic Tiger"', *World Politics*, 28, 2, June 2000, 157–93.

Ouchi, W.G., 'Markets, Bureaucracies, and Clans', *Administrative Science Quarterly*, 25, 1, 1980, 129–41.

Pappe, Ya., 'Rossiiskii krupnyi biznes kak ekonomicheskii fenomen: osobennosti stanovleniya i sovremennogo etapa razvitiya' ['Russian Big Business as an Economic Phenomenon: Some Specifics of Its Emergence and Development'], *Problemy Prognozirovaniya*, 1, 2002a, 29–46.

Pappe, Ya., 'Rossiiskii krupnyi biznes kak ekonomicheskii fenomen: spetsificheskie cherty modeli ego organizatsii' ['Russian Big Business as an Economic Phenomenon: A Specific Model of its Organization'], *Problemy Prognozirovaniya*, 2, 2002, 83–97.

Páralová, A., *Více Svobody, Méně Regulace [More Freedom, Less Regulation]*, Prague: Civic Democratic Party, 2004.

Pavlínek, P., 'Transformation of the Central and East European Passenger Car Industry: Selective Peripheral Integration through Foreign Direct Investment', *Environment and Planning A*, 34, 2002, 1685–709.

Pavlinek, P. and Pickles, J., *Environmental Transitions: Transformation and Ecological Defense in Central and Eastern Europe*, London and New York: Routledge, 2000.

Pearlman, M., 'Conflicts and Constraints in Bulgaria's Tourism Sector', *Annals of Tourism Research*, 17, 1990, 103–22.

Peck, J.A., *Workfare States*, New York: Guilford Press, 2001.

Pickles J. and Smith, A., 'Clothing Workers After Worker States: The Consequences for Work and Labour of Outsourcing, Nearshoring and Delocalization', in S. McGrath-Champ, A. Herod and A. Rainnie, eds, *Handbook of Work and Society: Working Space*, London: Sage Publishers, 2007 (forthcoming).

Pickles, J. and Smith, A., eds, *Theorizing Transition: The Political Economy of Postcommunist Transformations*, London and New York: Routledge, 1998.

Pierson, P., *Dismantling the Welfare State? Reagan, Thatcher and the Politics of Retrenchment*, Cambridge: Cambridge University Press, 1994.

Plehwe, D., 'Varieties of Transnational Capitalism?', paper presented at the 15th EGOS-Colloquium, Warwick 1999.

Polanyi, K., *The Great Transformation*, New York: Rinehart & Company, 1944.

Porter, M.E., *The Competitive Advantage of Nations*, London: Macmillan, 1990.

Potůček, M., 'Accession and Social Policy: The Case of the Czech Republic', *Journal of European Social Policy*, 14, 3, 2004, 253–66.

Radygin, A. and Entov, R., *Korporativnoe upravlenie i zashita prav sobstvennosti: empiricheskii analiz i aktual'nye napravleniya reform [Corporate Governance and the Protection of Property Rights: Empirical Analysis and Actual Directions of Reforms]*, Naychnye trudy IEPP N 36, Moscow: IEPP, 2001 (also available at http://www.iet.ru/publication.php?folder-id=44&category-id=116&publication-id=1719).

Rhodes, M. and Keune, M., 'EMU and Welfare States in East-Central Europe: The Political Economy of Adjustment', forthcoming in Kenneth Dyson, ed., *Enlarging the Euro-Zone: External Empowerment and Domestic Transformation in East Central Europe*, Oxford: Oxford University Press, 2006 forthcoming.

Říman, M., *Nový Růst: Modrá Šance Pro Podnikání [New Growth: A Blue Chance for Entrepreneurship]*, Prague: Civic Democratic Party, 2003.

Rugman, A.M. and Verbeke, A., 'Multinational Enterprises and Public Policy', *Journal of International Business Studies*, 29, 1, 1998, 115–36.

Seleny, A., *The Political Economy of State-Society Relations in Hungary and Poland: from Communism to the European Union*, Cambridge: Cambridge University Press, 2006.

Shafer, M., *Winners and Losers. How Sectors Shape the Developmental Prospects of States*, Ithaca: Cornell University Press, 1994.

Shafik, N., 'Making a Market: Mass Privatization in the Czech and Slovak Republics', *World Development*, 23, 7, 1995, 1143–56.

Silva, E., 'Business Elites, the State, and Economic Change in Chile', in S. Maxfield and B. Schneider, eds, *Business and the State in Developing Countries*, Cornell Studies in Political Economy, Ithaca: Cornell University Press, 1997, 152–90.

Silver, B., *Forces of Labor. Workers' Movement and Globalization Since 1870*, Cambridge: Cambridge University Press, 2003.

Sklair, L., *Assembling for Development: The Maquiladora Industry in Mexico and the United States*, London: Unwin Hyman, 1989.

'Slovenská Reforma Daní Je Mnohem Hlubší Než Česká' [The Slovak Tax Reform is Much Deeper than the Czech One], *Hospodářské noviny*, September 9 2004.

Smith, A., 'Informal work and the diverse economies of post-socialism', in E. Marcelli and C. Williams, eds, *The Informal Work of Developed Nations*, 2007 forthcoming.

Smith, A. and Stenning, A., 'Beyond household economies: articulations and spaces of economic practice in post-socialism', *Progress in Human Geography*, 30, 2, 2006, 190–213.

Smith, A., Begg, R., Bucek, M. and Pickles, J., 'Global trade, European integration and the restructuring of Slovak apparel exports', *Ekonomicky casopis* (Slovak *Journal of Economics*), 51, 6, 2003, 731–48.

Sobotka, B., 'Chceme Podpořit Růst a Prosperitu' ['We Want to Support Growth and Prosperity'], *Hospodářské noviny*, February 2 2004.

Stark, D., 'Path Dependence and Privatization. Strategies in East Central Europe', *Eastern European Politics and Societies*, 6, 1991, 17–54.

Stiglitz, J., 'Quis custodiet ipsos custodes? Corporate Governance Failures in the Transition', a paper presented at the World Bank's Annual Conference on Development Economics (ABCDE), Paris, June 1999, *Challenge*, 42, 6 (available at www.findarticles.com/p/articles/mi_m1093/is_6_42/).

Streeck, W. and Schmitter, P.C., 'Community, Market, State – and Associations? The Prospective Contribution of Interest Governance to Social Order', in W. Streeck and P.C. Schmitter, eds, *Private Interest Government: Beyond Market and State*, London: Sage, 1985.

Tőkés, R.L., ' "Transitology": Global Dreams and Post-Communist Realities', *Central Europe Review*, 2, 10, 13 March 2000, http://www.ce-review.org/00/10/tokes10.html.

Van Tulder, R. and Ruigrok, W., 'European Cross-National Production Networks in the Auto Industry: How Eastern Europe is Becoming the Low End of European Car Complexes', paper presented at the Berkeley Roundtable on International Economy 1997, http://www.ciaonet.org/conf/bri01/bri01eb.html.

TTPP, *Insiders, Outsiders and Good Corporate Governance in Transitional Economies: Cases of Russia and Bulgaria*, Regional Think Tank Partnership Program Working Papers Series, WP No. 2–5 (available at www.ttpp.info/library/library_.asp).

Uhl, P., 'Ksčm Zatím Jen Nadbíhá Nostalgii' ['So Far Ksčm Only Makes-up To Nostalgia'], *Právo*, November 22 2004.

Večerník, J., ed., *Zpráva O Vývoji České Společnosti 1989–1998 [Social Report of the Czech Republic in 1989–1998]*, Prague: Academia, 1998.

Vernon, R., *Sovereignty at Bay: The Multinational Spread of U. S. Enterprises*, New York: Basic Books, 1971.

Vernon, R. and Wells, L.T., Jr, *Economic Environment of International Business*, Prentice-Hall, Inc.: Englewood Cliffs, New Jersey, 1981.

Wallerstein, I., *The Capitalist World-Economy. Essays by Immanuel Wallerstein*, Cambridge: Cambridge University Press; Paris: Editions de la Maison des Sciences de l'Homme.

Weber, M., 'Chapter 2. The Spirit of Capitalism', *The Protestant Ethic and the Spirit of Capitalism*, 1905, London: Routledge, 2001.

Williamson, J., 'Democracy and the "Washington Consensus"', *World Development*, 21, 8, 1993, 1329–36.

Woodruff, D., *Property Rights in Context: Privatization's Legacy for Corporate Legality in Poland and Russia*, Working paper WP1/2003/01, Moscow: SU HSE, 2003 (also available at http://www.hse.ru/science/preprint/default.html#wp1).

World Bank, *World Development Report 1996*, New York: Oxford University Press, 1979.

World Bank, *World Development Report: From Plan to Market*, New York: Oxford University Press, 1996.

The World Bank Policy Research Dept, J.C. Brada and I. Singh, *Corporate Governance in Central Eastern Europe: Case Studies of Firms in Transition*, New York: M.E. Sharpe, 1998.

Wright, E.O., 'Working-Class Power, Capitalist-Class Interests, and Class Compromise', *The American Journal of Sociology*, 105, 4, 2000, 957–1002.

Yasin, E., ed., *Structural Changes in the Russian Industry*, Moscow: Publishing House of SU HSE, 2004.

Zemplinerová, A., 'The Importance of Foreign-Owned Enterprises in the Catching-up Process', in K. Liebscher, J. Christl, P. Mooslechner and D. Ritzberger-Grünwald, eds, *The Economic Potential of a Larger Europe*, Cheltenham, UK and Northampton, MA: Edward Elgar, 2004.

Zysman, J. and Schwartz, A., *Enlarging Europe: The Industrial Foundations of a New Political Reality*, Berkeley: University of California Press, 1998.

# Index

## Introductory Note

References such as '178–9' indicate (not necessarily continuous) discussion of a topic across a range of pages. Wherever possible in the case of topics with many references, these have either been divided into sub-topics (indented below the main heading) or the most significant discussions of the topic are indicated by page numbers in bold.